Milton's Teeth & Ovid's Umbrella

CURIOUSER AND CURIOUSER ADVENTURES IN HISTORY

Michael Olmert

A TOUCHSTONE BOOK
PUBLISHED BY SIMON & SCHUSTER
NEW YORK LONDON TORONTO
SYDNEY TOKYO SINGAPORE

TOUCHSTONE
Rockefeller Center
1230 Avenue of the Americas
New York, NY 10020

Copyright © 1996 by Michael Olmert
All rights reserved,
including the right of reproduction
in whole or in part in any form.

TOUCHSTONE and colophon are registered trademarks
of Simon & Schuster Inc.

Designed by Brian Mulligan

Manufactured in the United States of America

1   3   5   7   9   10   8   6   4   2

Library of Congress Cataloging-in-Publication Data
Olmert, Michael.
Milton's teeth & Ovid's umbrella : curiouser and curiouser adventures
in history / Michael Olmert. p.cm.
Some of the essays originally appeared in earlier versions in the column Points of origin,
published in the Smithsonian, 1981–1988.
"A Touchstone book." Includes bibliographical references.
Contents: Life : death, taxes, graffiti, hair, toothbrushes, teeth, hands — Leisure : football,
running, betting, the sporting chance, baseball talk, horse racing, lotteries, chess, cards,
cowboys — Celebrations : marriage, birth, vacation, hazing, graduation, April Fool's Day — Implements & symbols : tools, lawns, trees, keys, pets, place-names, dibs!, umbrellas.
1. History—Miscellanea. 2. Curiosities and wonders. I. Title.
D10.044 1996   96-1742
901—dc20.........................CIP

ISBN 0-684-80164-7

Portions of this book have appeared, in slightly different form, in *Smithsonian, Historic
Preservation,* and *Colonial Williamsburg.*

Excerpt from Wilhemina F. Jashemski's *The Gardens of Pompeii*
(1979) is reprinted courtesy of Aristide D. Caratzas, Publisher.

Excerpt from Tony Harrison's *The Trackers of Oxyrhynchus,* 1991, is reprinted courtesy of
Faber and Faber Limited Publishers.

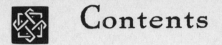 # Contents

Introduction:
From Manuscripts to Monkey Bones

1. Life

2. Leisure

3. Celebrations

4. Implements & Symbols

Acknowledgments

Special thanks to Don Moser, editor of *Smithsonian,* who invented the "Points of Origin" column for me. Early versions of a number of these essays first appeared in his magazine between 1981 and 1988. Thanks also to two other editors, Wayne Barrett at *Colonial Williamsburg* and Jeff Colin, former editor of *Historic Preservation,* who found space for me in their pages.

Thanks also to all the following:

At Williamsburg: Cary Carson, Jay Gaynor, Carl Lounsbury, Mark R. Wenger, Emma L. Powers, Edward Chappell, Ivor Noel Hume, Joanne Bowen, Harold Gill, Steve Mrozowski, Marley Brown, Linda Rowe, Kevin Kelley, Pat Gibbs, Lorena Walsh, Ken Schwarz, Thad Tate, John Ingram, Joe Rountree, Donna Shepperd.

At the University of Maryland: John Auchard, Theresa Coletti, Neil Isaacs, Barry Pearson, and Charles Rutherford, all of the Department of English; and Mark Leone of Anthropology.

At Historic St. Mary's City: Henry Miller.
At the Maryland Hall of Records: Lois Green Carr.
At Cleveland State University: Earl R. Anderson, Department of English.
At the Smithsonian Institution, National Museum of Natural History: Richard Thorington.
At North Carolina State University: Irwin Rovner, Department of Anthropology, and John C. Russ, Materials Science and Engineering.
At the National Eye Institute, NIH: Terrence Gillen.
In Lebanon, Ohio: John C. Quinn.

In England: Helen Paterson, who drove me out to Ashwell Church on a cold and windy day; Esther Potter, who gave me Pepys; and Freda Bates, who arranged for me to visit the chapel of Henry VII, Westminster Abbey, while it was under restoration.

Finally, thanks to Caroline Sutton at Simon & Schuster, Ann Marlowe, my agent and friend Leona Schecter, and, as always, to Meg.

Abbreviations

Baring-Gould	Sabine Baring-Gould. *Lives of the Saints.* 16 vols. Edinburgh: Grant, 1914.
Boller	Henry A. Boller. *Among the Indians: Eight Years in the Far West, 1858–1866.* Chicago: Lakeside Press, 1959.
Brown	*The Frank C. Brown Collection of North Carolina Folklore.* 7 vols. Durham: Duke University Press, 1952–64.
CWF	Colonial Williamsburg Foundation.
DNB	*Dictionary of National Biography.*
Ferguson	George Ferguson. *Signs and Symbols in Christian Art.* Oxford: Oxford University Press, 1954.
Frazer	Sir James George Frazer. *The Golden Bough: A Study in Magic and Religion.* 9 vols. bound as 13. 1913; repr. London: Macmillan, 1988.
Friedlander	Ludwig Friedlander. *Roman Life and Manners Under the Early Empire.* New York: Barnes & Noble, 1965.
Friedman	Albert B. Friedman, ed. *The Viking Book of Folk Ballads of the English Speaking World.* New York: Viking, 1956.
Hazlitt	W. Carew Hazlitt. *Faiths and Folklore of the British Isles.* 1905; repr. New York: Blom, 1965.
Horn and Born	Walter Horn and Ernest Born. *The Plan of St. Gall.* 3 vols. Berkeley: University of California Press, 1979.

Janssen   Johannes Janssen. *History of the German People at the Close of the Middle Ages.* London: Paul, Trench, & Trubner, 1925.

Landman I   Leo Landman. "Jewish Attitudes Towards Gambling: The Professional and Compulsive Gambler." *Jewish Quarterly Review* 57 (1966–67).

Landman II   ————. "Jewish Attitudes Towards Gambling, II: Individual & Community Efforts to Curb Gambling." *Jewish Quarterly Review* 58 (1967–68).

Leach   Maria Leach, ed. *Funk & Wagnalls Standard Dictionary of Folklore, Mythology, and Legend.* New York: Funk & Wagnalls, 1949.

Lewis and Short   Carlton T. Lewis and Charles Short. *Harpers' Latin Dictionary.* New York: Harper & Bros., 1878.

N&Q   *Notes and Queries.*

n.d.   No date.

OED   *Oxford English Dictionary.*

Opie   Iona and Peter Opie. *The Lore and Language of Schoolchildren.* Oxford: Clarendon Press, 1959.

PMLA   *Publications of the Modern Language Association.*

Pritchard   V. Pritchard. *English Medieval Graffiti.*Cambridge: Cambridge University Press, 1967.

Sitwell   Dame Edith Sitwell. *English Eccentrics.* New York: Vanguard Press, 1957.

Smith   Sir William Smith, William Wayte, and G. E. Marindin. *Dictionary of Greek and Roman Antiquities.* London: John Murray, 1901.

Strutt   Joseph Strutt. *The Sports and Pastimes of the People of England.* William Hone, ed. 1841; repr. London: Chatto & Windus, 1898.

TLS   *Times Literary Supplement.*

Mercedes Drain Olmert,

1918–1960

Introduction

From Manuscripts to Monkey Bones

THERE ARE SO MANY WAYS of getting at the past, so many texts. Not long ago, history depended chiefly on traditional sources, documents mainly—books, treaties, laws, newspapers, accounts of debates and court cases, the occasional memoir of a participant, fat authoritative tomes written decades or centuries after the events in question. For the most part, these were fine. Trouble was, such books were sometimes as much pronouncement as inquiry—the sort of imperiousness that stops us thinking about ambiguous or alternative pasts.

Today, of course, the historian uses an almost limitless set of tools and sources. Every scrap from the past is being harnessed to speak to us. Inventories of the contents of eighteenth- and nineteenth-century houses copied down for fire insurance policies help us recover how we lived, how we furnished and decorated our homes. Probated wills, used to settle estates, point to the exact period when the majority of farmers owned plows rather than hoes and could thus cultivate much more land—and contribute inevitably to agricultural runoff and water pollution and the siltation of rivers. Oral history and folklore preserve the old custom that the boy who finds a red ear of corn at a cornshucking gets to kiss all the girls; conversely, the girl who finds a red ear is liable to be kissed by all the boys. All such information is history; it's what we were.

Inventories, wills, oral history, and folklore are the sorts of records that cry out for interpretation. Yet this information went unheeded until recently, essentially for two reasons. First, these are historical "texts" that demand the voice of a scholar, a writer, to make them articulate. Second, they were elements of *little* history, the vernacular stories of ordinary people who seldom figured in Big History. These people might fall in battle or populate new continents, but they were silent when historians came to tell of the great movements in which they played a part.

So far, all the texts I've mentioned have to do with words. There are others, like art and artifacts and architecture, that also broaden and illuminate our pasts. But they especially require an interpreter.

The handsome brick residences of restored colonial towns are as elegant in their way as the pyramids of Egypt. They can be so imposing that we have a tendency to bow down before their majesty, to defer to the good taste of the eighteenth century. After all, these were people who could work so finely in Flemish bond brickwork and surround their homes with ornamental knot gardens; even their backyard "necessary houses" were painted in polychrome! But then along comes the bucket-toting historian, armed with ice water from archaeologists, property maps, letters, trial proceedings, and sketchbooks, saying, No, there were largely kitchen gardens in those backyards, not ornamentals, and the rest of the yard was filled with sheds where slaves lived, ramshackle structures that did not survive the test of time like brick. (The rich *do* have leverage over history. Certainly, it was the same story with the pyramids; we know far more about pharaohs than any other Egyptians.) Moreover, says the American colonial historian, necessary houses were probably not painted at all, merely whitewashed or, more roughly still, protected with some cheap tar product. They were structures well suited to their backyard site, a muddy place where bones, oyster shells, broken dishes, and other kitchen scraps would be thrown underfoot to harden the surface of the ground. And some necessaries were "three-holers," very bad taste indeed to modern notions of hygiene and privacy.

It's so easy to be overcome by nostalgia for the colonial era that we neglect its darker sides. Civility and savagery were the twin poles of eighteenth-century life. While celebrating the good and the elegant, the historian must not be afraid to explore the age's inhumanity. Yet we know it was overlooked. Using a census published in the *Virginia Almanack* in 1776, historian Kevin Kelley of the Colonial Williamsburg Foundation has shown that the population of Williamsburg was 52 percent African-American in 1775. For several decades after the town's restoration in the 1920s, however, blacks and slavery were scarcely mentioned.

The historian's job is to make sense of *every* text. It's not to sweep away thoughts of fine houses, but to fill out the past by bringing a voice to texts that have been silent before. Otherwise, for example, we might never have understood those antebellum plantations in the South constructed by African craftsmen. Their voices today are only available to us in the carved crocodiles and other African motifs they inserted among the classical acanthus leaves on those stately mansions.

How do you interpret such art? A subversive act on the part of a slave-craftsman? Or a collaboration between patron and artist, both proud to raise the nap on the threadbare cloth of classical pictorial allusion? Architecture is always about power, the presentation of self. Wouldn't the occasional slave owner want to demonstrate to his peers his control over his workers in this way, suggesting that his sway over them extended right back to the land of their birth? Or was it all done in fun, a celebration of the rich, exotic images that Africa and Africans offered, and still offer, the world?

Civility versus savagery? The point is not to come down on either side, but to articulate both voices that can be found in the eighteenth century, if not all of the past. History is about making texts sing. Henry Fielding (1707–1754) had the balance just right in his novel *Tom Jones*—itself an important historical text—and he did it with wit and power:

> It was Mr. Western's custom every afternoon, as soon as he was drunk, to hear his daughter play on the harpsichord.

THE BEST of texts are those that provoke. Even a bone fragment can make a mysterious text. At the house of John Brush in Williamsburg, archaeologists uncovered the jawbones of a West African green monkey, *Cercopithicus aethiops sabaeus*. The bones can be dated, from the debris layer they were found in, to about 1720. But why were they in Williamsburg? Was our monkey from one of the London plays or entertainments presented at the theater next door to Brush's home?

It's possible the monkey was the pet of a sea captain visiting Brush from the West Indies. Or that someone in the house with an interest in natural philosophy kept it for serious study, to consider its diet, to muse over its similarity to mankind. The theatrical explanation, the nautical explanation, and the scientific one all give us different sides of colonial life that might well have existed side by side. Must only one explanation be right?

Stand today in the Department of Archaeological Research at Colonial Williamsburg and turn over the tiny mandible and maxilla in your hand. Feel the power. Another thought occurs: The Brush house was staffed by a number of slaves. Was the monkey one of their pets? Green monkeys were brought as pets to the Caribbean with the slave trade. So many escaped, however, that these Old World primates soon went feral and still roam free on Barbados and St. Kitts.

Or was it dinner? Monkey was a regular source of protein in West Africa. Would African-American slaves in Williamsburg have eaten such an animal, one that so reminded them of their roots? The one thing we do know is that this monkey did not die of old age; its teeth were in good shape.

Moreover, the monkey was often a cult animal in Africa, its jaw-bones sometimes deposited at shrines as votive objects. Could these have been relics, smuggled across the great ocean, their power and their owner alike utterly lost to memory about 1720? If so, it makes these meager and yellowing bones, with their two struggling teeth, the final remains of some quiet devotion on the part of a real person. His luck may have failed, but surely not his gods.

As the monkey fragments exemplify, history has a great many texts. Oddly, the more texts we find—the more documents and artifacts, institutions and customs, habits and habiliments we uncover—the more historians are seen as *creating* new pasts rather than *containing* or controlling the ones we have. Where will it all end? It can be very disconcerting to those who want a fixed and final version of the past, History with a capital H. But as a great thinker said twenty-five hundred years ago, intellectual life has to do with questions, not answers. Or as novelist Penelope Lively put it in *Moon Tiger* (1987):

> Argument, of course, is the whole point of history. Disagreement; my word against yours; this evidence against that. If there were such a thing as absolute truth the debate would lose its lustre. I, for one, would no longer be interested. I well remember the moment at which I discovered that history was not a matter of received opinion.

HISTORIANS TODAY are drawn to ask questions that have scarcely been asked before, questions prompted by today's concerns. We have environmental problems, HAZMAT, all manner of erosion. What about the past? What was that fertile dance like, that first engagement between people and Nature in this New World? How did the two adapt—differently, or indifferently—to the presence and predations of each other?

They call themselves environmental historians or ecohistorians, this new breed of thinkers who conjure up the past and its view of the earth. They're as likely to use science—archaeobotany, pollen studies, or grubbing for the remains of intestinal parasites—as they are to use documents or artifacts. For them, the past is a text (in Latin, *textus* means a weave) and their job is to unweave the secrets of that tapestry.

Some of them look for history in the plaque on cows' teeth. Pick up an old cow's tooth. Note the yellowing along its sides, down near the gum line. It's plaque, the same buildup the dental hygienist removes from your mouth. Plaque on cows' teeth captures plant remains called phytoliths (the hard parts of plants), which clearly indicate the kinds of grasses the animals once grazed on. So we can tell whether they ate native grass or grasses introduced from Europe, i.e., whether the animals were for the use of a single family or were part of a market economy supplying meat for a town. This gives us a view of the colonial economy and environment that no written record holds out to us.

A pioneer in the analysis of phytoliths from archaeological sites is Irwin Rovner of North Carolina State University. Phytoliths are literally "plant-stones," the parts of grasses and plants that give them structure; consider them the "bones" of plants. Phytoliths of the three tribes of grasses, for instance, come in distinctive shapes. Those associated with the panicoid grasses (foxtails, tall-grass prairie plants) are often dumbbell-shaped, those from festucoids (wheats, moist-climate plants) oval or trapezoidal, and chloridoid (short-grass prairie) phytoliths saddle- or battle-ax-shaped. Phytoliths were first described in the 1840s. Although their potential as "texts," as microscopic indicators of ancient vegetation, was known in the 1890s, the idea of harvesting them from dental plaque had to wait until 1975.

Rovner works with cow teeth from datable archaeological assemblages of "faunal remains," the bones of animals thrown in trash pits after they were eaten. After cleaning the teeth with distilled water, he pries off bits of the dental calculus or tartar and dissolves these in dilute hydrochloric acid. He then prepares slides for viewing on a scanning electron microscope: phytoliths are extremely small, ranging from ten to thirty microns in length (a micron is a millionth of a meter). At this stage, Rovner's job is merely to look for the distinctive phytolith shapes to identify the presence of particular grasses.

The size of phytoliths is what makes them especially attractive. They're so small they're almost immune to mechanical destruction. And since they're all silica, they are in fact a form of opal. "Phytoliths are mineral particles," Rovner says. "There is no more durable evidence in all archaeobotany or archaeozoology."

Phytoliths from eighteenth-century cows in Hampton, Virginia, show how the fodder and pastures of grazing livestock change over time. Early in the century, cows are eating mostly native grasses, panicoids. "By about 1775," says Rovner, "the panicoids are disappearing. That is, to judge from what we are getting off the teeth, European fodder grasses have replaced the panicoids."

The other attractive characteristic of plants containing phytoliths is that they decay in place and are not carried on the wind for hundreds of miles like pollen. This was especially important for Hampton. Phytoliths in the town's soil differ from those on the cows' teeth. The soil shows mainly festucoid phytoliths, probably the result of introduced European lawn grasses, while the older cow teeth show mostly panicoid phytoliths. Which means that, even early on, city cows were being pastured outside town or were being fed with fodder carried in from outlying fields.

What happened to the panicoids? Says Rovner: "European grasses long ago adapted to being grazed by herbivores. Their defense was to add heavy doses of silica to the base of the plant so animals would eat only the tips of the blades, leaving the leaf ends to regenerate. Eastern North American panicoids did not have that adaptive history against grazers. Which means that festucoids eventually replace panicoids in pastures."

The plaque on cows' teeth can be used to measure historical water pollution as well. In addition to phytoliths, Rovner collects diatom remains trapped in the tartar. These are the surviving shells of algae that come into the cows' diet through their drinking water. Early teeth show only a few diatoms. By 1775 the plaque is enclosing many more shells, as many as twenty on a single slide under the microscope. Then, by the mid-nineteenth century, the diatom numbers drop off to where they were at the start of the eighteenth century. The implication is clear—and at the start of the eighteenth century, so are Hampton's streams and ponds. But by 1775 agricultural pollution has created algae blooms in all the available surface water. By 1850 the problem is over because the town depends on a food-market system in which animals are raised on rural farms where the water is crystalline. People in town no longer have cows. "It's a Polaroid of historic pollution and Hampton's response to it," says Rovner, "all from phytoliths and diatoms and postmortem dental hygiene."

> *The past is rubbish till scholars take the pains*
> *to sift and sort and interpret the remains.*
> *This chaos is the past, mounds of heaped debris*
> *just waiting to be organized into history.*

> —TONY HARRISON, *THE TRACKERS OF OXYRHYNCHUS*, 1988

BEFORE THE ARRIVAL of Europeans, native Americans grew corn and small plots of tobacco, which they used only in ceremonies. With a stone or wooden hoe they raked up tiny mounds that were seeded with corn and beans and squash so the climbing plants could grow up around the cornstalks. Tobacco too was a hill-cultivated crop. That is, you did not plow furrows and plant a continuous crop. Instead, seeds went into individual mounds of dirt. For the most part, this was the agriculture the colonists learned from the Indians. The switch from their failing European wheats to the native resilient corn (maize) kept them alive. But tobacco made them rich.

To a European visitor, the Tidewater farms of the seventeenth-century Chesapeake must have seemed scruffy. No manicured plots of amber grain, but irregular crops in uneven fields that were usually minimally cleared and burnt, often leaving tree stumps in place. Not exactly a green and pleasant land.

Domestic animals were allowed to roam the woods. Cattle and pigs and horses seemed to do all right, but sheep and goats were far too vulnerable to wolves. There simply was too much valuable work to be done tending the tobacco fields to allot any man-hours to shepherding.

Writing in 1644, John Lewger of St. Mary's City, Maryland, noted that of the eleven sheep he had, four had been eaten by wolves. Today at St. Mary's City, Henry Miller has studied the shallow burial of a ewe with the tiny bones of two near-term lambs still in its womb. It is a sad sight. Was this one of the sheep Lewger was keeping for Lord Baltimore, the proprietor of the Maryland colony?

Wolves were a problem, however, that was not beyond scope of man's retribution. County courthouses in the Tidewater began paying out bounties for wolf pelts and by the end of the century the wolf problem was eradicated. After 1700 payment of the wolf bounty had become as rare as the animal itself.

• • •

HENRY MILLER likes to refer to his work as "cultural ecology," looking at the relationship between human activity and natural processes. "I've always been fascinated," Miller says, "by such questions as, how did people make it in the New World, how did they use technology to be creative in the way they exploited the environment?" Although he's an archaeologist, a focus of his career has been probing how diet changed over time in the colonial Chesapeake.

For the seventeenth century, the agricultural system the colonists adapted from the Indians was beautifully sustainable, at least for small populations. The problem was that tobacco quickly used up the soil nutrients and fields had to be abandoned for long stretches of time. In the eighteenth century, as the population burgeoned, that system was no longer viable. Enter the plow.

Throughout the Tidewater, this new technology eased the transition to a grain economy, with its dependence on clear-cut fields and its attendant runoff. Lorena Walsh, a historian at Colonial Williamsburg, has studied just what the shift from seventeenth-century hoe cultivation to eighteenth-century plows meant. Looking at probate and inventory records, she found that before the Revolution, 10 percent of the population had plows. After the Revolution the number soared to 60 percent. In 1730 some 2 percent of the land was plowed; by 1800 that figure was 40 percent. The change caused so much siltation that formerly deep-water harbors at places like Port Tobacco on the Potomac and Londontown on the South River in Maryland were rendered useless in less than a century.

Walsh looks at documents. Miller fills out the picture by looking at the fish bones from refuse pits, often former cellar holes in basements or filled-in clay-extraction pits near building sites.

Miller's *locus classicus* is a tenant site in St. Mary's City, probably the home of tenants who worked as watermen and farmers. "From the 1640s up until the 1760s," he says, "when we look at the gill plates—the most resilient and easily identifiable part of the fish that survives—we see mainly drums and sheepsheads. All it took was a hook and a line; you threw it out and it rested on the bottom, and that was it. So why do they start, after 1760, going after the oyster toad fish and the shad, which are harder to catch, are less appetizing, and have less protein? The guess is that the others are no longer available."

To Miller, this indicates that the plow, coupled with the conversion of vast tracts of forest to farming, meant massive freshwater runoffs and siltation. This burden was too great for the oysters and worms and other creatures that were eaten by the bottom-feeding fish.

"The surprise," says Miller, "is that all the siltation probably created more marshland, but at the same time it altered the species composition of the Chesapeake. There's also no question that all the added freshwater runoff changed the salinity level of the water, and that helped change the kinds of fish that could be caught and eaten."

Consider oysters, a life-form that seems willing to grow and grow, at least until it encounters mankind. There are oyster-shell middens on the Potomac River, from about 500 B.C., that have samples at least a foot long: incredible, massive shells.

"We don't start out with those giant shells here," says Miller, "because St. Mary's had long been a cleared Indian settlement. The fact that it was cleared is what first attracted the *Ark* and the *Dove* in 1634."

Miller's trash pits tell us that from 1634, the start of the Maryland experiment, until about 1690–95, there's a decline in oyster size, from an average shell length of about 90 mm to 30 mm (3.5 to 1.2 inches). On a graph that registers shell size and population against time, it's obvious. Size declines as population rises. The colonists have harvested all the best oysters in the Potomac shallows around St. Mary's; there simply isn't enough time for large shells to grow. And then about 1695, when population drops off after the capital of Maryland moves to Annapolis, the shells found in the few remaining trash pits begin slowly to get larger again.

The rubbish pits also allow us to witness the evolution of the Chesapeake diet. There is, for example, a stunning revelation about the equality of meals across social class in the early seventeenth century. "There's a James River site," Miller says, "that contains both the Pettis Plantation and the Utopia Cottage site, the former a major-league Virginia planter, the other worked by tenants or possibly slaves. But the composition of the food bone—cattle, deer, fish—is identical at both households. This suggests meat is there for the taking and is not related to social status."

There is also the strange case of the disappearing fish. "Fish are a large part of the Indian diet," says Miller. "It looks like the colonists have adopted large chunks of that diet as their own, eating huge quantities of fish. But then there's a change. In the 1680s, fifty to sixty percent of the bones found in the pits are fish, but by the end of the eighteenth century throughout the Chesapeake fish are only three percent of the diet."

The question is, Is this change a simple response to declining natural abundance? Or a way of using diet to underscore social position, a rejection of the seventeenth century's subsistence or sharecropper cuisine, as if food were a sort of presentation of self, like fashion or architecture?

What fascinates me about [history] is that it owes nothing to fact. In that memory, atmosphere is more real than incident and everything is simultaneously actual and illusory.
          —BRIAN FRIEL, *DANCING AT LUGHNASA*, 1990

JOANNE BOWEN is a Williamsburg zooarchaeologist who specializes in interpreting faunal remains—animal bones—from the past, with an eye to what they can tell us about the raising, slaughter, and marketing of meat for the colonial table. Her data, like Rovner's and Miller's, come from refuse pits that contain "assemblages" of cow and sheep bones.

Her office is a scholar's boneyard—shelves and drawers groaning with antique bones from archaeological digs, plus a "reference" collection of modern animal bones begged and borrowed from local slaughterhouses. These days, faunal analysis depends on a relatively modern and clever observation: the age an animal died can be determined from its long bone development.

"The age at which a cow was slaughtered can tell us a great deal about colonial ecology," Bowen says. "Animal husbandry responds to market objectives. If people want to raise cows for milk, they slaughter their animals only after they've produced good cows and are no longer producing as much milk. So we'll find the bones of older cows. On the other hand, beef cattle are slaughtered as soon as they're mature and are no longer gaining weight rapidly. So, younger bones. . . . The age distribution of the animals killed at a site can shed a lot of light on the past. If people are raising animals for their own consumption, at a subsistence level, for oxen or beef or milk, they'll keep their animals a longer time. But if it's more of an enterprise supplying lots of meat for an urban setting like Hampton or Williamsburg, you'll see a different pattern in the age of the slaughter. There will be more younger animals."

Long bones are the key. Near each bone end there are "growing centers," soft cartilaginous sections that slowly ossify as the animal matures. By measuring how much the cartilage has hardened, Bowen can tell how old the cow was when it died.

"That's what the modern bone collection is for," she says, gripping a hefty cow femur. "I know that a bone with this level of ossification is about two years old."

Not that it's ever easy to peg the exact reasons for a younger killoff. For example, one of the by-products of a dairy is lots of calves, which drives the dairyman into harvesting veal. Again, lots of very young carcasses, but not necessarily associated with providing Williamsburg with meat commercially.

The point of all this age data is not merely to understand the origins of the colonial market economy. It also shows how the colonists used their land, and what the rural and urban setting might have been like. In the seventeenth-century Chesapeake, plantations focused on tobacco. If you'd taken the trouble, time, and money to clear a plot, you planted tobacco, not pasture. As the eighteenth century progresses, trash pits show more and more young bones, indicating a burgeoning beef-cattle business. This is also the time when urban areas are developing and tobacco farms are making way for more developed, contained pastures. Williamsburg must have been an attractive market.

The past is a mist.

—HAROLD PINTER, *MOONLIGHT*, 1993

HOW CAN WE imagine that there would be one settled History of the deep and abiding Past, when we find it nearly impossible to sort out what's going on in the here and now? People have long complained about this discrepancy.

Samuel Pepys, who was so troubled by history that he kept a diary (in cipher) for over a decade, was an early scourge of history's notorious unreliability. The year was 1667 and the burning question of the day was whether the duke of Buckingham would be destroyed in the political infighting:

> March 6th. Sir W. Penn told me, going with me this morning to White-hall, that for certain the Duke of Buckingham is brought into the Tower, and that he hath had an hour's private conference with the King before he was sent hither. . . .

Thence by coach to my Lord Crew's, where very welcome. Here I find they are in doubt where the Duke of Buckingham is; which makes me mightily reflect on the uncertainty of all history, when in a business of this moment and of this day's growth we cannot tell the truth.

NEVERTHELESS, this is a book about history. It's about the countless texts that bring the past to us—folklore, literature, phytoliths, pollen, monkey bones, and even a kind of personal archaeology that we scan for both the self-affirming anecdote and the scarifying time bomb. We swim in history.

The past is a resource. When we confront it, interpret it, the past has much to tell us about power, lifestyle, and the absolute presuppositions by which people live. It also tells us little things, of course, about what we once did or perhaps still do—when we find a red ear of corn. And that lets us in on how men and women once dealt—or perhaps still deal—with one another.

Epiphanies, however, only happen when we aggressively question history. In the end, no matter how many new facts and hard data we uncover about the past, the job of doing history always comes down to interpretation. Every generation finds itself in history, and finds it must then rewrite the history books to account for its priorities, its interpretive strengths and proclivities.

Point of view is no pitfall; it's a responsibility.

Children, I always taught you that history has its uses, its serious purpose. I always taught you to accept the burden of our need to ask why. I taught you that there is never any end to that question, because, as I once defined it for you . . . history is that impossible thing: the attempt to give an account, with incomplete knowledge, of actions themselves undertaken with incomplete knowledge. So that it teaches us no short cuts to Salvation, no recipe for a New World, only the dogged and patient art of making do.

—GRAHAM SWIFT, *WATERLAND*, 1983

Notes and Further Reading

For red ears of corn, see Brown, Item 8160. For the size of the African-American population, see Kevin Kelley, "The Demographic and Social Character of Williamsburg on the Eve of the Revolution," CWF memorandum, September 27, 1979. Dick Thorington of the Smithsonian's natural history museum identified the green monkey bones. Says he: "Green monkeys of West Africa are still common in the West Indies. They've gone feral. I'd be surprised if this one was not eaten; they certainly were in Africa." For more on the ecology of the Tidewater—siltation, rats, disease, clear-cutting—see my "Looking Into the Seeds of Time," *Colonial Williamsburg*, Autumn 1994.

For more on colonial market economies, see Joanne Bowen and Elise Manning, "Acquiring Meat in a Changing World," in *Archaeological Views of the Upper Wager Block, a Domestic and Commercial Neighborhood in Harpers Ferry*, ed. Jill Y. Halchin (Washington: National Park Service, 1994), 9-1 to 9-79. See also Henry M. Miller, *Killed by Wolves: Analysis of Two 17th Century Sheep Burials at the St. John's Site and a Commentary on Sheep Husbandry in the Early Chesapeake*, St. Mary's City Research Series No. 1 (1986).

For more on phytoliths, see Irwin Rovner, "Macro- and Micro-Ecological Reconstruction Using Plant Opal Phytolith Data from Archaeological Sediments," *Geoarchaeology* 3 (1988): 155–163. For Rovner's work on cow teeth, see "Extraction of Opal Phytoliths from Herbivore Dental Calculus," *Journal of Archaeological Science* 21 (1994): 469–473. See also his "Floral History by the Back Door: A Test of Phytolith Analysis in Residential Yards at Harpers Ferry," *Historical Archaeology* 28 (1994): 37–48.

Rovner's work has been aided by his partnership with John C. Russ, a physicist who designed artificial-intelligence expert-vision systems for recognizing and counting phytolith and diatom shapes on slides; see, for example, his "Object Recognition," chap. 9 of *Computer-Assisted Microscopy: The Mea-*

surement and Analysis of Images (New York: Plenum Press, 1990), 267-308. Philip L. Armitage was the first to suggest that phytoliths could be recovered from teeth; see "The Extraction and Identification of Opal Phytoliths from the Teeth of Ungulates," *Journal of Archaeological Science* 2 (1975): 187-197.

1. Life

DEATH

TAXES

GRAFFITI

HAIR

TOOTHBRUSHES

TEETH

HANDS

 Death

IT WAS ONCE firmly believed that the ghost of the last person to be buried had to guard the cemetery until the next village death, when the job could at last be turned over to a new ghost. Imagine then what happened—according to an eighteenth-century report from Argyll, Scotland—when two funerals were scheduled for the same day:

> Both parties staggered forward as fast as possible to consign their respective friend in the first place to the dust. If they met at the gate, the dead were thrown down till the living decided by blows whose ghost should be condemned to porter it.

Some things are worth fighting for. As this account suggests, the way we say a last good-bye to friends, relatives, and parents is one of them. History shows that man is determined to do the thing right, even though the funeral customs in effect at any one time or place seem to reflect centuries of ancient experience, involving accidents of religion, myth, superstition, art, and geography.

Take, for example, the matter of the funeral cortege. In modern times this involves automobiles, but with a single distinguishing feature: their headlights are on. (Note, in passing, that it's unlucky to count cars in a funeral procession—a belief that folklorists have recorded in modern North Carolina.) Today the lights indicate which cars belong in the procession, but they also have ancient roots.

Nighttime burial by torchlight was a Roman custom. Our word funeral is derived from the Latin *funes*, the waxed cords that were the wicks of classical torches. Even for the rare daytime burial among the Romans, a right reserved for important people, the torchlight procession was kept.

The torches also served as fire starters for the funeral pyre. (The Greeks and Romans practiced both cremation and inhumation— deposition of the whole body—at various times.) Cremation was practiced in two forms. In the first, the pyre was built over the grave itself, into which all the ashes would fall after the fire was doused with wine. In the second version of cremation, the bones that survived the fire would be gathered from the embers and stored in an urn, which would then be ceremonially buried.

A custom derived from the torches and pyres of the ancients that survived until recently is that of the funerary light tower. The best examples of these exist in southwestern France, where tall, hollow columns of stone, with an entrance at the bottom and a place for a light at the top, are used to indicate the sacred precincts of a cemetery. They are still called *lanternes des morts*.

Today's graveside ceremonies often include the placing of flowers or a pinch of dirt on the coffin. Virgil tells us the Romans put flowers on their dead, and Milton, Herrick, Gay, and Shakespeare all refer to the custom of laying flowers. Just after the line "With fairest flowers . . . I'll sweeten thy sad grave" from *Cymbeline* (1608), Shakespeare adds that in flowerless seasons, moss would do fine as a way to "winter-ground" the corpse, an allusion to the Jacobean gardener's habit of cold-mulching flowerbeds with moss.

Dirt thrown into a grave is considered liturgically to represent the biblical "ashes to ashes, dust to dust" notion, the cyclical nature of life and death. In the minds of many folklorists, however, the pinch of dirt was a reflection of the custom of burying gifts with the dead. Egyptian grave sites are famous for this, as are Roman and Greek sarcophagi. But even the most primitive societies practiced the bringing of gifts—as if to bribe the ghost of the dead. So the ceremonies surrounding burials and funerals are largely to protect the living from the discontented and suddenly envious dead. For some North American Indians, every relative is always sure to throw some article into the grave, if only a tiny bit of cloth. Among Christians, the custom declined to where a bit of earth would do. A southern folk custom is to bury any leftover medicine with the coffin, a tradition that seems to have a sarcastic edge to it—the worthlessness of the drugs has been proved with grim finality.

Graveyard dirt has special powers. An English writer in 1858 noted the usefulness of such dirt in determining whether the resident of a grave was wicked or good. If dust from a grave stirred in your open hand, it was thought the deceased led a wicked life, because "the wicked cannot rest anywhere, not even in the grave." Modern folklorists have recorded the use of graveyard dirt to dry up a well, to counteract an evil charm, or to hamstring an enemy by sprinkling it on the floor of his house.

At military funerals, the leaden grief is sometimes punctuated by a twenty-one-gun salute fired by a squad of riflemen (usually three shots each from seven soldiers). Invariably, just before this happens, the officer in charge discreetly leans over and warns the chief mourners to prepare for a loud report from the guns. And, just as invariably, everyone still flinches when the burst comes. Enough to wake the dead, you'd think.

But this is not merely an idle thought, for in it lies the key to the custom's origin: it *is* a last attempt at waking the dead. In the seventeenth century, before the widespread use of guns, a company of archers appeared at the funeral of a fallen comrade to shout three times over his grave. The Romans ritually made sure that death had occurred by calling the deceased's name three times and blowing horns. This practice is still kept today on the death of a pope.

The following newspaper account, from November 30, 1885, describes the triple shout at the great funeral of King Alfonso XII of Spain: "The Lord Chamberlain unlocked the coffin, which was covered with a cloth of gold, raised the glass covering from the King's face, then after requesting perfect silence, knelt down and shouted three times in the dead monarch's ear, 'Señor, Señor, Señor.' Those waiting in the church upstairs heard the call, which was like a cry of despair, for it came from the lips of the Duke of Sexto, the King's favorite companion. The Duke then rose, saying, according to ritual, 'His Majesty does not answer. Then it is true the King is dead.'"

Burial at sea is an option that seems to have been the funeral of choice for some societies, anathema for others. Odysseus' chief fear at one point in his wanderings is that he will drown, his body will be lost, and his soul will find no rest. By contrast, for the imperial years of England's Royal Navy, burial at sea was considered a major honor, and in fact contributed our present cliché "rise and shine." The idea is visible in the early nineteenth-century poem "On a Naval Officer Buried in the Atlantic":

No vulgar foot treads here,
No hand profane shall move thee,
But gallant fleets shall proudly steer,
And warriors shout, above thee.

And when the last trump shall sound,
And tombs are asunder riven,
Like the morning sun from the wave thou'lt bound,
To rise and shine in heaven.

On the long voyages of pilgrimage or trade in the Middle Ages, travelers who picked up mysterious diseases—or the plague—had sometimes to be disposed of overboard. This burial at sea gave rise to at least one significant place-name, Gravesend-on-Thames, which was the tidal limit on sea burials. During the Black Death, ships were forbidden to pass that point on their way up to London and were forced to unload downstream.

The final resting position of the corpse varies widely. Prehistoric graves often have bodies in a sitting position. Shakespeare's contemporary Ben Jonson was buried in Westminster Abbey vertically—so he would have a head start at the Day of Judgment. The Roman general Scipio Africanus ordered his burial so that he would face Africa and could continue to terrorize his arch adversaries, the Carthaginians.

Arctic Circle people have long practiced excarnation, exposing their dead till the flesh has been cleared away. It has to do with recycling the spirit back into Nature by way of the birds and winds that come to feast on it. (It also has to do with permanently frozen ground.) After the bleached bones are clean, they are solemnly buried. Returning the body to Mother Earth is so important that the folk motif known as the "grateful dead" is repeated across many cultures. The tale concerns a stranger who encounters a dead body and out of charity enables it to be buried. The ghost in corporeal guise then helps the stranger with anything he desires.

The custom of burying money with the deceased may have originated with the Greeks, who put coins in the mouths of their dead, coins intended to pay the ferryman Charon for the trip across the River Styx. The Romans changed the position of the coins to cover the eyes. Two other points about Roman funerals deserve mention because of their curiously modern viewpoint. A common Roman theme is the suggestion that death is a straightforward trip to nothingness, little more. A frequent Roman epitaph is the abbreviation *NF F NS NC,* for *non fui fui non sum non curo:* "I was not; I was; I am not; I care not." The other Roman custom was to have a sort of jester, an *archimimus,* accompany the funeral procession. His function was to mimic the dead man, to walk, talk, and act like him, to joke about him, even to wear a mask in his likeness.

The spirit of the *archimimus* lives on in the elaborate wake. In fact, the expense of funerals and wakes has been a recurrent concern because of the burden it placed on the public, especially the poor. Part of the reason for Roman laws limiting funerals to nighttime had to do with controlling the amount of panoply and feasting that could be put on. Private funerals were in danger of outdoing state ones. In England, all manner of strangers were expected to show up and eat and drink well at the funeral feast of even the poorest tenant farmer. Cockfighting and hunting were occasionally a part of the festivity, after which the body would be carted off to the cemetery, relatives and friends passing out drunk along the way.

Drinking, however, is what kept the wake on the minds of local divines: "The mourners," a sixteenth-century German noted, "mostly show mourning only in their dress, without any real grief in their hearts, as is evident from the feasting that goes on in the house, where costly viands and liquors are consumed in huge quantities until deep into the night; where the nearest relatives of the departed are forced to drink to intoxication for the good of the soul." Contrast that with the wake and burial of Thomas Hope, who died in 1793 in Petersburg, Virginia. He wanted, he said, "a Scotch burial, without parson's prayers or sermons; only give the attendants a repast, and acquaintance dirgie [a plain, sung funeral] at my expense."

The most surprising leftover from the customs and lore of death is the tale of the Widow of Ephesus, which furnished the basic outline for numerous folktales and was famously retold by Petronius and Voltaire. The widow is a woman of great beauty and faithfulness who vows to watch or "wake" with the body of her departed husband for five days and nights. As it happens, a handsome Roman soldier, who has been charged with guarding the cemetery against body snatchers, gradually falls in love with the woman, joins her in eating the ceremonial food, and even consummates the love match on the tomb of the departed. Unfortunately, during this dalliance, robbers steal a body from a nearby crucifixion site. Nothing daunted, the widow calmly substitutes the cadaver of her husband for the missing body, thereby preserving her new lover from certain death.

The necessity of not speaking ill of the dead has similarly given us a definitive tale, in this case an actual occurrence. The story concerns the infamous Mrs. Cresswell (1625–ca. 1699), a London prostitute and madam who left ten pounds in her will to the clergyman who would say her funeral oration, with the further condition that he say "nothing but what was well of her." At last, such a preacher was found. He opened his talk with a general discussion of death and concluded with: "By the will of the deceased it is expected that I should mention her, and say nothing but what was well of her. All that I shall say of her, therefore, is this: she was born well, she lived well and she died well; for she was born with the name Cresswell, she lived in Clerkenwell and Camberwell, and she died in Bridewell."

Notes and Further Reading

The funeral of Alfonso XII was covered in the *Daily News* (London), November 30, 1885, and reprinted in Hazlitt, 255. Hazlitt's book, by the way, is based on John Brand's *The Popular Antiquities of Great Britain* (London, 1813). Hazlitt is also the source (p. 254) of the Scots battle at the cemetery gates. For the importance of the "grateful dead" folktale, see Leach, 463–464. For the classical period, Smith is copious and reliable. Hazlitt, Brand, Leach, and Smith are mines of fascinating information, arranged alphabetically, that can be browsed over endlessly.

I'm a big fan of the short articles and letters printed in the antiquarian journal *Notes and Queries,* which began publication on November 3, 1849.

For the next seventy years it was a font for academics, divines, and independent scholars interested in archaeology, history, literature, classics, ethnology, folklore, philology, and anthropology. It continues today but is devoted solely to English literature. In this chapter, the poem on burial at sea is by H. F. Lyte (author of "Abide With Me"), printed in C. W. Penny's "The Sailor's Grave," *N&Q,* 5th series, XI:393–394 (May 17, 1879). See also John Pickford's "Flowers on Graves," *N&Q,* 8th series, III:314–315 (April 22, 1893) and Menyanthes' "Dust from a Grave," *N&Q,* 2nd series, VI:522 (December 25, 1858).

For graveyard dirt, see Brown, Item 5558 (to conjure wells) and Item 5501 (medicine buried with corpse). See also Item 5454 (counting cars in a funeral cortege). The quotation about German wakes is from Janssen, 406. For more on the Madam Cresswell story, see *DNB,* V:72. Thomas Hope's request for a Scotch burial is in *William and Mary College Quarterly,* VIII (1899–1900): 129.

Howard Colvin's *Architecture and the Afterlife* (New Haven: Yale University Press, 1992) elegantly traces the history of building as a memento mori. The modern funeral industry was skewered by Nancy Mitford in *The American Way of Death* (New York: Simon & Schuster, 1963) and in Evelyn Waugh's novel *The Loved One* (Boston: Little, Brown, 1948). The culture of death and dying has been thoroughly treated by Philippe Aries in *Images of Man and Death* (Cambridge: Harvard University Press, 1985) and *The Hour of Our Death* (New York: Oxford University Press, 1991).

 # Taxes

*But in this world nothing is certain but death
and taxes.*

—BEN FRANKLIN, 1789

THE TAX BURDEN that modern mankind groans under is no
newcomer to the list of life's complaints. We have been so chafed by
hateful taxes that no fewer than four historic milestones have been
tax revolts. Magna Carta, the English Civil War, and the American
and French Revolutions have all been about taxes. The truth is that
civil and religious leaders have *always* managed to collect money
from the people. A pattern of tributes, tithes, port duties, and excise
taxes on certain products is common to all cultures. Countless
Sumerian clay tablets and Egyptian granary receipts on limestone
flakes and papyrus attest to the practice.

Revenue collecting was so advanced among the Romans that
much of our diction relating to tax and accounting still corresponds
to theirs. The *fiscus,* the imperial treasury, took its name from the
Latin word for the money bags that separate tax accounts were held
in. An *exactor* was a tax collector, and an *assiduus* was an ostentatious tax or tribute payer, a word still used ironically.

Under Augustus Caesar, there was a separate military treasury
(aerarium militare) and public treasury *(aerarium saturni),* as
well as a special death duty of 5 percent that went toward military

pensions. There were even special names for special taxes, such as the *aedilicium*—the funds contributed by a province to sponsor the athletic games put on by a member of the ruling elite, an *aedile*.

So it was not for nothing that Queen Boudicea of East Anglia in Britain felt the fiscal strain and led a taxpayers' revolt in A.D. 61. Her remarks on that occasion are more than vaguely reminiscent of Patrick Henry's more than seventeen centuries later. "How much better to have been slain and to have perished than to go about with a tax on our heads! Yet why do I mention death? For even dying is not free of cost with them; nay, you know what fees we pay even for our dead. Among the rest of mankind death frees even those who are in slavery to others; only in the case of the Romans do the very dead remain alive for their profit. . . . "

Still, it was only a matter of time before Boudicea's descendants put on the cloaks of their Roman tax oppressors. In 1018 nearly a hundred thousand pounds was raised by King Cnut to bribe the Viking invaders away from the English coasts. Since the Anglo-Saxons considered the pirates "Danes," the tax was known as Danegeld. A few years later, the Danegeld was seen as so oppressive that the king's tax collectors were attacked and killed. In response, the king ordered the town of Worcester sacked—a penalty that must bring tears to the eyes of today's tax man.

Later taxes included a hearth tax, called a *fumage*, under which every household was required to pay for each of its hearths or chimneys. The year 1695 saw a similar window tax, a way of focusing the tax on the people with big houses—and pocketbooks. Architectural historians claim the tax produced a marked change in the design of buildings, to diminish the number of windows.

Port taxes seem to have been the most oppressive historically. Ships in trade, for example, were expected to pay such duties as *quayage, moreage, towage, terrage, strandage, anchorage, keelage, ballastage,* and *mensurage,* taxes whose names alone give some clue to their meaning. Not so clear are the taxes called *murage* (a city wall tax), *lastage* (payment for permission to load a ship), and *primage* (a harbor pilot's tax). There was even a payment called the *denier à Dieu,* God's penny, which enabled the tradesman to take leave of the customs agents and peddle his wares in another port.

Small wonder, then, that the English system of taxes was described as follows in 1769, on the eve of the American Revolution:

> The people are taxed in the morning for the Soap that washes their hands; at nine for the Coffee, the Tea, and the Sugar they use for their breakfast; at noon for the Starch that powders their hair; at dinner for the Salt that savours their meat; in the evening for the Porter that cheers their spirits; all day long for the Light that enters their windows; and at night for the Candles that light them to bed.

Probably the longest-running tax in western Europe was the tithe (literally a "tenth") extracted by the church. In fact, the parade toward modern taxation is largely the march from ecclesiastical and monastic tithes to municipal and national payments.

The system of tithing—giving a tenth of one's goods, produce, or cash to support religion—has ancient roots. At Olympia, site of the Greek athletic games, a statue of Nike was erected in celebration of a victory over the Spartans in 425 B.C. On the pedestal is inscribed an offer of one-tenth of the spoils from the war. Likewise, the Old Testament stipulates tithes from the faithful on grain, wine, and oil and later extends the tax to the fruit of trees, flocks, and herds. The New Testament is largely silent on the matter of tithes except for some criticism of the Pharisees for scrupulously and ostentatiously paying theirs. But that's the whole point about tithes: they're supposed to be freely given. It was not the least of the miscalculations of organized religions that they expected tithes to be openly granted without some little pride and strutting.

Although early theologians regarded the "expected" tithe as inconsistent with a sense of Christian charity, a church council at Macon in A.D. 585 firmly established it as a duty and set a punishment of excommunication for those who scoffed. Still, rules regarding the tithe varied wildly from parish to parish and from abbey to abbey throughout Europe. In some places, wheat would be cut, bundled, and left in the fields for the clergy to select every tenth sheaf.

Just such a custom was in place early in the nineteenth century, according to this 1865 letter: "When at a school near Shrewsbury, where the master was also rector of the parish, I can remember the schoolboys' assistance in the harvest collection, which was effected by placing a stick on every tenth sheaf in the cornfield, to be afterwards conveyed by the clergyman's team to his tithe barn."

Families sometimes brought their produce to the church or nearby barns. The great abbeys kept careful records of tithe contributions from the tenant farmers on monastic lands, and often cautioned gatekeepers to watch for "well winnowed and husked grain" and healthy cattle, sheep, and tithe-pigs.

It's in this connection that tithing has given posterity its greatest legacy. The tithe barns that dotted the medieval landscape required elaborate experiments to span their vast interiors. Architectural historians Walter Horn and Ernest Born saw in the tithe barn's wooden structure the rudiments of techniques that would later be tried in stone. These great buildings (typically three hundred feet long, seventy feet wide) are often cruciform in plan and have a central nave and two or four side aisles set off by pillars. Tithe barns were *ur*-cathedrals, fitting sites for the devout to bring and store the produce of their labor.

One such English tithe barn, at Great Coxwell, Berkshire, still exists and was considered by nineteenth-century poet and designer William Morris "the greatest piece of architecture in England." Perhaps the best commentary on the tithe barn comes from Thomas Hardy in *Far From the Madding Crowd* (1874):

They sheared in the great barn, called for the nonce the Shearing-barn, which on ground plan resembled a church with transepts. It not only emulated the form of the neighboring church of the parish, but vied with it in antiquity. . . . One could say about this barn, what could hardly be said of either the church or the castle, akin to it in age and style, that the purpose which had dictated its original erection was the same to which it was still applied. Unlike and superior to either of those two typical remnants of mediaevalism, the old barn embodied practices which had suffered no mutilation at the hands of time.

But not all tithes were payment in kind. The churchyard at Kirkby-Stephen, Westmoreland, was said to have a "very old" box tombstone, on which cash tithes were paid. It's on these premises— in the churchyard, on the church porch, or at the tithe barn—that another of the great customs connected with this tax appears: the tithe ale. Diarist John Evelyn records having attended one at a parish near Boston, Lincolnshire, on August 20, 1654. And William Cowper transfixed this social experience in his "Tithing Time at Stock, in Essex" (1790), a poem that neatly demarcates parson from plowman:

> *Oh, why are farmers made so coarse*
> *Or clergy made so fine?*
> *A kick, that scarce would move a horse,*
> *May kill a sound divine.*

Ales notwithstanding, the real problem with tithes was that they were so difficult to collect and enforce. Too many parishioners were on an honor system. Not always, though. A 1557 entry in the parish register at Whitney, Hereford, charges that each family bring in six cheeses annually to the church (three on the feast of St. John Baptist, three more on August 1), and further that this delivery be judged good and sufficient in the eyes of two "indifferent honest men" of the parish.

There was also the capricious nature of many tithe exemptions, vaguely akin to today's tax loopholes. One of the stranger exemptions fell to a family living in the parish of Renwick, Cumberland, whose forebears were said to have slain a "cockatrice" centuries ago. Plainly, the exemption was not commensurate with the exploit. A cockatrice, remember, was a great winged serpent that killed with its vision alone and whose killing range extended over great distances. In this case, a tax break was way too stingy a reward.

As with all loopholes, abuses were bound to occur. Perhaps the worst of them was the custom of selling the tithe rights of established parishes, abbeys, or colleges to investors. Churches were known to have sold their authority to collect tithes in perpetuity to raise cash to meet short-term needs. Under Henry VIII and the Tudors, tithe rights were also given away as government favors to powerful families, and sometimes resulted in the ironic prospect of lay owners who derived more income from church property than the church itself did.

This abuse was called "lay impropriation of tithes" and was apparently quite common, to judge from the number of court challenges that appeared over the centuries. Another custom was for parishes to sell the rights to the tithes that would be owed for the upkeep of a portion of the church—say, the chancel. Trouble arose when the new lay impropriators felt they actually owned the property itself, and so felt no compunction about "improving" it. There they built elaborate pews (with their backs to the altar), tombs, and memorials to themselves, sold seats to their friends, and entered and left the chancel by the priest's door.

A celebrated case in 1820 detailed the tribulations of a lay owner who was locked out of the church by the vicar to prevent him from remodeling the chancel. Nothing daunted, the man simply chopped a hole in the church roof, let himself down, and erected new seats. Truly, an assiduous *exactor*.

Notes and Further Reading

The Whitney cheeses are discussed by "C.J.R." in *N&Q*, 4th series, I:478 (May 23, 1868). For lay impropriation of tithes, see the contributions from Joseph Fisher in *N&Q*, 4th series, XI:374 (May 3, 1873) and from E. S. Taylor, *N&Q*, 2nd series, V:13 (January 2, 1858); for cutting through the roof, see H. T. Ellacombe, *N&Q*, 2nd series, V:96 (January 30, 1858). For the state of British taxation in 1769, see note by "W.P." *N&Q*, 8th series, IV:405 (November 18, 1893). The cockatrice is from "E.H.A." in *N&Q*, 2nd series, IV:490 (December 19, 1857).

Roman terms associated with taxation can be found in Lewis and Short. For English equivalents, see the *OED*. The list of port duties and other English taxes is available in Stephen Dowell's *A History of Taxation and Taxes in England*, 4 vols. (London: Longmans, Green, 1884). See also G. L. Harriss, *King, Parliament, and Public Finance in Medieval England to 1369* (Oxford: Clarendon Press, 1975).

For Egyptian tax records, see A. E. Samuel et al., *Death and Taxes: Ostraka in the Royal Ontario Museum* (Toronto: Hakkert, 1971). Horn and Born discuss tithe barns and tithing in II:222, II:282, III:113, and III:115.

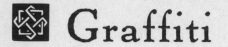 # Graffiti

EVERY TEXT CAN SPEAK to the future—even wall scratchings, the texts from the past we call graffiti.

Graffiti are, of course, a kind of vandalism, and have always been. And therein lies their power. They are the voice of the powerless, the midnight ravings of the crazed and subversive who feel they have no other outlet. The rich have terrific leverage over history—their art, buildings, and books dominate what we know about the past simply because good things, valuable things, well-made things outlast the vernacular and the ephemeral. Graffiti defeat that at a stroke, hitchhiking on the walls of the good to bring an alternative past to light.

Some otherwise anonymous Pompeians, for example, are known to us today because of what they wrote on tavern walls two thousand years ago. Wilhelmina Jashemski's comprehensive survey of the buried town includes the following, a few late-night jottings on the wall about a tavern owner and his watered-down wine:

> *Landlord, may your lies malign*
> *Bring destruction on your head!*

You yourself drink unmixed wine,
Water sell your guests instead.

Elsewhere in Pompeii, a tavern on the Via di Nola must have been the meeting place of the cloth fullers. We know this because a fuller named L. Quintilius Crescens celebrated a night on the town with his fellow workers by writing on the wall, "Crescens and his com panions sing to the fullers and the owl." Included with the text is a crude graffito of an owl, the sacred mascot of the fullers. The drawing is so shaky that another hand felt compelled to explicate it: "It's an owl."

Other Roman graffitists complained about their ill turns of fate at dice, and accused their hosts of cheating. Can you imagine someone trying that today at Las Vegas? Of course you can, and when you imagine that you're doing history. Rising, sore, from the craps table and walking directly to the lounge wall with chisel in hand? It's the past, and it's you.

Graffiti hold out clues to intimate details of daily life that do not survive in other ways. In England, scholar Violet Pritchard made a career out of collecting the incised scribblings on medieval churches and monasteries. Her *English Medieval Graffiti* is a classic that gives us, for example, two fourteenth-century churches that have dice scratched onto their walls. Gambling, it seems, was proper for church, especially in an era when popular entertainments—think of Chaucer or the medieval mystery plays—were a real part of religious life. There are countless chessboards and merels boards (a jumping game like checkers) cut into the sills and stone benches of monasteries.

The distinguishing marks of Pritchard's medieval graffiti are a solid draftsmanship and a dependable, sometimes elegant, Latin calligraphy. In fact, it's changes in handwriting styles and conventions—spelling, abbreviations—that allow historians to date these texts, along with the age of the buildings themselves. And there is something substantial about these medieval graffiti that the scratchings of later ages do not have. For this reason scholars believe that priests—the one segment of medieval society that could uniformly read and write—were responsible for most of them.

The church at Ashwell, Hertfordshire, is loaded with such texts. There is, for instance, a chilling record of the Black Death: *"Primula pestis in M ter CCC fuit L minus uno,"* which translates as "The first plague of the 1300s was in the year '50 minus one." Three feet lower on the inside wall of the church tower, another disaster: a mighty wind *(ventus validus),* a hurricane, that ravaged England on St. Maurus's Day, January 15, 1361, destroying buildings, blowing down towers, and killing a great many people. "The heavens thundered," wrote the chronicler: *"oc anno maurus in orbe tonat MCCCLXI."*

Even lower on the wall is a detailed incised drawing of a large, steepled abbey church or cathedral. It has been identified as either old St. Paul's in London, the one destroyed by fire in 1666, or Westminster Abbey. Ecclesiastical records show that Ashwell parish was a dependency of Westminster before the Reformation. In either case, this graffito gives the world a truly unique view of things that are changed.

In the south arcade of Ashwell, the second pillar has an interesting proverb: *"ebrietas frangit quicquod sapiencia tangit"*—"Drunkenness breaks what wisdom makes"—in an oddly sprawling fifteenth-century hand. Was the hand that wrote this palsied from drink?

Another class of graffiti is associated with a cry for attention, with people who are merely saying, "We were here." That impulse has been around as long as the handprints in the caves of Altamira and Lascaux. For every such bit of ancient graffiti the hand that wrote it is no more, an obvious fact that nevertheless adds a sublime note to our disapproval. To understand all is to forgive all.

The closer we get to our own day, with its legions of spray-painters, the less patient we are. The earliest negative reaction to graffiti known to me appeared in the pages of *Notes and Queries,* the clearinghouse for literary and archaeological tidbits, in 1859. The writer, who signed his contribution CL. HOPPER, was describing an intricate marble memorial, ca. 1355, in a Hungerford, Berkshire, church. Trouble was, Hopper was having a hard time reading the slab. After a few paragraphs, it came down to this: "The tablet has suffered much from wanton defacement, the first-mentioned square inscription being difficult to be deciphered. One of the spoilers has perpetuated his name and date near the bottom." **Willm Yong, 1616.** Think of it, in the year Shakespeare was dying, two counties away William Yong was hard at it with a sharp, pointed implement.

Sad to say, **Willm Yong, 1616**—surely one of the earliest graffiti goons ever to be assigned both a name and an exact date—had a great many imitators. A whole boatload of them, in fact, seem to have crossed the Atlantic and settled in Williamsburg, Virginia. There they did their thing on one of the finest of the town's buildings, the Public Records Office.

The PRO, just outside the walls of the Capitol yard, is a sturdy three-room affair meant to hold the Colonial Secretary, his deputies, and clerks in fireproof and verminproof security. It was elegantly constructed in Flemish bond brickwork with alternating glazed headers and with semicircular steps rising to an elaborate, almost ceremonial, doorway. The building was erected just after the 1747 fire that destroyed the first colonial capitol building and its papers.

Part of the building's charm is a delicate rubbed- and gauged-brick surround at the front door, a spot so inviting it inspired generations of Williamsburgers to do their imitation of **Willm Yong.** Here you can read many of the great names associated with the town's history, all incised deeply in the soft brick.

There's **J. Waller 1776.** That would be John Waller, the third child of Benjamin Waller, trained by his father as a clerk in that very

Public Records Office. There's also a **B WER,** probably Benjamin Waller, the lad who grew up to be a delegate in the Virginia statehouse. There's a **GWMaupin N89,** who must be George Washington Maupin, son of a keeper of the powder magazine; the year is signed Masonic style, with an N replacing the 17. So it goes, with nearly ninety entries, including the best of Williamsburg families— Pages, Blairs, Carters, and more. Some names, however, are much harder to identify, such as the ambiguous **AR 1774,** which could be either Alexander Reid, Abraham Roberts, Archibald Rose, or any of three Anthony Robinsons alive at the time.

Say this for colonial graffiti: They are finely wrought, most in all capitals or italic caps, some with delicate serifs on their tips making them easy to read. The lettering is as clear and precise as the town newspaper. Literacy has plainly spread beyond the priestly class of the middle ages. And all those **AR**s are still alive to us.

Notes and Further Reading

For English medieval graffiti, see Pritchard, 86 and 145. Appendix III, Ashwell Church, is by Bruce Dickens; see pp. 181–183.

See also Cl. Hopper, "Hungerford Family," *N&Q,* 2nd series, VIII:464 (December 10, 1859) and Wilhelmina Jashemski, *The Gardens of Pompeii* (New Rochelle, N.Y.: Caratzas, 1979), 179. The research files at CWF list the names and initials on the doorway of the Public Records Office; see RR 1372 Bullock, H1 272.

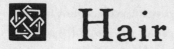 # Hair

THE DEBATE over how to wear hair—for both men and women—has coiled throughout recorded time. Should men's be short or long? Should women's be bound up in braids, hidden under a wimple, or allowed to flow in provocative tresses? Should men be bearded or clean shaven? As soon as any one generation gets a handle on these questions, its rebels and gainsayers magically appear, bearing either scissors or curling irons, to do pitched battle.

The English Civil War (1642–1651) is a case in point, and is clearly the watershed event in the history of modern hair fashion. As every schoolchild remembers, this bit of antique carnage pitted the Royalist forces under the elaborately coiffed King Charles I against the Parliamentary forces under Oliver Cromwell. The followers of Cromwell, largely Puritan in spirit, had their heads close cropped, an act of defiance to the curls and ringlets of the king's men. In the end, the rebellious Roundheads—as they were derisively called—conquered the dandified longhairs. And with that victory, the Roundheads left a palpable legacy. The majority of modern men have opted for short hair. It is quite possible that, had the Royalists won, not only would King Charles have kept his head, but my own locks would now be dangling down to the level of the keypad in front of me as I write.

But if the wig or the mane of elaborate curls connotes self-satisfaction and vanity, and cropping the hair is a symbol of reaction and intolerance, as the English experience shows, what can be said of shaving the head? Beginning about the eighth century, Christians adopted an earlier custom of shearing the hair of laymen about to be consecrated into the clerical state. This rite was called the "tonsure" (from the Latin *tondere,* "to shear") and gradually evolved into three forms.

In the eastern Mediterranean, the whole head was shaved or very closely cropped and was called the "tonsure of St. Paul." Farther west, in the Roman Church, the "tonsure of St. Peter" left its adherents with just a fringe or circle of hair about a bald center, a custom still followed by some monastic orders to this day. Both tonsures were a sign of penitence, humility, and obedience to church leaders. Since St. Peter was so firmly associated, in the minds of early Christian artists, with his triple denial of Christ on the night of his Lord's arrest, he came to be usually depicted with a tonsure. Theresa Coletti of the University of Maryland, a specialist in medieval illuminated manuscripts, points out that "in any group of figures surrounding Christ, such as at the Last Supper, the one with the tonsure is normally a penitent St. Peter."

This was an important sign for the devout. Since St. Peter's fault was rehearsed every year on Holy Thursday—indeed is still repeated daily in the sacrifice of the Mass—his sin symbolized the mistakes of all mankind. Through forgiveness, St. Peter triumphed over evil, a point that would be immediately clear to the faithful through the simple medium of the tonsure.

For the ancient Celtic churchmen—those defiant zealots who huddled in their beehive cells and protected medieval culture against the onslaughts of the Vikings and other barbarians—an even more radical tonsure was chosen. It consisted of shaving the top of the head in front of a line drawn from ear to ear. The hair in back was allowed to grow long, and certainly must have given those men a crazed appearance, which may have had something to do with their survival. In time, the tonsure became more than just a symbol of religious dedication. Chaucer used it to indicate the wisdom that was dispensed by clerics. At Canterbury in December 1170, the fatal blow that transformed Thomas Becket from archbishop to martyr was said to have landed on his tonsure. The location of the wound elevated a political act into the realm of sacrilege.

Shaving facial hair is surprisingly antique. Although the Gillette safety razor is a nineteenth-century invention and the straight razor descends from the Renaissance, a double-sided copper-alloy razor was recently found in a South London dig near Croydon. Shaped like a fan or a ping-pong paddle, it was dated to the Late Bronze Age, probably the eighth or ninth century B.C. Does this mean that early man was shaving? Probably, although the razors could have been ceremonial. The point is, modern cultural ideas about facial hair are hoary: the hairy face was wilder, more natural, masculine; and the smooth face more civilized, circumspect, feminine. The evolution toward a more rational, urban culture is on view in those Croydon razors.

In any case, a person's spirit was often thought to be embodied in his or her hair. The survival of such a belief is visible in the Scottish children's game called tappie-tousie, here described by an early folklorist: "One, taking hold of another by the forelock of his hair, says to him, 'Tappie, tappie tousie, will ye be my man?' If the other answers in the affirmative, the first says, 'Come to me then, come to me then,' giving him a smart pull towards him by the lock which he holds in his hand. If the one who is asked answers in the negative, the other gives him a push backward, saying, 'Gae fra me then, gae fra me then.'" Literally, tappie-tousie means "disheveled hair," from *tap* (the top of the head) and *tousie* (tousled or rumpled).

The game harbors a dim memory of the ancient custom of taking hold of a bondman's hair to receive him into servitude, a secular version of the religious tonsure. Further, because it was such a humiliation to have an enemy seize you by the hair, medieval Teutonic laws imposed stiff fines for this particular breach of the peace. On its face, the crime seems trivial to modern sensibilities, but even a cursory look at the weight of penitence and servitude behind the custom quickly shows why the fine in Saxony was 120 shillings for pulling someone's hair.

The belief that a person's spirit resided in the hair gave rise to countless folk customs. Among them: That you should bury your hair to prevent it from falling into the possession of your enemies. That a dead man's hair could be used to poison a rival. That if mice gathered your hair and used it to line their nests, you'd either get headaches or become an idiot (a Russian belief). In England, if a bird, especially a pie, made a nest of your hair, you would die. The Nandi, an East African tribe, shaved the heads of prisoners and kept the hair to ensure good behavior. They would return the hair only when the warriors were ransomed.

Nor are these customs restricted to times past. The Frank C. Brown collection of North Carolina folklore, compiled up through the 1960s, records numerous instances of human hair being used in charms, spells, and superstitions. "If you carry a lock of hair of a person, you will have power or control over that person." Likewise, "if a ten-penny nail and some hair is placed under the steps, witches cannot come into the house." More? "A spell was usually worked by means of a conjure ball buried in the victim's path. Bent pins and human hair seem to have been the commonest ingredients, though they were reported to contain snakes' tongues, lizard tails, ground puppy claws, and so on down the gruesome gamut." And finally, "a hair tied to a string, and placed prominently around a spring, will conjure a spring, and work harm on anyone drinking the water." This last was reported in the Durham, North Carolina, *Herald-Sun,* October 22, 1939.

Armed with this kind of understanding, it is instructive to take another look at the Samson and Delilah episode in the Old Testament. Samson, as a folk hero, is similar to the Roman Hercules and the Babylonian Gilgamesh. All three are strong and hairy men who undertake adventures outside their own societies, and all of them tangle barehanded with lions, animals as fierce and wild-maned as themselves. When Delilah enlists a confederate to cut her sleeping lover's hair, she is acting in accord with the recognized fact that strength is bound up in the hair, a belief exhibited in ceremonies ranging from England and France to India and Indonesia. Even the Aztecs cut the hair of sorcerers, to take away their strength and witchcraft, before executing them.

Christianity has elevated to sainthood four people whose connection with hair is essential. Mary Magdalene, the brazen beauty of the wild red locks, showed her conversion to the good life by drying the Savior's feet with her hair. She is often depicted clothed solely in her hair, like some devout Rapunzel. An Italian portrait of the fourteenth century shows her totally covered in hair, and in the sixteenth century Titian presented her mantled in a cloud of the red hair he gave his name to. Similarly, the virgin martyr St. Agnes, when she was stripped and driven naked into the streets of Rome by an outraged governor in A.D. 304, simply let down her abundant hair, which continued growing to cover her shame.

The fourth-century desert hermit St. Onuphrius so turned his back on the world that he neither shaved nor cut his hair, and wore only an apron of palm leaves. So fearsome was his hairy presence that a traveling abbot was almost driven away at the sight of this wild man, thinking him a satyr. Onuphrius's legend records that at his death, two lions came out of the wilderness—that's how wild and woolly the saint was—and docilely dug his grave.

But by far the most charming of all the sacred hair-raising tales appears in the legend of St. Wilgefortis, as told by the nineteenth-century scholar Sabine Baring-Gould: "The story of this Saint is almost too absurd to be given. She was the daughter of a king of Portugal. . . . Her father desired to marry her to the king of Sicily, but Wilgefortis had taken a vow of perpetual virginity. She therefore prayed, and a beard, mustache and whiskers, sprouting on her face, indisposed the prince of Sicily to accept her hand. Her father, in a rage, had her crucified." It must be said that enough people found the story sufficiently unabsurd that the saint's feast day is celebrated each year on July 20 and her statue in limestone adorns Henry VII's chapel in Westminster Abbey.

Another hair-religion link is found in the hair shirt. The wearing of these painful garments was seen by St. Jerome as a distinctive mark of penitence among Eastern monks and hermits. Others were not so sure. St. John Cassian denounced the practice as an ostentatious display of virtue. Typically, a hair shirt was made from mountain goat or camel hair and was called *cilicia* in Latin, named after the land where the cloth originated. Western European churchmen in time ceased to mention their shirts, considering them an occasion of pride. Thomas Becket was a model of discretion: his habit of concealing a hair shirt under his vestments was discovered only at his death.

Back in the realm of folklore associated with hair is the proverbial "hair of the dog that bit you." It is a commonplace of folk medicine, precursor of homeopathy, that a cure should be derived from the agent of the disease. For instance, dog liver or dog hair is applied to cure a dog bite. It follows that a small shot of schnapps the morning after should cure a hangover. The belief appeared in print in 1546:

I pray thee let me and my fellow have
A haire of the dog that bit us last night.

And what of no hair at all, baldness? In Caesar's case it is said that was the spur that drove him to great exploits, to gain the imperial laurel that would hide his lack of hair. In fact, his baldness was a badge of superiority, as witness this doggerel attributed to Caesar's troops:

Romans, lock up your wives,
Mind where they're bedded.
We've come back in triumph,
With a lecher bald-headed.

The all-time champion bald guy is one Matthew Robinson (1712–1800), the eighteenth-century character captured by Dame Edith Sitwell in *English Eccentrics* (1957). In middle age, Robinson became Lord Rokeby. Freed from his family's chains, he set out to distinguish himself. Though completely bald, he grew a beard that extended to his knees. He once received a visitor in his bathhouse face down on the floor, his beard poking out from between his armpits. He was known as a wild hermit who bathed himself and his hair daily in the sea near Hythe no matter what the weather until he fainted and had to be dragged from the water by his servants. Late in life, Lord Rokeby redeemed his reputation by penning a series of well-received political pamphlets.

His sister, Mrs. Elizabeth Montagu, the elegant friend of Dr. Johnson and Horace Walpole, was so relieved that she wrote the following, in an age where a great beard was a sure sign of obdurate eccentricity: "Julius Caesar exercised his valor in early youth, that he might hide the defect of baldness under the conqueror's wreath. I think Mr. Robinson's [Lord Rokeby's] hair wants an honourable cover as much as any baldness can do, and I am glad he has covered it with bays. There is no man in the world to whom such a proof of talents is more important. If a man shows genius, people think all his oddities are the excrescences of genius."

Notes and Further Reading

The Bronze Age razor is among the finds discussed by Geoff Potter in "15-17 Brighton Road, Croydon: The Investigation of a Prehistoric and Roman Site," *London Archaeologist* VII (1994): 234. Caesar's baldness is celebrated by Suetonius in *Lives of the Caesars,* I, §51. For St. Onuphrius see Baring-Gould, 6:150, and Ferguson, 137. St. Wilgefortis appears in Baring-Gould, 8:488–489. See John Butler, *The Quest for Becket's Bones* (New Haven: Yale University Press, 1995) for details of the martyr's death wound.

North Carolina folklore has a great deal to do with hair; see, for instance, Brown, Items 5549, 5555, 5614, 5620, and 5655. Hair is also important in Frazer, and in T. F. Thistleton Dyer's *The Folk-lore of Shakespeare* (New York: Harper & Bros., 1884). For "hair of the dog" see Leach, 474.

C. R. Hallpike's "Social Hair," *Man* 4 (1969): 256–264, is a solid discussion of the psychology behind hair symbolism. The hair shirt is explored in a contemporary context in J. F. Powers's *Wheat That Springeth Green* (New York: Knopf, 1988); I am indebted to Neil Isaacs for this citation.

A version of this chapter appeared in *Smithsonian,* November 1982. Shortly thereafter, I received a letter from Benjamin Boyce of Duke University, who offered a number of interesting contradictions on the issue of hair and the English Civil War. "The Puritans were indeed called Roundheads briefly in the mid-1640s, especially by hostile pamphleteers. But Lucy Hutchinson (born 1620) says it was only the extremists among the king's enemies who adopted the rule of 'a quarter of an inch to the skull.' If one may judge from contemporary portraits, men often wore their hair long enough just not to cover the lobe of the ear. Almost the only man of the time whom I have found painted with a short-cropped head is, oddly enough, that fierce royalist Archbishop Laud. (His head was removed on the block by order of the Puritans in 1645.)"

▧ Toothbrushes

WE ARE ACCUSTOMED to brushing our teeth every day. We know it to be a healthful ritual that preserves our teeth and gums and widens our smile. Its benefits are personal as well as social. But an archaeologist working among the remains of eighteenth-century Annapolis has suggested a new view of how and why we came to all this brushing and flossing and fussing. Toothbrushes, it turns out, were instrumental in easing us into the Industrial Revolution.

Mark Leone and his team of urban archaeologists have been digging under the streets of Annapolis since 1981. Among over a million artifacts, they've found numerous toothbrushes. Considered as a group, these artifacts illustrate how the rational mind-set of the eighteenth century not only gave us the seeds of our Constitution but also fostered a society that was eager to leave its agricultural past and settle into the urban clock-watching ways of the factory hand.

Leone considers archaeology part of anthropology, which attempts to reconstruct or understand culture, not history. Its emphasis is not on what some few people, if any, knew, but on what everyone had to know—sometimes intuitively, sometimes subconsciously—in order to act at all. To Leone, a toothbrush is a cultural artifact, not just a bit of history poking up from the past.

Eighteenth-century toothbrushes suggest a new emphasis on personal hygiene and the notion of the self-maintained individual. It's important: to have workers arrive on time and do a job, they have to develop discipline. So society emphasizes toothbrushes and a lot of other things like combs, clocks, cups, and toilet equipment to help people make themselves orderly. A study of fifteen Annapolis toothbrushes dating from 1750 to 1820, done by archaeologist Paul A. Shackel, shows how these implements themselves became more standardized. Made of either pig bristles or horsehair, their bristle holes get progressively more similar in diameter, depth, and arrangement on their handles as the century wears on.

The toothbrush is a late invention. The word first appeared in English print only six decades or so before the first Annapolis examples—in the autobiography of Anthony Wood, who speaks of buying a toothbrush from a certain J. Barret in 1690. From mid-century until the late 1700s, the Annapolis toothbrushes show hand-drilled holes that are irregular and unpredictable in their placement. But by about 1800, the holes are cut in tighter and more controlled patterns and the handles are smoothly turned on a lathe. Soon the brushes become so regular they are indistinguishable. People seem to be carving their initials on them to keep track of their own. (Even our third president took part in this. The polished-bone handle of a toothbrush clearly marked THOS JEFFERSON was uncovered in a 1988 dig near the Governor's Palace in Williamsburg.)

Over time, toothbrush designs clearly show the rise of mass production and standardization. Adam Smith predicted this: As population rises, workers specialize in certain products, turning them out more efficiently by making more and more exact copies. In turn, the people who buy and use such products expect them to be standardized and familiar. Owning them makes people feel a part of a larger whole, a society.

That larger whole, in colonial Annapolis, was a new class of people who were willing and eager to work for someone else. Toothbrushes had become part of a complex of ideas and artifacts that
engendered the basic working habits of capitalism. This is the part
of our history that Americans know the least about, but ought to be
most interested in, since most of us still make money for someone
else. "It's what Annapolis can show most clearly," Leone says, "because this was always a city devoted to the pursuit of profit."

Indeed it was. Colony capital, shipbuilding center, and seaport,
Annapolis had its own tea party in 1774, just months after the famous event in Boston harbor—a more virulent one, too, for the An-
napolitans of the day burnt the ship to the waterline as well as
steeping Chesapeake Bay in English tea.

A display of eating utensils from beneath Annapolis also speaks
volumes on the transformation of colonial society. In the exca-
vating, Leone and his colleagues noticed that, as the eighteenth
century progressed, communal eating from plates and bowls disappeared, being replaced first by randomly sized plates and then by
matched sets of chinaware. At first this seems paradoxical, because
china sets remind people at every meal that they're individuals as
well as members of an emerging new kind of society.

"The function of this sort of individualism within colonial capitalism," says Leone, "is to convince people that they're autonomous
and have a will. The table settings show that even the poor are
pulled into this way of thinking, whereas realistically they're not autonomous. They've been absorbed into capitalism as productive
rent payers, workers, and consumers."

In this way, people were willingly teased away from the slow and
inexorable routines of the growing season, which may have been
crowded with chores but were also cyclical, comforting, pre-
dictable. The idea was to create a new lifestyle, a new ethos, a new
way of dealing with the disruption in what used to be the daily
round.

According to probated wills preserved in the Maryland Hall of Records and studied by Lois Green Carr, Annapolis went through a major realignment of wealth holding after 1720. Leone thinks this means that the rich dominated the middle class and the poor. Eighty percent of the wealth was held by 15 percent of the people by 1735.

"Within less than a generation," Leone says, "the Annapolis rich had aggrandized themselves dramatically at the expense of people who were literally their neighbors. The money came from financially disenfranchising the middle class. The city's wills show that the middle classes were tapped out."

When that happens today, there's constant murmuring and resistance: "It's the economy, stupid." The question is, Why wasn't there a rebellion then? Why didn't the American Revolution happen forty years earlier than it did? The answer has to do with the fact that the rich had begun to introduce a number of new practices—including the toothbrushing and the mealtime etiquette—that buttressed the idea that everyone was an individual. Everyone could succeed, indeed prosper, if he or she would exercise an appropriate degree of personal discipline.

Another surprising factor that tended to justify the position of the moneyed class among Annapolis society of the day was a growing patrician interest in natural science. An example of such activity was a rare greenhouse hypocaust that's still visible today under the Governor Calvert House, now a restored inn. Based on classical Roman models, the hypocaust was a sort of forced warm-air heating system that artificially provided a salubrious climate for plants in a greenhouse.

There are colonial hypocausts elsewhere—at Wye Island in Maryland, at Dumbarton Oaks in Georgetown. But this one is remarkable because it's one of the earliest in America (built between 1720 and 1730, abandoned about 1750). The greenhouse and hypocaust were associated with the governing Calvert family. For them it was part of "rule by ostentation," as Leone calls it. When the position of the newly rich was tenuous, they tried showmanship to bolster it.

This was dabbling, not science at all, Leone thinks. It was a form of prestidigitation, a way of demonstrating that you had a right to control society because you could control Nature. You could take a pineapple from the tropics and grow it in temperate Maryland.

The horticultural element is paralleled by archaeological remains of other scientific playthings: clocks, weathervanes, barometers. These are the political instruments of those who hold wealth insecurely, not the decorative arts of the old rich with taste. Like their massive houses, they are symbols rather than implements.

Notes and Further Reading

For more on Annapolis, see my article in *Historic Preservation,* June 1986. The discovery of Jefferson's toothbrush is discussed by Marley Brown III in "Thomas Jefferson's Toothbrush," *Colonial Williamsburg,* Winter 1988–89: 12-13.

See Mark P. Leone, "The Georgian Order as the Order of Merchant Capitalism in Annapolis, Maryland," chap. 7 of *The Recovery of Meaning: Historical Archaeology in the Eastern United States,* eds. Mark P. Leone and Parker B. Potter, Jr. (Washington: Smithsonian Institution Press, 1988), 235–261. See also Paul A. Shackel, *Personal Discipline and Material Culture* (Knoxville: University of Tennessee Press, 1993).

The historian E. P. Thompson was a pioneer in the cultural study of the working classes; see his "Time, Work-Discipline, and Industrial Capitalism," *Past and Present* 38:56–97.

 # Teeth

IF THE TOOTHBRUSH is a symbol (and a text), then teeth certainly are. They form a defensive barrier for the inner you against the world. And they go before you do. Losing a tooth is a small intimation of mortality.

The Latin for tooth is *dens, dentis.* In classical architecture, for instance, the boxlike projections running in a row beneath a cornice are called dentils. Although they were intended to symbolically represent the tips of the roof rafters, they more accurately resembled teeth, just as the projections on a gear wheel or a saw do: they're all teeth.

One of the masterpieces of medieval art, *The Martyrdom of St. Apollonia* by the French court painter Jehan Fouquet (1420–1481), deals with teeth, specifically their extraction. Apollonia was put to death in A.D. 249 in Alexandria, but not before having her teeth pulled out one by one. Not surprisingly, in later centuries she was invoked by people with toothaches, and became the patron saint of the first dentists, the barber-surgeons.

Her iconography also was used to name the dentist's tooth-pulling tool, the pelican. Medieval people thought the pelican was a bird that pierced its breast to feed its young with its own blood.

The image was everywhere in the Middle Ages, in stained glass, in manuscripts, on the limestone cathedrals. The pelican's blood-stained chest became a symbol of martyrdom and so the instrument for pulling Apollonia's teeth, drawn extra large by Fouquet, was called a pelican. To drive home the point, the artist included the pelican bird in the bottom of his painting.

The connections between teeth and language are many. The Romans thought the mouth a magical part of the body, for only there were a person's bones visible. The teeth were a species of bone to them. The Latin word for mouth is *os,* same as the word for bone—think of osteoporosis or osso buco. There were Latin names too for specific teeth: *primores,* the front teeth; *canini,* the canines; and *maxillares,* the jaw teeth, grinders.

The Romans also had toothpowder *(dentifricium)* and tooth-picks *(dentiscalpium)*, as well as false teeth. We know this last from both archaeological remains and Roman law. Whereas one statute forbade excess expense at funerals as wasteful, another allowed the gold settings of false teeth to be burned as part of cremation rites.

Teeth occur in a surprising number of classical metaphors and proverbial sayings. *Albis dentibus deridere aliquem* means to show the whites of one's teeth, or to laugh heartily at a fool. *Vinere sub dentum* means to come under the teeth or jaws of some evil force. And *dentem pro dente,* a tooth for a tooth, is how the Gospel of Matthew describes Old Testament justice in the Vulgate; the phrase occurs in Exodus and Deuteronomy as well.

"To look a gift horse in the mouth" appeared in print in an English proverb in 1546, although the exact phrase then was "given horse." The year 1663 saw the first appearance of "gift horse." The expression "tooth and nail" was used by Sir Thomas More in 1534, and Tennyson sang of "Nature, red in tooth and claw" in 1850. As a metaphor for resolution in the face of impossible odds, Shakespeare has Henry V cry, just before the battle of Agincourt, "Now set the teeth, and stretch the Nosthrill wide."

The parade of such conceits is endless. "Hen's teeth" are rare indeed and a "colt's tooth" signifies childish and wanton behavior. The mammoth Bowie knife was known as an "Arkansas toothpick"—one of the high points of American slang, closely followed by "tooth carpenter" as an epithet for a dentist.

In A.D. 17 an earthquake in Asia Minor uncovered many fossil relics. From these remains a huge tooth, over a foot long, was sent to Rome for Emperor Tiberius to marvel at. When that monarch was then asked if the rest of the body should be sent along, Tiberius respectfully declined to further disturb the repose of what he took to be the bones of a race of giants.

That same wisdom, unfortunately, cannot be attributed to the greedy men who took part in the obscene search for the bones of poet John Milton in London in 1790. On August 4 of that year, the floor of the parish church of St. Giles Cripplegate submitted to the spade. Before long, a lead sarcophagus was uncovered; the wooden coffin that was once inside it had completely decomposed in the years since the poet's death in 1674.

From a contemporary account of the disinterment, we learn that the bones and hair were remarkably well preserved, although the rib cage collapsed when the shroud was touched. But by far the greatest treasures for the defilers were Milton's teeth. According to the original account, "Mr. Fountain told me that he pulled hard at the teeth, which resisted, until some one hit them a knock with a stone, when they easily came out. There were but five in the upper jaw, which were all perfectly sound and white. . . . Mr. Laming told me that he had, at one time, a mind to bring away the whole under-jaw, with the teeth in it; he had it in his hand, but tossed it back again."

To this day, we have no idea what happened to those teeth. Just one month later, however, in September 1790, it was reported that upwards of one hundred such teeth were for sale in London, reported to be "the furniture of Milton's mouth."

In the realm of folklore, there has always been the problem of what to do with the teeth you lose during life. Nineteenth-century Armenians, for example, preserved their lost teeth for the Day of Resurrection by hiding them in the cracks of church walls or hollow trees. Such places were deemed holy. Among some Aborigines of Australia, a boy's cast-off milk teeth were intimately bound up with his future health. In New South Wales, one or two of a boy's front teeth would be knocked out in an initiation rite. The teeth were then inserted in the bark of a tree overhanging a river. In time, if the teeth fell into the water, fine. But if they were overrun by ants, the child would be subject to mouth disease later in life.

Although the tooth fairy appears to be largely a modern invention, it echoes many such early folk superstitions, all of which seem to bow in the direction of the tooth's magical property. Folklorists in the nineteenth century noticed the widespread custom of tossing cast-off teeth into the fireplace in Sweden, Switzerland, and Britain. In Lancashire and Norfolk, the custom was to fold the tooth in a piece of paper, sprinkle salt on it, and then consign it to the flames. The loss of the tooth in the fire would prevent its being eaten by a dog—a fate that would cause a dog's tooth to sprout in the jaw.

In 1870 a Yorkshireman related that the penalty for not burning a tooth was to be forced to search for it after death in a pail of blood, in hell. Another informant painfully recalled the frantic and fruitless search for a little cousin's tooth, dropped in a plowed field at twilight. Imagine the horrors this belief could conjure up in the pliant minds of children.

Another lost-tooth custom, decidedly less threatening, cautioned children to keep their tongues out of the cavities left by recently departed teeth. If that feat could be accomplished, so the belief ran, the child would be rewarded with a bright golden tooth in its stead. This idea was found in both New Jersey and London in 1853 and 1854.

And what of the pain of toothache? Magical cures for this

abound in the past. An Egyptian medical papyrus directs that the lower jaw of a tortoise be worn as a preventative. (Homeopathic magic, according to Frazer: "like cures like.") Pliny the Elder (A.D. 23–79) suggests that toothache sufferers "stand under the open sky on the living earth. . . . Grasp the head of a frog. Open his mouth and spit into it, ask him to take away the toothache and then let him go alive."

It was crucial to be careful about teeth, because a rotten tooth was a vulnerable point in the body's defense. A case in point is the bad tooth of Molly Bland, the ruby-lipped heroine of the American folk ballad "Springfield Mountain." The song can be dated to a real event that occurred on August 7, 1761, when young Timothy Myrick of Springfield Mountain, Massachusetts, died within hours of receiving a rattlesnake bite while cutting hay. His tragedy was the occasion for several morose but popular songs that almost at once began to cry out for parody. The result was a string of humorous versions of the song.

According to the lyrics, Myrick "scarce had mowed half the field,/ When a pesky sarpent bit his heel." After dispatching the snake with his scythe, Timothy ran to his girlfriend Molly, crying out for help. The song continues:

Now Molly had a ruby lip
With which the pizen she did sip.
But Molly had a rotten tooth,
Which the Pizen struck and kill'd 'em both.

The ballad holds out a somewhat less than conventional moral: "And mind when you're in love don't pass/ Too near to patches of high grass."

Notes and Further Reading

Fouquet's miniature *The Martyrdom of St. Apollonia* is reproduced in *The Hours of Etienne Chevalier* (New York: Braziller, 1978). Fouquet painted the same scene in MS 71 of the Musée Condé, reproduced in Millard Meiss, *The Limbourgs and Their Contemporaries* (New York: Braziller, 1974), plate 207.

For teeth folklore, see *N&Q,* 4th series, VI:131 (August 13, 1870) and 341 (October 22, 1870). On the new-grown golden tooth, see Oxoniensis, "Teeth Superstition," *N&Q,* 1st series, IX:64 (January 21, 1854); for "False Teeth Among the Romans," *N&Q,* 2nd series, XII:417 (November 23, 1861) and 481 (December 14, 1861). Other folk accounts are in Brown and in Frazer. Latin and English tooth vocabulary are from the *OED* and Lewis and Short.

"Springfield Mountain" is in Friedman, 302–307. For the desecration of Milton's tomb, see Sitwell, 304–319.

See also Christopher Lawrence, "Extracting Expertise," *TLS,* December 26, 1986, a review of Elisabeth Bennion's *Antique Dental Instruments* (London: Sotheby, 1986). The question Lawrence raises is important: How does the historian elevate artifacts like dental instruments out of the realm of the quaint and into useful history? He suggests that, in this case, it is instructive to view high-style (and now valuable) luxury instruments as part of a rising profession's impulse to see itself as requiring and deserving "important" tools. Dentistry was becoming a serious *profession* above the muck of the farrier or the barber-surgeon. Elegant tools were the proof of that.

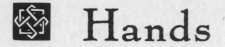 # Hands

IN 1792 the celebrated Captain Philip Thicknesse died, but not before leaving one of the world's most unusual wills. He stipulated that his right hand be cut off and delivered to his inattentive son, Lord Audley. The rebuke was, as the will said, "to remind him of his duty to God, after having so long abandoned the duty he owed to a father, who once so affectionately loved him."

Thicknesse was right to do so, because the hand has forever been a symbol of friendship, trust, and duty—as the recreant Lord Audley doubtless found out.

Consider the handshake, for example. Traditionally this ritual is thought to be a sign of peace and goodwill. After all, we do it with the right hand—a *weaponless* right hand—as if to say that we welcome another's friendship and guarantee not to wield force against him or her, at least for now.

Actually, the handshake has been on my mind ever since I recovered from a mild bout of scarlet fever, a flu-like illness that reddens the skin on the palms of your hands. Later the skin flakes off as it would after a bad sunburn. For weeks I shrank from shaking hands with strangers for fear of alarming them. But they wouldn't hear of it. That's exactly the point about handshakes. Far from being merely a negative expression ("I won't hurt you, for I have no weapon"), the act is instead positively friendly ("I gladly take your hand, heedless of any illness you may have, for I *trust* you").

Truly, the handshake is an ancient and honorable custom. Its oldest instances had to do with conveying power from god to man. In Babylonia it was customary for the king to shake the hands of a statue of Marduk, that civilization's chief god. This act, which took place annually on New Year's Day, served to transfer authority to the potentate for another year. So persuasive was the ceremony that when the Assyrians defeated and occupied Babylonia, the invading kings also felt compelled to submit to the ritual.

Since kings were ordinarily thought to receive their special powers from the gods, it follows that the king's job in turn was to pass a sense of this divinely acquired security on to his people. The idea is embedded in the old English legal custom of "hand-grith," whereby the monarch's protection of his subjects was guaranteed "under the king's hand." Similarly, on medieval feudal estates it was the custom for tenants swearing fealty to a new lord to have both their hands clasped tightly between those of their new master during the ceremony. But there might have been more to this custom than a mere transference of power. In 1775 an early folklorist speculated that the reason for this was to prevent the lord from being murdered during the investiture, and that this horror had actually happened at some time in the past.

Perhaps the most miraculous of handshakes occurs in the legend associated with Wilfreda, a British saint and abbess of the convent at Wilton, who lived in the tenth century. It is reported that her beauty so inflamed King Edgar (959–975) that he pursued her vigorously, even to the door of her church. When the king caught up with her, he dropped to one knee, took her hand, and plighted his troth. Evidently Wilfreda thought little of the idea—so little, in fact, that she retired directly into the church, leaving only her hand in his royal grasp.

Symbolically, hands are important in all manner of sacred and profane art. In Christian works, the presence of God is often shown, in little, by depicting only his hand. A hand with three fingers upraised signifies the Trinity, while a hand with a ray of light or the palm outward shows God's blessings on creation. In Judaism, an entire chapter of the ancient book of rabbinical instruction, the *Mishnah,* is devoted to *Yadaim,* hands. It deals with the cleanliness of hands and their use in ritual. Holy blessing was so firmly associated with the *Cohanim,* Cohens or priests, that uplifted hands were often inscribed on their tombstones. For Islam, raised hands are called the "hands of Fatima," a symbol of good luck connected with the mystical number five—for the five members of the Prophet's family, the five daily prayers, and the five pillars of the faith.

In classical literature, clasped hands were not only a symbol of power, they could also be a formidable obstacle to other forces, even natural ones. Ovid relates how the mother of Hercules, Alcmena, was forced to travail in childbirth for seven days because her enemies sat before her house with clasped hands. Pliny the Elder tells us that no one was allowed to sit at a government or business session or a religious ceremony with clasped hands; otherwise the outcome of the meeting could be hindered or rendered worthless. Pliny also warns against interlacing your fingers anywhere near a pregnant woman or a sick man who is being given medicine. In this century, scholars in Louisiana and North Carolina have recorded how unlucky it is, for example, to shake hands across a fence: "Set your foot on my dirt before you offer your hand."

Among some primitive peoples the hand was associated with powerful taboos. The Maori ostracized anyone who had handled a corpse. So did the Shuswap of British Columbia, who were further forbidden to touch their own bodies for several days. Warriors of the Theddora tribe of Australia and the Dyaks of Sarawak used to eat the palms of their enemies. To prevent the ghost of a suicide from haunting, the ancient Athenians used to cut off the hand and bury it apart from the body. And when the Kurnai of Australia saw the southern lights in the sky, they would swing a dead man's severed hand at it, intoning, "Send it away! Do not let it burn us up!"

But there are more relaxed uses of the symbolic hand as well. Among the Bering Strait Eskimos, a very special hand is depicted on masks, utensils, and weapons to signify unity with Nature. This is the hand with a hole in its palm, a reminder that at least some game should be allowed to escape from the hunt, so it may return to the wild and propagate an eternal supply of food.

Since kings' hands have always held special taboos, it is fitting that they should have special powers as well. In Europe it was commonly held, well into the eighteenth century, that the disease of scrofula, or the King's Evil, could be cured by a regal touch. Dr. Johnson, the great lexicographer, was thus touched as a very young child by Queen Anne on one of her royal progresses. Later, when Boswell asked the greatest intellect of his day if he remembered the occasion, Johnson replied that he had "a confused, but somehow a sort of solemn recollection of a lady in diamonds, and a long black hood."

During his reign Charles I cured a hundred patients on a visit to Scotland, and Charles II touched nearly one hundred thousand cases during his tenure. History is silent on his cure rate. William of Orange, however, scoffed at the practice. Once, when he deigned to touch a pleading sufferer, he added: "God give you better health and more sense."

Curiously, a marvelous touch is imputed not only to royalty but to hanged men. Folklorists call this the "hand of glory" and its powers are legion. Nursing mothers brought babies to the gallows to have the executioners stroke their infants with the hands of executed criminals. Eighteenth- and nineteenth-century English newspapers attest to similar practice. An 1845 account says that "scarcely had the soul of the deceased taken its farewell flight . . . than the scaffold was crowded by members of the 'gentler sex' afflicted with wens in the neck, with white swellings in the knees, &c., upon whose afflictions the cold clammy hand of the sufferer was passed to and fro." The hand of glory was also an important part of the burglar's kit. A French text of 1751 says that the hanged man's hand could stupefy every sleeper in a house so that intruders could go about their work undisturbed.

Children worldwide have arcane uses for handshakes. As Iona and Peter Opie observed in *The Lore and Language of School Children,* youngsters cement bargains and reunite friendships by shaking hands and having a third child break the grasp with a blow. In Glasgow, the Opies report, the third party says "Cut cheese" while doing so.

A similar handshake occurs when children unintentionally say the same words at once. They join pinkies and shake hands three times. In addition, in Italy for example, they may count to three and then let go, crying out either "flic" or "floc." If again they say the same thing, each is allowed a free wish.

The hand is also involved in one of the oldest games on record, a clenched-fist game in which the players try to guess how many fingers an opponent will show on a certain signal. The game is called morra, and was played by both the Egyptians and the Romans. An English manuscript of 1341 depicts a game under way.

"Growing up in New Haven," says Neil Isaacs, "I learned to play the game in first grade, and have impressed Italian friends with it ever since. Each player throws zero to five fingers from one hand, and simultaneously calls the predicted *total* of fingers. Half the fun of the game is the histrionic duet of Italian numbers."

Fur trader Henry A. Boller reported that he often noticed morra, called the "game of hand," being played by the Assiniboines, an offshoot of the Sioux nation, along the upper Missouri in the late

1850s; the game seemed so engrossing that the braves would rather play than eat, chanting "heh-ah-heh" as they gambled on each thrust. The game also figures in a famous *bon mot:* "An honest man," said Cicero, "is one who would play morra in the dark."

With all this weight of history and tradition associated with hands and handshakes down through the ages, it's easy to see how the greatest of artists would want to grab hold of it. So it was with Shakespeare. In *Julius Caesar* he uses it to the hilt, literally. The scene immediately follows the grisly murder in the Capitol. Brutus enjoins his fellow conspirators to "bathe our hands in Caesar's blood/ Up to the elbows." Then Mark Antony enters. Says he: "Let each man render me his bloody hand:/ First, Marcus Brutus, will I shake with you." The violation of the handshake trust is so palpable here you can feel its power. Trust is wasted on such people, Shakespeare is telling us. What's needed now is simple justice.

Notes and Further Reading

Captain Thicknesse can be found in Sitwell, 184. St. Wilfreda is in Baring-Gould, 10:140–143; her feast day is September 9. For hands in Judaism, see *The Mishnah*, ed. Herbert Danby (Oxford: Clarendon Press, 1938); see also *N&Q*, 6th series, IX:160 (February 23, 1884). Cicero's joke about morra, *"quicum in tenebris mices,"* is in *De Officiis* (London: Heinemann, 1968), iii.19.77 (p. 348). For the Assiniboines, see Boller, 129 and 201.

For the Bering Strait Eskimos, see my article in *Smithsonian*, May 1982; on the hole in the hand, see p. 54. The bargain-sealing handshake and the pinkie game are from Opie, 130, 312, and 325. For shaking hands across a fence, see Brown, Items 3588 to 3590. Material on the Babylonians, Dyaks, Kurnai, Maori, and Shuswap is from Frazer. Hazlitt, 301, explains the "hand of glory." For clasped hands, see Pliny, *Naturalis Historiae* (London: Heinemann, 1963), xxvii.17 (p. 43).

A version of this chapter appeared in *Smithsonian* in March 1984. In the May issue (Letters, 22–24), Gary C. Vitale of Springfield, Illinois, wrote to wonder if the story of St. Wilfreda's courtship was related to the American

Midwest's custom of "mittening." He explained: "Long lines of boys reached from either side of the church door, extending sometimes to the middle of the street; and then the girls came out and ran the 'gauntlet.' First one boy and then another would sidle up to a girl, his arm bent in a V, signifying 'Can I see you home?' If the girl saucily jerked away, the whole platoon of fellows would yell, 'You've got the mitten!' and guy the poor devil till he wanted to jump into the creek. But if she grabbed his arm, he was a hero."

2. Leisure

FOOTBALL

RUNNING

BETTING

THE SPORTING CHANCE

BASEBALL TALK

HORSE RACING

LOTTERIES

CHESS

CARDS

COWBOYS

 # Football

THE YEAR IS 1439. In Calais, British and French negotiators have gathered to discuss truce terms to stanch the Hundred Years' War, already 102 years old and counting. During a lull in the discussions, the participants take to the field for a friendly game of football.

That was their first mistake. The archbishop of Rheims, the French chancellor, dove into a scrimmage pileup and came out with a "shinner," a nasty leg bruise. But the real blow was probably to ecclesiastical decorum. It's hard to take anyone seriously who's wearing a miter and hopping around on just one pin. As for the other mistakes engendered by the conference, the bottom line is this: The war continued for fourteen more years.

By contrast, the barely organized warfare known as football had been going on for centuries at that time. Herodotus tells that balls were invented by the king of the Lydians as a diversion for his people during a famine. (Think of that the next time you buy a limp stadium hotdog.) Over the ages, ancient ball games developed along lines related to the size of the ball and also whether it was to be hit or caught with a racket, a bat, the hands, or the feet.

Some unacknowledged genius, who stipulated that the ball could be either kicked or picked up and run with across an imaginary goal line, invented medieval football. In practice, the game must have resembled modern rugby. But it was not until the nineteenth century that football evolved into its three distinct types: soccer (what the British call Association Football, in which no hands but the goalie's may touch the ball); rugby (a back-formation from soccer in which all players can pick up the ball); and American football (a highly patterned form of rugby, with discontinuous action, in which the players wear heavy padding).

Although reminiscent of rugby, medieval football was played on a much larger scale. It was a team sport in the broadest sense: Whole villages formed sides to contend for either a ball or another totem—a bull's head, say, or a flitch of bacon. The winners would bear home the prize and would be acknowledged as victors, at least until the next game.

Football owes its origin to regular seasonal festivals, whose modest purpose was to bring together village and manor tenants for communal work, such as harvesting or sowing, shearing or slaughtering. The game was to be a kind of reward for work well done. But it also served darker, sacrificial purposes. In the Haxey Hood game, played in Lincolnshire in the thirteenth century, teams of villagers strove to gain possession of a coil of rope encased in a sack (the Hood) and return it to their homes. To anthropologist E. O. James, "it seems very likely that originally the Hood was the half or head of a bull sacrificed to fertilize the newly plowed fields, and therefore eagerly sought by those who could secure it to vitalize their crops." In an astounding parallel with modern sport, a ceremony before the game in the town churchyard acted to rile up the populace before they rushed to the fields to tussle for the real or imagined head of a bullock. To early mankind, such a game acted out the annual tilt between the seasons, in this case between deathly winter and regenerative spring.

Football has been firmly associated with the springtime festival of Shrove Tuesday in numerous accounts throughout medieval England. In Chester, the shoemakers' guild donated the leather ball for the annual game; the town hall was designated as the terminus of the game's play. In 1540, because of the violence associated with the game, it was replaced by a simple footrace from a nearby road crossing to the town hall. Shrovetide (pre-Lent) ball games in the fields near London were recorded in the thirteenth century. At that time, football was an afternoon diversion, an energetic capper to a morning spent at the Shrovetide cockfights. Variants continued to be played well into the twentieth century. On February 13, 1923, a game was played at the duke of Northumberland's Alnwick Castle. According to an eyewitness, the opposing sides were the two parishes of St. Michael's and St. Paul's. At Ashbourne in Derbyshire, the "Up-Towners" played the "Down-Towners." The field was three miles long and crossed a river.

This sort of communal participation was the single most important feature of early football. Victory seems to have been taken as a kind of insurance that a good growing season and harvest would follow the spring planting. A similar game, of ancient origin, is still played in Afghanistan for the honor of competing clan members; the game is called buzkashi. Played on horseback, its object is to gain control of a carcass of a goat or calf and carry it across a goal line. The game is described as barely organized chaos (involving up to a thousand players), and aptly demonstrates the violence into which medieval agricultural football could descend.

Moreover, football seems to derive violence not only from its agricultural past but also from much more arcane anthropological traditions, including the custom of kicking the head of a deposed ruler. In the eighteenth century, a motion to discontinue the troublesome Shrove Tuesday football at Kingston-upon-Thames was put down on the grounds that the players were rightfully commemorating an ancient victory over the Danes. It was said the players were kicking the decapitated king's head about the town in derision.

This is just what happens in the fourteenth-century poem *Sir Gawain and the Green Knight*, when members of King Arthur's court play football with the severed head of the mysterious invader. The Green Knight, of course, gets the last laugh, as he casually bends down, grabs his own head, replaces it on his shoulders, and rides off into the night. Scholars reckon this as one of the earliest literary allusions to football.

In France, the game was played with a ball of bran or hay that was delivered by the lord of the manor for the field hands to contend for. The communal spirit was important there too, for often age groups, parishes, sexes, or clergy and laity were pitted against one another. The game was called *la soule* or *soulette* and resulted in the same unpredictable violence and mayhem recorded in England. In Italy, the game was played in the arena at Padua as a kind of Lenten festival involving twenty to forty players. Playing inside old Roman amphitheaters, a circumscribed locale, accounts for the Italian game's reputation as a more civilized pastime than elsewhere in Europe. In England, special subsets of participants were sometimes involved. At times, only guild members or apprentices contended. At Inverness, Scotland, the annual football game pitted married women against the single girls.

It was a dangerous game. In 1303 an Oxford student and footballer was killed during a game in the High Street. In 1321 Canon William de Spalding was absolved by Pope John XXII for accidentally killing a friend who fell against his sheathed knife during a football game. In 1381 fines were set against the organizers of a football game for the tenants at Southwick and Wearmouth; it was said the game was the occasion of "grievous contention and contumely." In 1409 London forbade the collecting of money for new Shrovetide footballs.

During the two centuries between 1300 and 1500, attacks on the game began to mount. Royal decrees were leveled at the game, with obviously little success, in 1314, 1349, 1389, 1401, 1457, and 1491. St. Andrews University in Scotland utterly forbade football to its students. In 1518 the archbishop of Dublin set an automatic eighty-pence fine for clerics who played football. It's in this wild context that Kent's rebuke of Oswald in *King Lear* makes sense: "You base football player," he says, and then he knocks him down.

In spite of such round condemnation, however, football prospered. As a nineteenth-century historian suggests, the unadorned "rush and struggle of the rude and manly game" was the key to its survival. We find the game enshrined still today in several undeniably medieval settings. In the choir of Gloucester cathedral, a fourteenth-century wood carving on a seat, called a misericord, shows two youths contending for a ball. One player is about to punt. In the medieval folk song "Sir Hugh," the play is reminiscent of Pelé:

> *He kick'd the ba' with his right foot,*
> *And catcht'd it wi' his knee.*

One other thing. Medieval sport had no referee. We must have been different back then. Certainly medieval man came from a sporting tradition. Plato and Homer encouraged play. And most writers, up to and including John Milton, made use of games and sports in their poems, plays, books, and sermons. Even the ordinarily dour St. Thomas Aquinas smiled on sport.

So it is with the medieval sport of football, a game of ancient tradition still played at the change of the seasons. E. O. James again:

> From the cradle to the grave, and from season to season, in the primitive and peasant cultures the entire group, domestic and social, have been united as a harmonious whole in a common activity, welded together by collective emotions as a corporate unified entity.

Football was just such a common activity. The expectation of competition, achievement, and pleasure at contending for the ball played an important role in bringing people together for their feudal and agricultural duties. The absence of such a legitimizing underlying rationale may be what causes the problems that surround the game today. In any case, problems have been a long time a-building. In 1583 the Puritan pamphleteer Philip Stubbes saw it all too clearly:

> As rather a friendlie kind of fyghte than a play or recreation . . . for doth not everyone lye in waight for his adversarie seeking to overthrow him and picke him on his nose, though it be on hard stones, on ditch or dale on valley or hill . . . he careth not, so he have him down?

Notes and Further Reading

The archbishop of Rheims's injury is recounted in *Thomas Beckington's Journal*, printed in *Proceedings and Ordinances of the Privy Council* (London: Public Records, 1835), V:363. See also V. B. Redstone, "Social Conditions of England During the Wars of the Roses," *Royal Historical Society Transactions*, new series, 16 (1902): 195. Philip Stubbes's *The Anatomie of Abuses* has been often reprinted since its appearance in 1583. The song "Sir Hugh" is in Friedman, 63.

For Shrovetide football, see John Stow, *A Survey of London* (1603; repr. Oxford: Clarendon Press, 1908), I:92. For buzkashi, see G. Whitney Azoy, *Buzkashi: Game and Power in Afghanistan* (Philadelphia: University of Pennsylvania Press, 1982). The game is also discussed in Jacob Bronowski's *The Ascent of Man* (Boston: Little, Brown, 1973), 82. For Arthurian football, see Francis P. Magoun, Jr., "Sir Gawain and Medieval Football," *English Studies* 19 (1937): 208–209. Magoun has given us a very fine book in his *History of Football from the Beginnings to 1871* (1938; repr. New York: Johnson, 1966). E. O. James's book is *Seasonal Feasts and Festivals* (London: Jerrold, 1961).

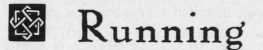 # Running

JOGGERS. Runners. Marathoners. Surely these are thoroughly modern maniacs, on whom history can shed little light. But the fact is that the printed record—newspapers, essays, even stage plays—has so much to say about the great road racers of the past that the bulk of today's runners seem almost anemic by comparison.

By the early sixteenth century, the ability to cover ground quickly on foot had given rise to a special class of servants, the footmen. We think of them today as junior butlers, but for some two centuries, from the seventeenth to the end of the eighteenth, the footman's job was specific: He was to run alongside his lord's coach to make sure it was not overturned by ditches or tree roots, and to run ahead to prepare for his master's arrival at the next inn.

In 1614 Sir Thomas Overbury, the essayist and great collector of seventeenth-century "characters," noted several things about a *foote-man:* "He will never be a staid man, for he has a running head of his owne, ever since child-hood." Overbury liked to play with words, as you can see. "Hee lives more by his owne heat then the warmth of cloathes," which any jogger will tell you. And finally:

Tis impossible to draw his picture to the life, cause a man must take it as he's running; onely this. Horses are usually let bloud on S. Stevens day: on S. Patrickes hee takes rest, and is drencht for all the yeare after.

Overbury was neither exaggerating nor punning by asserting that footmen were always on the run. Their lives were consumed in accompanying their betters around the countryside or in training for upcoming travel. Indeed, the pace must have been staggering.

In passing, Sir Thomas has let us in on another custom, that of bleeding horses on St. Stephen's Day, December 26. The reasoning was clear: Since you bleed humans to rid them of toxic humors in the system, why wouldn't the same work with animals? Thus, in 1580:

Yer Christmas be passed, let horsse be let blood,
For manie a purpose it doth them much good,
The day of S. Steven, old fathers did use,
If that do mislike thee, some other day chuse.

Because running footmen were in effect a species of chattel, as were all servants, they too were to have a day of therapeutic rest. According to Overbury, St. Patrick's Day was selected. History is silent on the reasons for choosing that day, but the answer may be bound up with the number of Irishmen who excelled at the trade. In hagiography, horses have as much to do with St. Stephen as footmen have to do with St. Patrick, which is precisely nothing.

It was only a matter of time before gentlemen made a more obvious connection between footmen and horses—that you could race them and wager on the outcome. From early in the seventeenth century, we have evidence that this was done. The best of such runners were called celeripedians according to the early lexicographer Henry Cockeram, whose *English Dictionarie, Or Interpreter of*

Hard English Words was published in 1623. And in a 1625 tragedy by John Webster, an offhand remark uncovers the training regimen of racing footmen:

> *I have heard of cunning footmen that have worne*
> *Shoes made of lead, some ten days 'fore a race*
> *To give them nimble and more active feet.*

The world-class expert on running footmen and pedestrians (or peds, as they were also called) is Earl R. Anderson of Cleveland State University. Anderson is an Anglo-Saxonist and also a marathoner whose passion for running has led him into the tangled wood of sport history. Using sources as disparate as old newspaper accounts, lawbooks, and eighteenth-century novels, Anderson set to work uncovering the history of eighteenth- and nineteenth-century wagering on races between footmen.

Anderson is fond of a nineteenth-century story associated with the duke of Queensberry. His Grace the duke was said to have been the last English nobleman to keep running footmen and often tried out candidates for his employ by timing them from his balcony. He also had them try out by running in his livery or household uniform. (Footmen are variously described in old accounts as wearing feathered hats, jockey caps, or red silk petticoats with gold fringe, and carrying long canes topped with removable silver balls that were said to hold white wine for soothing parched throats.) One time, when the duke had decided to hire a certain runner, he announced to him, "You'll do very well for me." "Your livery will do very well for me," replied the man, according to a writer to *Notes and Queries,* and he "gave the duke a last proof of his ability as a runner by then running away with it."

Anderson's research shows that the commonly respected and achieved distance for running footmen was sixty miles a day. As early as 1608, a footman in a London stage play is addressed as

"Three-Score-a-Day" and later as "Seven-Minute-Mile." Such men would be the ultramarathoners of today.

But even they would be overshadowed by the exhibition peds of the eighteenth and nineteenth centuries. In 1773 the legendary Foster Powell covered the 402 miles between London and York in five days, eighteen hours. He coursed the same route again in 1790 and 1792, attracting large crowds as he went, and cut two and a half hours off his time. In the 1880s, six-day races were a major spectator sport in America, with fans dropping by the indoor arenas at 1 A.M. to check on the progress of their favorites. The victors in those contests often covered more than a hundred miles a day. Apparently the trick was to sleep as little as possible; about four hours was the optimum! Anderson points out that the races were mercifully kept to six days to avoid breaking the Sabbath.

Peter Lovesey's murder mystery *Wobble to Death* (1970) covers this milieu, which was as hard on the athletes as Nero's Rome once was:

> The Press accounts of the race had followed a well-established pattern. For the first day or two it was described as the 'Islington Mix'; by the third day, 'Herriot's Wobble'; and at the end of the week the 'Cruelty Show at the Agricultural Hall'. As the eventual result became more certain, reports dwelt instead on the state of the blistered survivors. And the more harrowing the details, the larger the attendance.

Nor is the tradition of great athletes who write books about their exploits a modern idea. An English writer and long-distance walker named Thomas Coryate (1577–1627) seems to have started the trend. Coryate boasted of walking from Venice to England and then ended his days with a trek from Europe down through Mesopotamia to India, where his feet and his life gave out. The book that detailed his wanderings was oddly titled *Coryats Crudities, Hastily*

Gobbled Up in Five Months Travells in France, Savoy, Italy, Rhetia, Helvetia, High Germania and the Netherlands (1611). What made the book memorable, in addition to his endurance and eccentricity, was his introduction of a new form of technology to English life: the dining fork, all the rage in Italy.

Because of all this celebrity, Coryate's village church back in Odcombe, Somerset, proudly displayed a pair of his long-distance shoes, where they are reputed to have hung from 1612, at the start of his second trip, to some time early in the eighteenth century when they mysteriously disappeared. For over a century, the shoes were venerated much the same as the gear of modern sports heroes.

Literary interest in running extends back to Homer and the swift-footed Achilles. And the funeral games in the twenty-third book of the *Iliad*, said to be among the highest achievements of all sports history, include a short race won by a devout Odysseus. His patron, Athena, had caused his closest opponent to slip on ox dung near race's end; Odysseus had friends in high places.

The great long run in history, of course, was the twenty-two miles between the plain of Marathon and Athens. The most famous retelling of this story appears in Robert Browning's 1879 poem *Pheidippides*, titled for the Greek athlete who made the trip. (Actually, Browning's lines conflate several stories found in the classical sources, in which the runner's name is variously given as Thersippus, Eucles, or Philippides.)

The time was September of 490 B.C. and the Persian army was about to crush the Greeks, according to the account in Herodotus. The Athenian generals, huddling before the fight, dispatched the athlete Pheidippides on foot to Sparta (about 160 miles) to ask for aid. He covered the distance in two days; not bad, nearly the level of the best nineteenth-century peds. Browning recounted the scene like this:

Like stubble, some field which a fire runs through,

Was the space between city and city: two days, two
  nights did I burn
Over the hills, under the dales, down pits and up peaks.
Into their midst I broke: breath served but for
  "Persia has come!"

Unfortunately, Sparta turned a deaf ear to his plea. Pheidippides then ran back to Athens with the bad news. Then off again to fight at Marathon. Finally, he ran back to Athens to deliver the word on the upset victory at Marathon. Browning again:

So to end gloriously—once to shout, thereafter be mute:
"Athens is saved!"—Pheidippides dies in the shout
  for his meed.

In 1896, at the first modern Olympiad, the so-called marathon race was reinvented. Since the games were held in Athens, the very course Pheidippides ran was used again. It is fitting that a Greek athlete took the laurels that day. What is not so fitting is that Pheidippides was commemorated by just his twenty-two-mile trot, since the frantic dash from Athens to Sparta and back was so much more important and demanding.

Today, the Olympic marathon distance is 26 miles, 385 yards, because at the fourth Olympiad—held in London in 1908, the first Olympics held outside Athens—the royal grandchildren wanted to see the start of the race. So it began on the lawn at Windsor Castle, continuing on to the stadium at Shepherds Bush, precisely 26 miles, 385 yards.

And what of Pheidippides, who is called the *hemerodromos* ("all-day runner") in Herodotus? Is he really the one who "died in the shout" on delivering the news? Probably not, chiefly because Herodotus does not mention that stirring finale. And we know Herodotus would have killed for such a story.

Instead we can credit Browning, a self-taught Greek scholar who brought together several classical tales to create a new legend for his 1879 poem. It was perfect for its time, a tale that combined nationalism and athleticism in a way that was characteristic of the Victorian sports revival. Such is the power that poetry once had.

Notes and Further Reading

Special thanks to Earl R. Anderson for talking with me. See Earl R. Anderson, "Freak Races," *Running Times,* March 1982, 21–24, and his "The Running Footmen of 19th Century England," *Running Times,* March 1981, 17–20. A scholarly version of some of the same historical material is in Anderson's "Footnotes More Pedestrian Than Sublime: A Historical Background for the Foot-Races in *Evelina* and *Humphrey Clinker,*" *Eighteenth-Century Studies* 14 (1980): 56–68. The story of the duke of Queensberry comes from William J. Thoms, "Running Footmen," *N&Q,* 2nd series, I:9 (January 5, 1850).

For the character of "A Foote-Man," see *Sir Thomas Overbury,* ed. W. J. Paylor (Oxford: Blackwell, 1936), 53. On bleeding horses, see Hazlitt, 57. The Webster play is *Appius and Virginia.* Interesting Victorian notes on Browning's poem can be found in Edward Berdoe, *The Browning Cyclopaedia* (London: Allen & Unwin, 1891), 333–337.

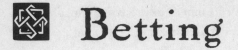 # Betting

SO THERE I WAS, eating a solitary pub meal in the Green Man & French Horn, in St. Martin's Lane, London, awaiting the start of Mozart's *Così Fan Tutte* next door. That opera, as you know, is based on a Neapolitan wager involving romance and fidelity. As I considered this, however, my eye chanced on a discreet wall plaque across from my seat. Under the title "Betting, Gaming & Lotteries Act of 1963" it warned: "With the permission of the manager only cribbage, dominoes and certain games *of pure skill* may be played for small stakes."

Far from being merely a sign of the times, this seemed to compress into twenty-one words most of the history of wagering, encompassing the notions of controlling the stakes and prescribing the games to be bet on, and even hammering home the distinction between games of skill and games of chance.

Certainly, people have been betting on the outcome of a vast range of activities for ages. The Old Testament recounts in detail the wager of Samson's wedding feast. A foreigner and a Jew, Samson was about to marry a Philistine woman. To prove himself, he bet thirty of her wedding guests that he could out-riddle them. The stakes: thirty linen tunics and thirty festal garments. The riddle: "Out of the eater came something to eat. Out of the strong came something sweet." The allotted time: until the seven-day marriage feast was over. Samson had proposed that particular riddle because he'd slain a lion on the way to his wedding and its carcass had been filled with honey by a swarm of bees. Over the next few days, Samson's bride constantly implored him for the riddle's answer. When he relented and told her the secret, she betrayed him to her compatriots. As a result, Samson was bound to go to Ashkelon, kill thirty men, and hand over their garments to the Philistines. Then, "in his anger he went back to his father's house," the Bible says, and the unnamed girl married Samson's best man.

Although this wager is associated with betrayal, bloodshed, and loss, both the riddling game and the idea of betting are vindicated here because they prevented Samson (for a time at least) from denying his people and his God. Partly because of this precedent, for some rabbis of the Middle Ages gambling was neither forbidden nor considered a sin. Cheating and manipulating the results were sinful, but games solidly dependent on chance were allowed.

Among the Greeks, a rare example of a bet on a sporting event is found in the coverage of the chariot race run as part of the funeral games in the *Iliad*. During that race, the course at one point took the five competitors out of the spectators' view, because of a hollow in the terrain. When the spectators began to bicker over which driver was in the lead, a wager arose. The stakes were a tripod or cauldron, a common enough prize for Greek athletes, but hardly for gamblers.

Both Samson's bet and the Homeric wager are examples of betting on games of skill. The competitors were wagering respectively on their skills at riddling and at doping out the abilities of horses and charioteers. By contrast, games of chance—dice rolls and coin tosses being the most common—involve only the immutable laws of probability.

In the long parade from ancient to modern times, this distinction between games of chance and of skill has been invoked countless times. The Romans, under the Code of Justinian, forbade games of chance and tolerated those of skill, as long as the stakes involved were not excessive. The reasoning was undoubtedly that chance introduced too much margin for cheating. Thus, loaded dice and weighted coins are commonplace in classical and medieval archaeology, as are marked cards in the Renaissance. The plea rolls from London courts show that there were nine indictments for loaded dice entered between 1364 and 1381. This is the sort of historical reality that lies behind the sign at the Green Man & French Horn.

By contrast, in the United States the bias at gambling resorts is against games of skill and toward chance. Take the dedicated black-jack players who are able to count cards and memorize odds to defeat the casinos. The resorts maintain files on such players and ban them from their tables. A spokesman for an Atlantic City gaming house has contended that such people abuse what the law says should be a game of chance by turning it into a "game of skill." On the other hand, the state legislators of California have acted against chance in favor of skill. All forms of poker considered variants of "draw" are legal, while "stud" poker is illegal. The idea, established over a century ago under the state's gaming laws, is that draw is a game of skill; stud is just dumb luck.

History is replete with attempts to ban gambling of both kinds. The medieval church often tried to curb betting, not because it was an outright sin but because it inclined men to sloth, encouraged them to play rather than pray, and led them to haunt taverns, a source of other distractions such as gluttony, drinking, wenching— and cursing if they fell under a string of losses.

The result was a mixture of censure and tacit approval for betting. At St. George's Chapel, Windsor, a fifteenth-century miseri-cord—a wood carving on a choir seat—shows two men quarreling over a dice game; one slices the air with his dagger while the other grips his attacker's face. And yet, the respected Bolognese physician and mathematician Girolamo Cardano (1501–1576), who wrote a treatise on dice play, saw gambling as a proper test of patience, "for a good man will refrain from anger even at the moment of rising from the game in defeat." Because of his interest in betting and chance, Cardano was able to pioneer the science of probability. He even had some kind words for card counters: "Those . . . who know merely by close attention what cards they are to expect are not usually called cheats, but are reckoned to be prudent men."

The church has its own history of gambling. All Saints Parish Church of St. Ives, Cambridgeshire, England, holds an annual dicing on its altar. The stakes are six Bibles, awarded to the best of twelve child dicers, in a game that began in 1675 with a bequest from one Dr. Robert Wilde. In 1879 there was an official inquiry into the "scandal" of dice throwing inside the church, but as the purpose was to get Bibles into the hands of poor children, it was allowed to continue.

To their credit, civil and religious authorities were also worried about the poverty that attended ill-fated bettors. Roman laws tried to stop the lower orders from gaming while turning a blind eye to patrician betting. In the face of terrible Roman poverty, the poet Juvenal satirized the wagering of the rich: "None approach nowadays the gambling table with the purse; they must carry with them their strong box. What can we think of these profligates more ready to lose one hundred thousand than to give a tunic to a slave dying with cold?"

It was much the same in England. The royal uncle John of Gaunt in 1375 lost forty-five pounds at dice. But at Great Horwood, Buckinghamshire, in 1515 no tenant farmer could play dice or cards "except at the time of the Lord's Nativity." At Coventry in 1553 the same games were forbidden to laborers, journeymen, and apprentices. While Cardinal Wolsey was attempting to have all the cards, dice, and bowling pins of the common people burnt, there is a record of Henry VIII losing nine pounds at "shovel-board."

Over the next century, matters began to get so far out of hand that even Charles II's mistress Nell Gwynne was able to lose £5,000 in one evening. But the greatest century, by far, for huge bets was the eighteenth. On January 9, 1752, Horace Walpole reported that George II and the royal family played at hazard, a dice game, in which there was more than £11,000 on the table. The king won three guineas; his son the duke won £3,400.

Charles James Fox (1749–1806), the Whig statesman and supporter of the colonial cause, was an inveterate (and bad) gambler who is said to have dropped £200,000 during his lifetime. Gibbon reports that he once played for twenty-two hours straight, with an average loss of £500 per hour. And the earl of Carlisle, George III's commissioner for colonial affairs, once lost £10,000 at a sitting.

As for America, William Byrd II, the proprietor of Westover, a grand estate of 179,000 acres on the James River, appears guilt-ridden and foolish after losing twelve pounds gaming with friends. Then, according to his secret (written in cipher) diary, he went out and lost another twelve pounds the next night. He also bet two bits (a quarter of a Spanish dollar) that an acquaintance would not try to cross a frozen river, and in 1711 lost two guineas on a seven-mile footrace. "Gaming is amazingly prevalent in Williamsburg," said a visitor to the city in 1777.

Over the years, people have managed to wager on a mind-numbing range of events. There was the Victorian gentleman who stood on London Bridge offering newly minted gold coins to passersby at a penny each. He bet he'd get no takers, and won. Or Lord Corbet of Sundorne Castle, Shrewsbury, who wagered his vast estates that his was the handsomest leg in England. After winning, he commemorated the event with a painting depicting the great gam showdown.

And on July 1, 1777, an infamous wager had to be settled before the Court of King's Bench, involving the sex of the courtier the

Chevalier D'Eon, a Frenchman who was all the rage in London—a sort of neoclassical *Crying Game*. Although D'Eon had been baptized male, his demeanor and carriage were such that most of fashionable London quickly divided into two opposing camps, one claiming him to be a man, the other to be a woman. Huge sums were wagered. The court case was brought by a plaintiff named Hayes, who had laid a hundred guineas, at seven to one, that D'Eon was female.

The judge, after wishing publicly that he had the power to make both sides lose, admitted that wagers were legal and agreed to hear the case. But because the evidence was "too indecent to be mentioned," he declared that the only question to be put to the witnesses was "Do you know D'Eon to be a woman?" It mattered not how they knew; perjury would be the quick and simple result if things turned out differently later.

The plaintiff was awarded £700, 40s., and raked in another £3,000 on side bets. Immense sums were said to depend on the verdict for other bettors. As for the chevalier, she passed the rest of her days in dwindling notoriety, and finally died in 1810, aged eighty-two, having been—for one brief, glittering moment—the toast of the sporting crowd.

Notes and Further Reading

Samson's wedding bet is in Judges 14. The wagering on the chariot race in the *Iliad* (23:485 ff.) is discussed in E. Norman Gardiner, *Athletics of the Ancient World* (Oxford: Clarendon Press, 1930), 22. The Windsor wood carving is in G. L. Remnant, *A Catalogue of Misericords in Great Britain* (Oxford: Clarendon Press, 1969), 8. On the gambling resorts, see Tom Zito, "Blackjack Legend Banned," *Washington Post,* March 1, 1979.

On dicing in church, see Everard Home Coleman, "Casting Dice in St. Ives Church," *N&Q,* 8th series, II:50 (July 16, 1892). The London Bridge wager is from *N&Q,* 2nd series, II:427 (November 29, 1856). See also William Bates, "Celebrated Wagers," *N&Q,* 1st series, I:247–248 (September

23, 1854). On the rabbis and gambling, see Landman I:298–318.

For Great Horwood, see Warren Ault, *Open-Field Farming in Medieval England* (London: Allen & Unwin, 1972), 137. On George II's big night, see *Horace Walpole's Correspondence with George Montagu*, eds. W. S. Lewis and Ralph S. Brown, Jr. (New Haven: Yale University Press, 1941), 125. For more on Augustan gambling, see Thackeray, *The Four Georges* (London: Dent, 1949), 361 and 408. See also Pierre Marambaud, *William Byrd of Westover, 1674–1744* (Charlottesville: University of Virginia Press, 1971), 198–199. The Chevalier D'Eon story is from the *DNB.*]

The Sporting Chance

HANDICAPPING has become commonplace in modern life. We do it at the racetrack and on the golf course, and less rigidly in the classroom and around the family hearth, where younger siblings are traditionally given leeway in games and conversation. Similarly, on the American frontier, the Colt .45 was considered the "great equalizer" for good guys and bad guys of wildly unequal physical stature.

But the systematic use of fair play and giving the little guy a break is not a modern idea. It has roots deep in the Middle Ages, a time when a body of local laws and customs grew up to regulate the everyday exchange between man and neighbor, serf and lord. For example, when the village workers on the Essex manor of Borley were needed to help with the hay harvest, each man was entitled to as much mown grass, for each day he labored in the field, as he could manage to lift with just the point of his scythe. Similarly, each man delivering oats in his cart could keep as much grain as he could "thrice take with his hand."

Likewise, fourteenth-century tenants of the Frauenkloster abbey near Zurich were allowed to settle disputes over the extent of their poultry runs with a throw of a sickle. (Neighbors have always been a problem.) The statute said that fowl could roam as far as the homeowner could throw, but with a special provision. Each man had to stand on the roof ridge of his home and throw with his left hand. The law was silent on the question of natural lefties. It's possible that few self-respecting villagers would admit to being "sinister" southpaws. In the same century, tenants at a German estate were allowed to let their hens and chickens wander as far as the hausfrau could throw an egg. She was allowed to use her veil as a sling to give the heave added distance.

What we see here are laws and customs that give legal status to athletic prowess. Take the matter of removing wood, even dead branches, from royal or ecclesiastical forests. Ordinarily, this was strictly forbidden. But there was an exception. Local villagers were allowed to keep the wood they had illegally taken, so long as they carted the contraband more than an ax throw from where they had cut it before the forester arrived. Again, the law seems to handicap in favor of the oppressed: the forester was obliged to throw left-handed. But the matter did not end there, according to rules set down by the bishop of Strassburg in the fourteenth century: "Then may the forester, if he will, follow after the cart, and thrust his right hand under his girdle, and with his left hand drag from the cart what wood he may, until he come to the man's own toft. So far may he go; but, if he follow the man into his toft, and the peasant then turn round and smite the forester on the head, even unto death, then shall no judgement be passed upon him for that deed."

G. G. Coulton was the first historian to comment extensively on the inclination of the Middle Ages toward the "sporting chance" in daily life. In fact, he coined the phrase to use as a chapter title in his richly detailed book *The Medieval Village* (1926).

In practice, such local customs acted to take the hard edge off some extremely punitive and arbitrary rules. A criminal could have six weeks and three days of freedom if, on his way to prison, he could spot a monk out of his cloister and catch him by the cowl. A common prison term was the length of time that a man would take to consume two bushels of wheat—a rule that likely transformed many a light eater into a trencherman.

Even the athletic ability of a peasant's livestock could be called to account. One measure of length was "as far as a tame hen can go at a single flight, which is reckoned at three hundred of a man's paces." As for the tithe fowl that tenants were required to render to their landlords yearly, both goslings and sick hens are mentioned specifically in the manorial customs. A gosling could be rejected if it was not old enough or strong enough to pluck grass by itself without falling down. And even a sickly hen had to be accepted by the lord of the manor if, when the animal was startled, it could jump the garden fence.

Boundary rights were settled according to an ax or hammer throw from recognizable landmarks. Legal rights might extend out into a lake "as far as a man can ride in his saddle from the shore." Or riparian rights might extend a barge-pole reach up the beach from water's edge, a rule which called on good balance and upper-body strength.

The peasant who wished to move to another manor or another village was ordinarily not allowed to do so. Medieval farming was labor intensive, as they say these days, and the alert steward or reeve would do his utmost to keep his field hands at home. The result was a contest that pitted a tenant's fully laden cart and his oxen against the steward in a tug-of-war. If the oxen won, the man and his family moved on; if the steward, using one hand, could prevail, the family was obliged to stay.

The whole matter of poaching is intimately connected with gamesmanship and the sporting chance. Since virtually all animals (except vermin) were protected by statute to provide meat and sport for the upper classes, any hunting or trapping at all was considered poaching. Game management being unknown, this ruinous concept forced many a poor serf to watch helplessly as the cosseted deer and hordes of rabbits chewed up his tender sprouts. Eventually the game laws became a contest of wills between tenant and lord, with wild variations in enforcement. Even the statute books seemed to connive at this standoff. Some regulations allowed peasants to keep hunting dogs if the animals' foreclaws were cut, to render them less effective—but certainly not useless—as hunters. In support of limited access to the bounty of God's forests, a thirteenth-century German authority demanded "that no man might be maimed or slain for poaching." The complaint indicates that severe punishments were in fact being meted out. Such penalties added considerable threat to the sporting chance, likely causing the quest for rabbits to become the heart-stopping equivalent of a big game hunt.

Elsewhere, at certain times of the year a sheep or pig would be loosed in a field for the mowers to tussle for. Whoever caught it could keep it. It mattered little that this game was mainly providing entertainment for the ruling classes, or that it pitted the mowers against each other. The game held out the possibility of temporary gain for a tiny percentage of its participants and so it was tolerated, perhaps even welcomed. The parallels with modern college and professional sports and with state lotteries are unmistakable.

For cases that involved disputes between lord and servant, the corpus of "sporting chance" laws had special provisions. For example, the abbot of Glastonbury gave his serfs one sheaf of wheat from each cartload they cut. But the rules for settling arguments about the size of the sheaf were much more extensive and complicated than the original, rather simple, allowance. Thus, "if any sheaf appear less than is right, it ought to be put in the mud, and the hayward should grasp his own hair above his ear, and the sheaf should be drawn mid-way through his arm [i.e., inside the bend of the elbow] and if this can be done without the defiling of his garments or his hair, then it is adjudged to be less than is right; but otherwise it is judged sufficient."

This is indeed a game, one apparently weighted in favor of the abbot. Only a perfectly clean hayward (a representative of the abbot after all) would qualify the hungry peasant for more grain. Obviously, it would take an extremely steady hand to get even the smallest of bundles through his crooked arm without dirtying the hayward. But if the typical peasant realized his disadvantage, there is no record that he recoiled under the benign yoke of this and countless other sporting chances. At least the system held out the *promise* of more than he felt entitled to, even if the peasant usually lost.

With such exchanges a regular part of daily living, it is easy to see how the idea of life as a game became so conventional a part of language and literature. Life resembles a game because its outcome is always uncertain. A miniature painting in the pages of the famous 1409 prayer book *Les Grandes Heures du Jean, Duc de Berry* illustrates this well. Here, a juggler balances a plate on a long pole above his chin; his other hand manipulates a rod to spin the dish. While he concentrates on the magic taking place in the air over his head, a dragon slithers into the picture from below, about to devour the acrobat's foot. Life is like that.

Notes and Further Reading

Sports Illustrated on December 23, 1985, p. 162, reported that Bill Dance, a two-pound rooster, took first place in the featherweight division of the Fourteenth Annual Chicken Flying Meet in Gallipolis, Ohio, with a flight of 180 feet.

G. G. Coulton's *Medieval Village* was published by Cambridge University Press. See also P. Vinogradoff, *Villainage in England* (Oxford: Oxford University Press, 1892). Other Coulton volumes, easy to get hold of and valuable for their details of medieval life, are *From St. Francis to Dante: Translations from the Chronicle of the Franciscan Salimbene, 1221–1288* (1907; repr. Philadelphia: University of Pennsylvania Press, 1972); *Life in the Middle Ages* (Cambridge: Cambridge University Press, 1935); and *Social Life in Britain from the Conquest to the Reformation* (Cambridge: Cambridge University Press, 1919).

⧉ Baseball Talk

"SPEAK TO ME!"

When Horatio says that to the crotchety ghost in *Hamlet,* he represents us all. For in that same breath he's also acknowledging Shakespeare's greatest strength—his engaging, entangling, and mesmerizing language. There's magic in that web of words.

But baseball, who would have thought it too would be all about language? Chatter is what they do on the diamond and in the stands—the fielders among themselves, the players in the dugout to the solitary batter at the plate, the announcer to the airwaves ("Oh, Doctor!"), and the fans to the heavens. If we had to be reverential and silent, as we are in church, we'd never go out to the ballpark.

So the connection between *Hamlet's* "Speak to me" and "Hummmm in there. Swinnngg, batter!" is clear. There are countless phrases and images and allusions we use to pepper our recollections, debates, and writings on baseball—so many, in fact, it could be argued that the game is merely a vast experiment stemming from somewhere deep in the DNA just to prompt evolution in our language, our imagination, our perception. Well, sort of.

The list of baseball catchphrases is long and endearing. Listen to them: Texas leaguer, southpaw, bush league, Tinker-to-Evers-to-Chance. There are also the less familiar—like "dial 8," a Wally Pipp, or simply the letter *K*—that have the weight of history behind them.

The derivation of "southpaw" is obvious once you remind yourself that baseball is a summer game. To provide shade for the infield box seats—the expensive ones—most parks were oriented so the pitcher threw into the west, into the afternoon sun, while the paying customers luxuriated in the cool shadows. Chicago's West Side Park was thus open to the east, so a pitcher's left hand would be his southern hand, or southpaw. It was here that the humorist Finley Peter Dunne, also one of the first baseball reporters, regularly used the term, starting in 1887.

And what of a Texas leaguer? Down there, the fields were so huge, and without fences, that the outfielders used to hang deep. Deep enough that it was almost impossible to hit a ball over their heads. But that only made it easier to drop one in front of them. Unfortunately, the term became derisive, implying a cheesy, ill-gotten hit. In the 1890s a former Texas player, Art Sunday, became known for those little hits, said to be an impertinent holdover from his Lone Star days.

In Canada, a Texas leaguer is a *ballon à l'entre-champs,* a "hit between the fields." I like that, but it hardly translates. In fact, it is not the Québecois but the Latinos that seem to be making the most of the poetic possibilities of baseball talk. For them, a fly ball is a "little dove," a *palomita.* A catcher is a "stopper," *parador,* and the pitcher, *lanzador,* a "launcher." "Gardeners" *(jardineros)* play in the infield, while "forest rangers" *(bomberos)* patrol the outfield.

"Bush leagues" refers to the hinterlands of sport, where there was little money for maintenance. Grass grew tall in the infield gardens and a grounder rustled like a hedgehog through the vegetation. A "dying quail" is a flare or a "humpback liner" and a "chicken" is a foul ball, the latter term appearing in an account of a San Diego game played in July 1880. A "frozen rope" is a ball hit so hard its line of flight is straight and low. I've heard Joe Garagiola speak of homers hit so deep you had to "dial 8" to get them back. (The reference is to hotel phones, where 8 is long distance.) The splendid baseball film *Bull Durham* gave us a homer that went so far it "had a stewardess on it."

Consider, too, the eleventh letter of the alphabet. Everyone knows "Dr. K" was New York Mets pitcher Dwight Gooden. He was called that because of his 24-karat stock-in-trade, the rally-quenching strikeout. But when and how did K come to signify "strike out" on score cards?

Actually, K became the scorer's symbol for strikeout a surprisingly long time ago. For this we can thank Henry Chadwick, amateur ballplayer, sportswriter, and baseball editor of the *New York Clipper*. For a time near the turn of this century he was known as the "Father of Baseball." Chadwick was a prolific writer, and the old card catalogue at the Library of Congress contained almost an inch of slips that detailed his many books on lawn bowling, chess, ice skating, curling, American cricket, yachting, and rowing. But baseball, to judge from the number of book titles alone, was his first love, and he turned out separate volumes on hitting, base running, and pitching.

That card catalogue also suggests that Chadwick was the sentimental favorite of at least one anonymous librarian. Each of his book titles is printed on a standard card bearing Chadwick's name at the top, and next to it the year of his birth, 1824. After April 20, 1908, though, his death year was carefully added to each card in thick black ink, in Henry's case a lengthy and lugubrious task.

In the early 1860s, Chadwick came up with a new system for helping newspapermen and official scorers keep track of games. More important, the system enabled them to efficiently transmit game summaries over the old telegraphs. Published as *Chadwick's Association Score-book* and endorsed by the National Baseball Association in 1865, the system gradually took hold and was widely reprinted, notably in *De Witt's Baseball Guides,* published annually from 1869.

Letters were the key to Henry's system. A meant a putout at first base, B at second, C at third. F was a caught fly ball, and L a caught foul. K signified "struck out," as Henry wrote in 1883, because "it was the prominent letter of the word strike, as far as remembering the word was concerned." S was probably avoided to prevent confusion with the *s* in sacrifice or shortstop.

It is no coincidence that Henry was also chairman of the rules committee of the first National Baseball Association and editor of the DeWitt handbooks. That publication later evolved into the statistical compendia known as *Spalding's Official Baseball Guides,* which Chadwick edited from 1881 until his death.

Later in the century a number of competing systems came into use. The printing and selling of seasonal schedules, scorecards, and even tables of percentages, for calculating won-lost records and standings, became a big business (there are several shelves of them in the Library of Congress). In 1887, for example, a Stockton, California, publisher favored a system in which a strikeout was an S with a circle around it. But gradually, although much of Chadwick's system fell into disuse, his K became accepted.

And what about a backwards K? Put that in a scorecard and it means not only a strikeout but a humiliating "called" third strike. Batter just stood there like a "wooden Indian" or a "Statue of Liberty," he did. Now recall that Mets fans at Shea Stadium used to fly K flags whenever Gooden was on a rampage. The real surprise is not that the symbol exists, but that no one ever unfurled sarcastic backwards-K flags for some of the great home-run swatters, most of whom strike out far more often than they achieve round-trippers.

The names of countless men enrich the diction of sport, but none is as thought-provoking and wistful as that of Wally Pipp. He was the Yankee first baseman who got a headache one fine June day in 1925 and so let a rawboned newcomer called Lou Gehrig play in his stead. Bad career move. So today, a player taking a day off is risking a "Wally Pipp," gulping down what turned out to be "the two most expensive aspirins in history."

And then there is Tinker-to-Evers-to-Chance, the magnificent double-play combination of the Chicago Cubs. In 1908 the club won the pennant with an infield of Joe Tinker at shortstop, Johnny Evers at second base, and Frank Chance at first. The surprise is that they were not monumental that year at all, combining for a meager sixteen double plays (the record, 217, is held by the 1948 Philadelphia A's). Ah, but they had art as well as sport on their side. New York columnist Franklin P. Adams shuffled the trio into the pantheon of sport with just a few brief lines:

> *These are the saddest of possible words:*
>   *"Tinker to Evers to Chance."* . . .
> *Ruthlessly pricking our gonfalon bubble,*
> *Making a Giant hit into a double,*
> *Words that are heavy with nothing but trouble:*
>   *"Tinker to Evers to Chance."*

A "gonfalon," a word that dates from Renaissance Italy, is a flag; and in the world of baseball it's the only flag that counts, the championship pennant.

To my mind, games become vital and riveting only when you know and love the diction and history. It all raises delightful speculation: Why are there no northpaws? And if there are "speed merchants," then why not "error merchants"? I myself have known one or two of those.

Of course, you can think too much about all this. Hitters—and writers—get themselves in trouble that way, trying to outguess the opposition. As one batter (in Mark Harris's *Bang the Drum Slowly*) said: "Knowing what is coming is only half the trick. You have still got to hit it."

Notes and Further Reading

The card catalogue at the Library of Congress is no more. My stumbling on Henry Chadwick's slips in those dark wooden trays was the inspiration for this piece, but it's all been replaced by a hard disk. So long, serendipity.

Peck & Snyder's Amateur Score Book, For the Coming Season (New York, 1883) contains an introduction by Chadwick, "On Scoring in Baseball." See also *Cosgrove's Symbol Score-Book for Baseball Games* (Stockton, California, 1887). *De Witt's Baseball Guide for 1872,* edited by Henry Chadwick, also has an essay by him on scoring; its cover is printed *De Witt's hand books, no. 1.* All three of these books are in the Library of Congress.

For the foul ball as a "chicken," see Henry Schwartz, "1871: The First Baseball Game Downtown Was No July 4 Picnic," *Downtown* (San Diego), June 28, 1984. In Brooklyn in the 1950s, a dying quail was an "egg ball," according to Terry Gillen, and a ball that was deflected by telephone wires was termed "hinders," invariably pronounced "Hindu." Joseph McBride's *High & Inside: The Complete Guide to Baseball Slang* (New York: Warner Books, 1980) can be read with pleasure.

Part of this chapter, on Dwight Gooden and K, first appeared in the *Washington Post,* May 4, 1986.

▣ Horse Racing

BEFORE 1780 a horse race was only a horse race, and a Derby was just a man. His name: Edward Smith Stanley, twelfth earl of Derby. But by spring of that year, big changes were about to occur.

Derby and Sir Charles Bunbury, a friend and fellow breeder of fine horses, were founding a new race, a springtime test of the fastest three-year-old Thoroughbreds in all England. But before the first test could be run, on the yawning expanse of flat earth known as Epsom Downs, the contest had to be named. The question was, Which of the two partners would it be named for? A coin flashed in the air . . . and landed in Derby's favor. A good thing, too. Otherwise we'd all be trooping out to Churchill Downs every May to see the Kentucky Bunbury. In fact, derbys have become so splendid a test of horses that more than a hundred such races are now annually held, worldwide. And they were almost called bunburys. (Perhaps as consolation, Bunbury's horse Diomed *did* win that first derby.)

Horse racing is a very old business. The Romans and Greeks had spectacular horse-racing competitions, and even built hippodromes especially for the sport. But their horses pulled chariots. The emphasis was on the skill and bravery of the drivers, not on the horses themselves. Plato once wondered why anyone would want to mortgage his life to the mastery of such a trivial activity. And though there was a great deal of wagering on the outcomes, the sport was really a way of encouraging the arts of war: the horse and its chariot rider were formidable.

A winning tradition at the hippodrome was also thought to enhance prestige and encourage trade. The little Greek city-state of Agrigento on the south coast of Sicily put its all into developing horses and drivers for the Panhellenic games. They were so successful that archaeologists still recognize their coins by the racing chariots they bear.

To England goes the laurel for developing both the Thoroughbred and the regulations that govern the modern racing world. There were meets at London's Smithfield market as early as 1174, and Hyde Park was having regular races by 1637. The new king, Charles I, patronized the racing at Newmarket in 1625 and probably awarded Newmarket's first Gold Cup in 1634. His son Charles II was an even greater horseman who jockeyed his own steeds, authored rules, and worked to settle racecourse disputes.

One of the earliest accounts of a racecourse appears on a broadside in the Bodleian Library, Oxford. Dated May 26, 1662, it's loaded with details. Race length? Five miles of plowed land, harrowed twice, seeded with hay. Heats? Three. Number of judges? Also three—one to weigh the riders and enforce the weight limit of ten stone or 140 pounds (this judge also presided at the finish line), a second judge to make sure all the horses reached the halfway mark before turning back, and a third to see to a fair start. To the winner went a cup worth a fiver (at a time when a well-paid schoolmaster made about ten pounds a year) donated by the race underwriter, the marquess of Newcastle. The entry stakes were ten shillings for each horse. The winner kept both the cup and his entry fee. Second place took the rest of the stakes.

Flat racing (on straightaways without jumps) was the invention and mania of the upper classes from its very beginning. They owned the land and had courses laid out all over East Anglia in the seventeenth century.

Such people worry about decorum. There were constant cautions against violence: "If any rider whip another rider, or his horse on the face, or pull back another's bridle, he shall lose the cup." What we'd call substance abuse was also monitored: during the half-hour rubdown between heats, the horses were only to receive "faire water." Jockeys were to be weighed between heats, and were allowed to lose no more than two pounds in perspiration ("wastage"). Rules like these echo down the straightaways of racing history. The constant repetition of them argues that they were regularly violated. The sport of kings? And gentlemen? Well, whenever money and wagering has been involved, men—pedigreed or not— have always sought ways of increasing their odds. Even the jockey of King George IV was discovered to have thrown a race.

The rough-and-tumble race known as the steeplechase was a far different matter. Originally, these cross-country meets were run over obstacles from one village steeple to the next. They were organized by the hunting crowd, who wanted to prevent the Thoroughbred owners—who had their own flat races—from dominating all the hunting races. The first recorded steeplechase dates back to 1752 in Ireland: a four-and-a-half-mile course from Buttevant Church to St. Leger Church.

Aristocrats like Newcastle and Derby had sired flat racing, but steeplechases soon became big moneymakers for publicans, tavern owners, and brewers. From the very start, the steeplechase became the haunt of lower-class louts, a gigantic booze-up. The contrast was clear. By the 1880s, steeplechasing was "the recognized refuge of all outcasts, human and equine, from the legitimate turf."

The two reputations are now totally reversed. As everyone knows, American steeplechases and point-to-points are the province of the weekend horsey set, the Upperville country squires—or at least people who would like to appear country squires—most of whom wouldn't be caught dead bellying up to the two-dollar window at Bowie or Santa Anita.

Historically, there are two surprising outcomes of this rage for racing. First, horse breeders over a century ago gave the world the fashions we now call sports clothes. Without horses and horsemen, Ralph Lauren and the people who make loafer snaffles would be out of business. The idea: If you can't be a country squire, you can at least look like one.

Second, the primary appeal of the newspaper in the late eighteenth century was its ability to publish race results from far and near. Track news was the foremost product of early journalism. Sod the Battle of Yorktown, who won yesterday at Epsom?

Since the horse is not native to North America, it was from Spanish conquistadors that American Indians got their mounts, which came mainly from the wild descendants of horses lost by Cortés and de Soto. Over the centuries, horse racing grew to become a favorite pastime of the Plains Indians. The fur trader Henry A. Boller, who lived among the Gros Ventre Indians along the upper Missouri from 1858 to 1862, recorded one such scene:

Five or six young men are galloping away, in the direction of the creek, fully a half mile distant. They are naked, with the scanty exception of a breechcloth, and control their spirited ponies with a lariat tied around the lower jaw.

From the tops of the lodges eager eyes are directed towards the starting-point and a few brief sentences announce to the expectant throng that the riders are coming this way. In one moment the competitors are spread out in line. The next they are hid from view by an intervening roll of the prairie, but the quick strokes of their horses hoofs grow rapidly more distinct.

I like that a lot, especially the bit about the horses dipping out of view in the terrain. It's exactly how Homer describes the chariot race on the plains below Troy in the *Iliad.* Boller loved these Indians, and depicted them in epic colors. The race continues:

> The friends of the competitors yield to the impulse of the moment and make bets, throwing down robes, blankets, and guns in the most reckless manner. The riders lean forward until they lie almost flat upon their horses, yelling, thumping their heels into their sides, and using the heavy Indian whip with a will.
>
> Gathering all his energies for the decisive moment, the Crow-that-Flies shoots far ahead of the rest, and careers on at full speed until within a few feet of the edge of the precipitous bank of the river. Then, checking his horse so suddenly as to throw him back on his haunches, he wheels sharply around and canters back to receive the congratulations of his friends.

Not that all of Boller's accounts of Indian races ended so congenially. At Fort Berthold, North Dakota, a winning steed was once killed by an arrow through its heart, fired by a disgruntled loser. Left for the ravenous village dogs, the carcass was picked clean before dawn the next day.

Early American patriots were so incensed at wasteful luxury in the Colonies that they constantly tried to curb horse racing itself, never mind the wagering that attended it. On October 20, 1774, the Continental Congress sought no less than the eradication of "every species of extravagance and dissipation, especially all horseracing, and all kinds of gaming, cock-fighting, and other expensive diversions and entertainments."

They had in mind something like the excesses of Virginian John Carter (1732–1806), owner of the plantation called Shirley on the James River. He had a great silver bowl crafted with the image of his favorite horse, Nestor. Carter filled it with champagne and gave it to Nestor after every race.

Horse racing had become a fixture on the social calendar of every American town. In the days before *Eyewitness News,* the horse race was an important place for governing officials and politicians to display themselves before an admiring populace. Every village had its racecourse laid out. In Annapolis, they raced outside the west gate of the city on relatively flat ground, almost within the shadow of the colonial capitol.

Just east of Williamsburg, Virginia, on land now occupied by a railroad right-of-way, was its municipal course. English visitor John Smyth surveyed the scene in the 1770s: "There are races at Williamsburg twice a year. Adjoining to the town is a very excellent course, for either two, three or four mile heats." Winning horses would take a purse of one hundred pounds the first day of the meet, Smyth said, and fifty pounds each day thereafter. But those were just the race stakes; side bets considerably spread the action about, "the inhabitants, almost to a man, being quite devoted to the diversion of horse-racing."

It's easy to see why we're still addicted to horses. Up close—chomping green grass out of our flat palms—they seem human, childlike. But from a distance they're all power, blinding speed. Pizarro's horses so terrified the Inca nation that 24 million people could be overcome by 167 men and 27 horses, the armored personnel carriers of the sixteenth century.

Certainly, horses can be big, scary machines. Not for nothing do the Four Horses of the Apocalypse announce the crack of doom (and get transmogrified by Grantland Rice into the lethal backfield of Notre Dame football). Not for nothing did the Venetians steal the four bronze horses from Constantinople's hippodrome in 1204 and mount them atop St. Mark's Basilica. It was all the same at those first London race meetings, just outside the city gates in Smithfield, in 1174:

The horses are so eager for the race that their limbs tremble and they chafe at the delay; they cannot stay still. At the signal they leap forward. . . . You would think that, as Heraclitus says, the whole world was moving. . . .

Notes and Further Reading

William Nack is the best writer covering horse racing today; his farewell to Secretariat, "Pure Heart," *Sports Illustrated,* October 24, 1994, is perfect. Bill Barich's *Laughing in the Hills* (New York: Viking, 1980) is another fine writer's take on the human need for horse racing. For the almost ineffable logic of horse racing and wagering, read anything and everything by Andy Beyer.

Banstead Downs was the seventeenth-century name for an area south of London that ran from Croydon to Farnham and included Epsom, later the site of the Derby. Samuel Pepys mentions in his diary entry for May 27, 1663, that he regrets missing the great "horse-race and foot-race" at Banstead. Epsom was mainly known for its mineral waters, which were dehydrated and marketed elsewhere as Epsom salts.

For the Bodleian broadside, see C. H. Firth, "Racing in the Seventeenth century," *N&Q,* 7th series, VI:421 (December 1, 1888). For racing regulations, see "J. M.," "Horse Races on Leith Sands, Sept. 5, 1723," *N&Q,* 4th series, VIII:349 (October 28, 1871). For Indian racing, see Boller, 165 and 288.

For steeplechases, see Roger Munting, *Hedges and Hurdles: A Social and Economic History of National Hunt Racing* (London: W. H. Allen, 1987). See also Roger Mortimer, *The History of the Derby Stakes* (London: Michael Joseph, 1962).

On racing at Williamsburg, see John Ferdinand Dalziel Smyth, *A Tour in the United States of America* (London: G. Robinson, 1784), I:17–21. See also John W. Reps, *Tidewater Towns* (Charlottesville: University of Virginia Press, 1972), 180 and 313n.

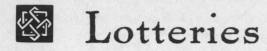 # Lotteries

WHEN IT COMES TIME to consider the value of lotteries, the argument, in effect, inclines toward one of two people: either Leslie Robins or Tessie Hutchinson.

Who?

In July 1993, Robins hit the lottery, raking in $111 million, the largest single winner in U.S. history. You can put him down as a big plus in favor of the idea.

On the downside, there's the pathetic figure of Hutchinson, the antiheroine of Shirley Jackson's powerful 1948 short story "The Lottery." Tessie, you will recall, rashly selected the paper slip with the black spot, won her village lottery, and was stoned to death for her trouble, proclaiming all the while, "It isn't fair, it isn't right."

Actually, the fairness of lotteries is the best thing about them. We have, all of us, looked to their unimpeachable equity and randomness for years, ever since our school days. Back then, the process of choosing up sides to play team games, or deciding who was in and who was out, often depended on little lotteries counted on our fingers, on the fall of a tennis racket, or on the last hand able to grasp and swing a baseball bat. Even doggerel was enlisted to help make seemingly random selections, by reciting what folklorists call "counting-out rhymes." Typical is this example chanted by a Welsh girl: "Ip, dip, dip,/ My little ship,/ Sailing on the water/ Like a cup and saucer,/ But you are not in IT."

The modern rebirth of interest in lotteries is easy to fathom. They *appear* to be a painless way for governments to stay solvent—even though player profiles show lotteries to be a regressive tax that takes far more from the poor than the rich. Still, every dollar dragooned out of private purses via the lottery is one that does not have to be raised through a hateful tax. So the argument goes.

Oddly enough, this line of reasoning was found persuasive by one of our Founding Fathers. Thomas Jefferson, in a famous essay penned in February 1826, saw the lottery as "a salutary instrument" and a "tax . . . laid on the willing only, that is to say, on those who can risk the price of a ticket without sensible injury for the possibility of a higher prize."

Jefferson's purpose in writing the essay was to prompt the Virginia legislature to let him run a private lottery so he could sell off the bulk of his lands around Monticello. To his mind, the lottery was virtually the only way of selling large and expensive parcels of agricultural land, especially in a depressed tobacco-and-wheat economy with little cash and fewer buyers. "This method of selling," Jefferson noted sadly, "was formerly very much resorted to, until it was thought to nourish too much a spirit of hazard."

As a result of that spirit, in 1769 the legislature began to control all lotteries in the Virginia Colony. After the founding of the United States, Jefferson observed between 1782 and 1820 close to seventy instances in which the legislature put its stamp of approval on lotteries to raise money for schools, bridges, mills, and roads as well as for general state revenues. In a 1791 case, a lottery was held simply to allow a nervous author enough money and leisure to finish a book. "This, then," Jefferson urged, "is a declaration by the nation, that an act was not immoral, of which they were in the habitual use themselves as a part of the regular means of supporting the government; the tax on the vendor of tickets was their share of the profits, and if their share was innocent, his could not be criminal."

In not condemning them outright, Jefferson was following the conventional wisdom regarding lotteries that had been handed down from classical and medieval times. Far from being a debased game, lots were a way of divining the future and of giving the gods a palpable voice in everyday affairs.

The lottery derives from the ancient game called lots, a choosing or selecting game. Herodotus is the first to mention lots and he does so in connection with the reign of the ancient Lydian king Atys. During the same famine in which the king is reported to have invented ballplaying and dicing as diversions for his hungry populace, the resourceful monarch was forced to divide the people into two groups. He made them draw lots to determine who would stay and who would leave.

By the time of Herodotus, lots or "sorts" seem to have become a commonplace of Greek public life. Elections at Athens by lottery (sortition or κλήρωσι) were thought to be more equitable and less likely to encourage political dynasties. In fact, the lottery was familiar enough to serve in the title of a lost play by the comic dramatist Diphilos. Called the *Kleroumenoi,* "The Lot-Drawers," its plot involved two slaves who draw lots to decide which man shall have the hand of a fair maid. We only know of the play today because it was transposed into Latin by Plautus as his play *Casina.*

So too the luck of the draw figures in Homer, where the funeral games in honor of Patroclus began with a chariot race. The five competitors cast their lots in Achilles' helmet to determine their starting places. Among the Greeks, it was the custom to shake the container holding the lots until one fell out. The owner of that lot was declared the winner. In this case, the lot belonging to Nestor's son Antilochus was the first out. He took the pole position, but lost the race.

In Roman life, lots were a religious rite, part of a standard kit for predicting the future. Roman sorts also were made of wood or bone, with short verses inscribed on them (not unlike fortune cookies). These were to be drawn out of an urn (by a child occasionally). Some lots, like a famous set discovered near Padua, even had holes drilled into them so they could be kept on a string and at hand. By Cicero's time, however, the casting of lots had fallen out of favor in Roman religion. Said he: "The whole scheme of divination by lots was fraudulently contrived from mercenary motives, or as a means of encouraging superstition and error."

In addition to religious uses, lots also served important political and social ends. For example, judges who were to pronounce sentences for publicly condemned criminals were selected by lot. Julius Caesar was so selected to condemn Gaius Rabirius, a political enemy. For their drinking sessions after meals, the Romans would select from among the guests a master of ceremonies (the *magister* or *arbiter bibendi*) to preside over the evening's toasts. He was chosen by casting lots. The Romans also held lotteries to dispense gifts, which could range from slaves to nuts. Martial refers to this custom in a series of 350 epigrams, one for each of the gifts likely to be given out.

The idea of casting lots as an aid to decision making received a curious mixture of approval and censure from medieval officials. There is, of course, the biblical case of Jonah. When Jonah's shipmates were seeking a reason for the great storm that threatened their lives, they cast lots. Since the draw clearly pointed to Jonah as the object of God's anger, he was thrown overboard.

This scriptural approval gave rise to an odd species of lottery that was allowed to take place within the medieval church itself. Caesarius of Heisterbach, a thirteenth-century writer, spells out this sanctuary custom, known as choosing "Apostles by Lot." In this ceremony, the devout would select from among twelve tapers, one for each apostle, randomly laid out on the church altar with the saints' names hidden from view. Caesarius tells of a woman who was said to have received a deathbed reproof from St. Andrew because she once discarded his taper in order to have a chance at another saint. Another woman was stricken with palsy for a year because she threw the taper of St. Jude behind the altar. Both wanted, apparently, a more useful and effective (and more popular) patron for their special prayers.

Caesarius notes that even this lottery had biblical precedent. St. Matthias, he points out, was chosen by lot to replace the lost Judas. Still, says Caesarius, "I have heard at Cologne a learned priest publicly reproving such elections in church; 'all apostles,' said he, 'are equally holy.'"

From all this, it seems clear that lotteries were seldom regarded as intrinsically evil. As is often noted about the history of games, it's only their abuse that causes them to be condemned.

There was, however, a tendency in the late Middle Ages to see lots as a flirtation with witchcraft. Writers of the fourteenth century made a distinction between those who practiced *sors* and those who practiced *sortilegium*. The former could legitimately be involved in such activities as dividing property or deciding which of two beggars would get limited alms. By contrast, *sortilegium*, the profane dependence on either God's or Satan's power to control the fall of the lot, was almost always banned.

The *sortilegia* work as follows, according to Thomas Aquinas: "By observing which of several sheets of paper, with or without writing upon them, a person may happen to draw, or by holding out several unequal sticks and noting who takes the greater or the less." Similar attempts at divination were possible by casting stones or dice onto the "points" of the backgammon board or, frequently, with the random opening of books, such as the Bible or the *Aeneid*, believed to have mystical and fortune-telling powers.

Lotteries have an important place in literature. In addition to the Bible, where lots are cast for the sacred garments on Golgotha, there is the singular instance of the *Canterbury Tales*. In that poem, lots are drawn to decide which pilgrim will tell the first tale. In a way then a lottery is the mainspring of Chaucer's whole fiction. Note too how a winning ticket in a Mexican lottery brings about the action in B. Traven's *Treasure of the Sierra Madre*. Is it purely coincidental that this novel is a modern version of Chaucer's "Pardoner's Tale"?

By far the greatest problem with any lottery is the dearth of winning tickets, paper slips, or broom straws. This is unfortunately true whether you're trying to ease the national tax burden or just trying to stake out your own plot on Easy Street. So it's nice to know that someone has thought out an appropriate response to the agony of this particular kind of defeat. On April 24, 1752, the *Virginia Gazette*, a newspaper printed in Williamsburg, published "A Meditation . . . by an unsuccessful Adventurer in a Late Lottery." In it, the anonymous writer, possibly a sore loser, confidently asked:

Why frets my Soul because of a Blank! or why doth it lament at having missed of a Prize? Suppose I had got one of the Ten Thousands, what then?—Why then, slap dash down at a Blow, with the whole Catalogue of my Wants. But soft Would not the Destruction of those Wants be the Generation of others? . . . At this Rate, what would be gained by a Ten Thousand Pound Prize?—Nothing—Or, what have I lost by a Blank?—Nothing at all.—Why then, a Blank is as good as a Ten Thousand Pound Prize. . . . Then what are they who rejoice at a Prize? Prize Fools. And what are they who grieve at a Blank? Blank Fools.

Tell it to Leslie Robins.

Notes and Further Reading

For sorts *(sortes)* and sortition, see *Dictionnaire des Antiquités Grecques et Romaines*, eds. Charles Daremberg and Edmond Saglio, 5 vols. (Paris: Hachette, 1877), IV:176; see also *Oxford Classical Dictionary*, eds. N. G. L. Hammond and H. H. Scullard (Oxford: Clarendon Press, 1970), 1003; also Hazlitt, 557, and Smith, 687. On some golden bowls given away during the Saturnalian lotteries, see Friedlander, 279. On the lots found at Padua, see Smith; see also John Edwin Sandys, *A Companion to Latin Studies* (Cambridge: Cambridge University Press, 1935), 749–750. The Cicero quotation is from *De Divinatione* (London: Heinemann, 1922), II.xli.85 (p. 467). The Aquinas quotation is from *Summa Theologica*, II.ii.95. Caesarius of Heisterbach's tale of "Apostles by Lot" is reprinted in G. G. Coulton's *Life in the Middle Ages* (Cambridge: Cambridge University Press, 1935), 69–70. The Williamsburg lottery meditation is reprinted by Jane Carson in her *Colonial Virginians at Play* (Charlottesville: University of Virginia Press, 1965), 84. For "Ip, Dip, Dip," see Opie, 377–378. Finally, for how Chaucer's narrator Harry Bailly rigs the draw so the knight tells his tale first, see my "Chaucer's Little Lotteries: The Literary Exploitation of a Medieval Game," *Arete: The Journal of Sport Literature* 2 (1984): 171–182.

Chess

NO GAME has been as influential in cultural history as chess.

The thirteenth-century *Chess Book*, a Latin collection of observations on playing chess by a Dominican monk, was one of the most popular books of the Middle Ages. It was copied, plagiarized, and recycled in countless editions, in many languages, and in both poetry and prose. It was such a hot commercial property it was the second book printed in English (at Bruges by Caxton in 1476), under the title *The Game and Playe of the Chesse.*

Chess had such a following that Shakespeare refers to the game fifty-seven times, while his contemporary Thomas Middleton spent time in the clink for writing a play called *A Game at Chesse* (1624). It was much more than just another chess allegory, however. At heart it was a thinly veiled attack on court politics and the Spanish ambassador; that's what got Middleton tossed in jail.

Violence has something to do with the appeal of chess. There are countless examples of assassinations attempted, and accomplished, while a victim ponders over a chess move (in the same way that gunslingers were killed at card games on our frontier). And there is the legendary example of Charlot, son of Charlemagne, who killed the son of a Danish warrior, using the chessboard itself as his fell weapon. About 1200, Walter Map, archdeacon of Oxford, tells of a similar taunt over the chessboard that led to a vicious revenge, involving the eyes and genitals of a player being splashed down on the board among the chessmen. This bloody act was accompanied by one last taunt: "Mate!"

Actually, the popularity of chess is not hard to understand. Its play was reminiscent of the clash of armies, with their kings, knights, and foot soldiers. More important, the game also reflected the struggle up and down the medieval social structure: protection, promotion, misfortune, elimination, death, and loss. It was the perfect metaphor for life itself. Although it was essentially a mind game, it spelled carnage and mayhem.

Early chess took two forms. In the first, players contemplated long and hard over their moves; medieval commentators regularly complained about the interminable length of these games. In the second form, however, dice were used to speed up the moves, just like in backgammon. Much more frequent, then, were contemporary complaints about the use of dice with chess.

In Italy in A.D. 1062 Cardinal Damiani condemned chess, its play, and wagering on its outcome. He seemed to regard it as just another dice game. The cardinal was probably right to do so, for until 1475 the dice remained. A vestige of the dice play is still present today in the practice of beginning each game with a kind of lottery to determine who plays with white and who with black pieces. Player one places both hands behind his back, holding a pawn of each color. Player two then chooses a hand. If he selects white, he gets the decided advantage of having the first move.

Chess had its origins in the East, probably in India, and was brought to Europe by the Arabs through Spain. Much of the history of chess can be inferred linguistically from Arabic. For example, according to scholar H. J. R. Murray, whose definitive *A*

History of Chess was published in 1913, the Persian/Arabic word *shah* was used for the important kinglike piece on the chessboard. But it also was a term used during the game to signal that the king was in danger. In Latin *shah* evolved to become *scacus,* the name of the game, and the verb *scacare,* "to check." Our word "checkmate" is likely derived from the phrase *shah mat,* "the king is dead."

Similarly, the Arabic elephant, *al-fil,* became our bishop, while their chariot, *rukh,* became our rook. At the same time, the Eastern cavalrymen were transformed into medieval knights and oriental foot soldiers adopted the Latin *pedo* (foot) and became pawns. The Arabic *firs,* the equivalent of our queen, was a much less powerful piece than it is in modern chess. In its one-square moves (except for an opening) and in its vulnerability, it resembled today's king. Nor could the bishops make the long diagonal moves that they do today. This meant that knights and rooks were the most powerful pieces on the board. In fact, the name queen itself was given to the old *firs* piece simply because of its position on the board next to the king. The Arabic *firs* lives on today in our words vizier and viceroy.

It is also fair to say that the changes in this age-old game brought about by a few centuries of play in Europe greatly improved it. European refinements—from A.D. 800 to 1100 in the movement of the pieces and their relative power were critical to the game's popularity. Meanwhile, the game slowly conquered the Continent, reaching England about the time of the Norman Conquest.

The changes tell us something of the medieval view of chess. In Muslim chess, the *firs* had been a sort of commanding general to the *shah.* In medieval Europe, the change from commanding general to queen was paralleled by changing the eight infantrymen to eight pawns, peasants in fact. As a result, the Eastern game of battle strategy became one that dealt with the social order as well.

Overall, chess history seems to divide neatly into three phases. Muslim chess in Europe extends up to about A.D. 1000, then comes medieval chess until about 1475, when modern chess, totally without dice, begins. This completely supersedes the older versions by the mid-sixteenth century.

The impetus to improve the play of chess can be traced to the collecting of so-called chess problems, notably in a manuscript from about 1250 or 1275 called *Bonus Socius* (Good Fellowship). The fact was, the slow and inconclusive nature of medieval chess, without dice, led to a great many draws. That reduced the game's attraction to the gambling crowd, and the publication of chess problems in an early kind of self-help manual aimed to overcome this defect. *Bonus Socius* presents 194 chess games and gives advice on other board games as well. The book survives in many manuscripts.

The thirteenth century also saw the first attempt to attach some moral purpose to chess, a sure sign of the game's popularity. This appeared as the work of the Dominican Jacobus de Cessolis, whose *Chess Book* is a compendium of allegorical interpretations of the game. For him, chess is an apt representation of the capabilities and duties of every rank in human society as it moves through the game of life. A king, for example, presides over his kingdom but has to be protected by the people, his pawns and knights. Pawns have a right to promote themselves after a lifetime of sacrificial duty. A queen is free to move as either a rook or a bishop "since she is the representative and personal advisor of the king." De Cessolis also includes a lengthy session on the virtues that are necessary to each station in life. A queen, for instance, needs only *castitas* (chastity) for obvious reasons and *sapientia* (wisdom) for the education of princes. Highest among the classes of pawns are the plowmen, who are blessed with loyalty and truth.

This monastic imprimatur was certainly high praise for a game. Even civil authorities seemed to smile on chess. In the twelfth century, the Spaniard Pedro Alfonso included chess among his list of seven aristocratic skills. (The others: riding, boxing, fowling, swimming, archery, and poetry.) Apparently the royal houses of Europe took this advice seriously. Louis XIII of France learned the game when he was six years old. In 1341, Edward III of England entreated his hostess, the countess of Salisbury, to keep a valuable ring she won from him over the chessboard one relaxed evening before an expedition against the Scots.

The medieval church seems to have adopted a rather casual attitude toward chess for the most part. Perhaps it was following de Cessolis in this. What is more likely, however, is that of all possible recreations, chess alone reflected the monastic spirit by putting a premium on reflection and meditation during the course of play.

But too much of a good thing was distinctly possible. When Archbishop Peckham found too many monks at chess during his January 1281 visitation to Cokesford, he perpetually banned the game and ordered three days of bread and water for anyone caught at it again.

Among the Jews, chess was generally regarded as a thoughtful and sober game, following the tradition that it was invented by King Solomon. At Cremona in 1576 all players of games of chance were condemned, except for chess players when they were not playing for money. Eventually the game evolved into a regular Sabbath recreation. In fact it was customary, up to the sixteenth century, for Jews to have a special set of silver chessmen for Sabbath play.

As de Cessolis discovered, medieval chess was admirably suited to portraying the game of life. In it, all ranks and stations had their moments, and success or failure seemed to depend as much on skill in manipulating the pieces as it did on luck. The alert preacher would want his audience to learn from this that the winner's success might last only until his next game, and that the loser might yet end up victorious. The implication was that winners must ever be vigilant to gain heaven. Losers still have time to work on their game.

Because of all this approval, medieval art is rife with chess. Most famous is a set of sixty-seven walrus ivory chessmen now in the

British Museum but originally found on the Isle of Lewis in the Outer Hebrides, discovered there along the eroding shoreline one fine June day in 1831. Remarkably, the set suggests that the game was regally played in the Far North as early as 1150. And there are countless other examples of illuminated manuscripts, stone carvings, misericords, and ivory mirror-backs, all showing the game in play.

By far the single most common image connected with chess is that of Death as player. In modern times, this stark evocation of the Middle Ages was in part responsible for the success of Ingmar Bergman's film *The Seventh Seal* (1957). In it, a knight plays chess with a hooded Death in a valiant attempt to forestall his demise during the plague. The medieval stained-glass window "Death Calls for the Archbishop" in St. Andrew's Church, Norwich, is similarly constructed around a chess game. There, as part of the church fabric itself, a wan prelate—the third highest ecclesiastical office a man could hope for—struggles for his life with an abstraction. The message is clear: If *he* could not forestall the end, what shall *we* do?

Why should the Middle Ages choose a mere game to show the encounter between Death and mankind? Because chess was no trifle. It had a clearly defined set of rules, just like life. Its action and actors were lifelike. It was life in little. The lesson behind the image was simply that Death has a terrifying finality. Its inexorability is rivaled only by the endgame in chess when one's opponent is a great player. Plainly, Death is a grand master.

Notes and Further Reading

In Woody Allen, Death plays gin rummy. See "Death Knocks," *The Complete Prose* (London: Picador, 1993).

H. J. R. Murray's 1913 history of chess is magisterial; it will not be superseded.

Bonus Socius was translated by James F. Magee, Jr. as *Good Companion* (Florence: Tipografia Giuntina, 1916). The *Chess Book* is available as "Jacobus de Cessolis: *Libellus de Moribus Hominum et Officiis Nobilium Ac Popularium Super Ludo Scachorum,*" ed. and trans. Sister Marie Anna Burt (dissertation, University of Texas, 1957).

For the walrus or narwhal ivory chess pieces, see Michael Taylor, *The Lewis Chessmen* (London: British Museum, 1978). For violence at the chessboard, see *Master Walter Map's Book De Nugis Curialium,* trans. Frederick Tupper and Marbury Blanden Ogle (New York: Macmillan, 1924), 242. For more on Middleton, see Bernard M. Wagner, "New Allusions to *A Game at Chesse,*" *PMLA* 44 (1929): 827–834. For Jews and chess, see Landman I:304, and Landman II:44.

In London in the 1850s there was apparently a salon near the Strand where you could hire people dressed up as chess pieces ("five shillings each player per game") and move them about on a large chessboard laid out on the floor. See "M.C.," "A Novel Game of Chess," *N&Q,* 2nd series, III:338 (April 25, 1857). "M.C." claims to have actually participated in such a "living chess" game, moving his pieces by calling out instructions from a pulpit at one end of the board. It was "very perplexing to the player, and from the fidgetting of the individual chess-men he was in momentary expectation of seeing some of his pawns, or pieces, take huff and walk off the board without leave."

And, finally, this is Raymond Chandler's view of chess, from *The Long Goodbye* (1953): "She hung up and I set out the chessboard. I filled a pipe, paraded the chessmen, and inspected them for French shaves and loose buttons, and played a championship tournament game between Gortchakoff and Meninkin, seventy-two moves to a draw, a prize specimen of the irresistible force meeting the immovable object, a battle without armour, a war without blood, and as elaborate a waste of human intelligence as you could find anywhere outside an advertising agency."

 # Cards

*"He calls the knaves, Jacks, this boy!" said Estella
with disdain.*

— DICKENS, *GREAT EXPECTATIONS,* 1861

PLAINLY, young Pip faces a lifetime of trouble. When he uses a low-class word while playing the child's card game Beggar-my-Neighbor, the mistake speaks volumes about Pip's status and prospects in the world. "I determined to ask Joe," he later relates, "why he had ever taught me to call those picture-cards, Jacks, which ought to be called knaves. I wished Joe had been rather more genteelly brought up, and then I should have been so too." Cards may seem a trivial pursuit, but in fact they're eloquent.

Although Beggar-my-Neighbor is an easy child's game of battle, it cannot be very old. Why? Because cards are a comparatively modern invention. It's strange, really. Most card games are so simple, you'd think they were around forever and that the simplicity betrays eons of refinement and experiment. The theory—in play as in Nature—is that complex games evolved from easy ones. Just like we evolved from blue-green algae. But not in this case.

Dice and board games? They are truly ancient, and came to us practically ready-made from Egyptian and oriental sources. Muslims imported chess from medieval India. That's why it's always a surprise to discover that playing cards arrived so late.

Cards were a thirteenth-century development that originated on the Continent and slowly migrated to England. Chaucer, who wrote at the end of the fourteenth century and whose poetry is loaded with references to games of all sorts, does not mention cards. If cards were at all common in England, Chaucer would have found a way of using them.

Continental references to cards are, however, nearly as old as Chaucer, who died in 1400. The most important of these is the notice in 1393 that a French painter was to be paid for decorating a pack of cards to console the mad King Charles VI. There are few earlier references. Cards were being played in Italy in the 1320s. In France a 1341 manuscript of *Le Roman de Renard le Contrefait* refers to the playing of *cartes,* while a 1350 chronicle of life at the court of Charles V records a rebuke to certain pages for wasting their time at cards. A pack of fifty-two cards is described in Switzerland in 1377. Belgian card playing is documented in 1379. And cards appeared in Nuremberg, Germany, in 1384.

In England, the important dates for card history are 1461, when Edward IV forbade card playing except during Christmas, and 1463, when an embargo on foreign-made packs went into effect to protect British card makers and to stem the outflow of the island's money. Indeed, the fifteenth century in England was the watershed century for the popularity of cards. The inveterate letter writer Margery Paston complained on December 24, 1484, that cards were gradually replacing caroling and other traditional Yuletide customs—much as mothers today complain about the execrable practice of watching televised football at Thanksgiving and Christmas.

To this day the face cards are still decorated with English court costume of that century. The jack, for one, wears the precise court herald's getup. By contrast, wrote anthropologist and games expert Stewart Culin in 1898, "England appears to have at once adopted the French suit marks." That's why we have hearts, diamonds, clubs, and spades, rather than the sausages, cats, parrots, and horses of old German card makers. The English names of the suits, however, are partly of Spanish descent.

The Spanish connection is vital because cards, like chess in the very early Middle Ages, came to Europe through Spain, the great cultural meeting ground between Europe and Islam. An Italian scholar noted the linguistic evidence in 1379. "Cards," he said, "came from the land of the Saracens, and are called *naib* by them." The Spanish word for cards is still *naipes*.

Etienne de Vignolles, a supporter of Joan of Arc, is credited with originating the modern suits: spades, diamonds, clubs, and hearts. His instincts seem to have been to give the game a social and moral dimension, much as we have already seen with the history of chess. Thus the *pique* or lance (pike) represents the aristocracy. The *carreau*, an arrowhead or diamond paving stone, represents the townsmen. The *trefle* or cloverleaf stands for fodder, the peasantry. And the church is represented by *coeur*, a heart, the symbol of charity or love. By 1628, when the Worshipful Company of Makers of Playing Cards was incorporated in London, the heart had become something far more secular. The guild was created to once again protect English manufacturers from foreign card imports. Its punning motto: *Corde recto elati omnes*, "All are exalted by a good heart."

Oddly enough, an English lottery game called Ragman's Roll seems to have contributed to the development of cards. A simple pastime, this was an acting-out or reading game in which the players—children and adults—would write verses or stock characters on slips of paper and then randomly pull them out of a rolled-up manuscript. At the time, manuscript sheets were pasted end to end and rolled, rather than gathered as pages into book form. The manuscript at game's start must have had the appearance of an old rug with countless tag ends sticking out. Ragman's Roll also gave us the modern word "rigmarole," a catalogue of nonsense. In diplomacy and law, a difficult treaty or legal document, rolled up with many seals and ribbons hanging out of it, was also called a Ragman's Roll in honor of the child's game. In time, the game was simplified by writing the verses and characters on sheets and dealing them out as if they were cards. Because of this, some historians believe Ragman's Roll to be the immediate precursor of modern cards.

The conventional view, however, is that cards developed from chess. Nineteenth-century historian Thomas Wright saw cards as "the game of chess transferred to paper, and without a board. . . . Cards, while they possessed some of the characteristics of chess, presented the same mixture of chance and skill." In addition, card games could be incredibly simple and brief and portable—all features of gambling games.

It's clear that playing-cards really satisfied the needs of the time better than chess. Card games provided a means of gambling far superior to any board game, and they gradually took the place of chess as the favorite game of the leisured classes. The reform of chess late in the fifteenth century—whereby the use of dice to determine moves was abandoned—delayed the triumph of cards for a time, but by the end of the eighteenth century chess fell finally from the position it had held in the Middle Ages.

Economics played a large part. We know that the manufacture of cards (using woodcuts) was closely tied to man's first steps at printing with movable type. Some scholars suggest that the anonymous printer known as the Master of the Playing Card may have been Gutenberg himself, and that the technology of printing cards may have been a trial run for his first Bibles. Printing made cards widely available to the masses.

The joker seems to be a Victorian invention, though it too is related to the printing and manufacture of card decks. When cards began to be mass produced, the makers used to add a blank fifty-third card on the top as a sort of protective layer for the pack. But after thrifty and inventive players began to use the card, it became a fixture in most decks. Ironically, though decorated with the likeness of a lowly court jester, it often became the highest trump card.

The reputation of cards and cardplayers has suffered since the beginning. Surely this is because a certain amount of deception is encouraged by the rules. Today we call this bluffing. In the sixteenth century the Italian statistician Cardano called it "ambush":

> There is a difference from play with dice, because the latter is open, whereas play with cards takes place from ambush, for they are hidden.

Cardano goes on to enumerate several species of card cheating, including the use of marked and unshuffled decks, mirrors, and kibitzers. He takes special pains, however, not to indict card playing itself.

This seesawing between good and evil—nothing that God created can be wholly evil, said Augustine, because God is incapable of doing evil—is a direct holdover from the Middle Ages. In fact, anyone who really wanted to play cards could usually find a justification for it.

Almost at the beginning of card history, in 1377, the Dominican John of Rheinfelden wrote a treatise that moralized, or explained, the pastime in religious terms. The church figured that it was better to tap into its popularity rather than to try to ban it completely, an impossible task anyway. Still, the peace did not last long.

On January 22, 1397, cards were banned to Paris laborers on workdays. Late in the fifteenth century, the duke of Clarence threatened to dismiss any member of his household who played cards for money. Monastic leaders constantly railed against card playing, though not as often as they complained about other forms of gambling. The visitation records—the results of ecclesiastical fact-finding parties—for Southwell Minster mention the abuses of religious card players in

1484 and 1499. And some medieval rabbis forbade cards on the grounds that the sheets of paper the card faces were painted on were pasted together with a nonkosher glue.

In the literature of the Middle Ages cards do not figure much, in contradistinction to chess. The lack of a firm moral perspective on the game may account in part for its scant mention. There is, however, a modern American folk song or folktale that has a connection with the old moralization of cards that John of Rheinfelden composed in 1377.

The tale recounts how a soldier, caught playing cards in church, defends himself before a court-martial by using all the numbers associated with a deck of cards to put him in a reverential frame of mind. For him, the ace represents God; the deuce, heaven and hell; the trey, the Trinity; etc. In the 1950s and 1960s, most Americans knew it from the musical versions recorded by radio comedian Phil Harris or country and western stars like Tex Ritter or T. Texas Tyler. At heart, however, the story is nearly identical to Rheinfelden's of 1377—or that of the heretic and martyr Hugh Latimer. "The first card declared that thou should not kill," Latimer says, explicating a card game he calls "triumph." It's clearly a divine game because, he assures us, it's one that the dealer, the players, and even the "standers and lookers" can win. Bishop Latimer did not, however. He was burned at the stake in Oxford on October 16, 1555.

In all its forms, the tale aims to exonerate card playing from the criticism usually leveled at gambling. In fact it is a kind of a secular casuistry that comes across either as sincere (from a preacher) or as parody (from a gambler obviously putting one over on dull and moralistic companions). So the old medieval ambiguity about whether cards are good or bad still lives. Just remember this: Augustus Toplady wrote "Rock of Ages" (1775) on the back of a six of diamonds.

Notes and Further Reading

A chapter in my "A Man May Saye Ful Sooth in Game and Pley: The Tradition of Sport in Middle English Literature" (dissertation, University of Maryland, 1980) is devoted to the history and lore of cards. For further reading, see David Parlett's *A History of Card Games* (Oxford: Oxford University Press, 1990) and the *Journal of the International Card-Playing Society*. A brief illustrated history is Roger Tilley's *Playing Cards* (New York: Putnam's, 1967). See also Strutt, 48 and 423–437. The work of early Smithsonian expert Stewart Culin is solid and was consulted for this and the previous chapter; see *Chess and Playing Cards: Catalogue of Games and Implements for Divination,* 2 vols. (Washington: Smithsonian, 1898), 940–941.

For the card-playing moralist, see D. K. Wilgus and Bruce A. Rosenberg, "A Modern Medieval Story: *The Soldier's Deck of Cards,*" in *Medieval Literature and Folklore Studies,* eds. Jerome Mandel and Bruce A. Rosenberg (New Brunswick, N.J.: Rutgers University Press, 1970), 291–303. For Hugh Latimer's "Sermons on the Card," see his *Sermons,* ed. George Elwes Corrie, vol. 27 (Cambridge: Parker Society, 1846), 3–24.

For Gutenberg and cards, see Helmut Lehmann-Haupt, *Gutenberg and the Master of the Playing Cards* (New Haven: Yale University Press, 1966). See also the Gutenberg chapter in my *The Smithsonian Book of Books* (Washington: Smithsonian Institution Press, 1992).

For Ragman's Roll, see T. Wright, *A History of Domestic Manners and Sentiments in England During the Middle Ages* (London: Chapman and Hall, 1862). For Jews and cards, see Landman I:306–307; see also Landman II.

A powerful—perhaps the best—account of the frisson of high-stakes poker is by A. Alvarez, *The Biggest Game in Town* (Boston: Houghton Mifflin, 1983). By far, the greatest scam game is the fictional one in Mark Harris's *Bang the Drum Slowly* (New York: Knopf, 1956). It's TEGWAR, "the exciting game without any rules," played by baseball players in hotel lobbies on the road against fans. The players, fleecing the dolts, make it up as they go along.

 # Cowboys

THE SCENE has a haunting familiarity. In a desolate landscape far from the nearest town, a band of fifty men, mounted and armed to the teeth, await a lonesome traveler, in this case a treasury agent and prominent government figure. Closer, closer the rider comes, and as he clears the last hillock and descends into a little draw, the ambush is on. . . .

The locale here could well be Tombstone, Abilene, or Dodge City—the Wild West of nineteenth-century America. But it's not. This action was played out in Leicestershire, England, a few miles from the sleepy village of Melton Mowbray. The date was January 19, 1326. And the band in waiting was the notorious Folville gang—Eustace, Robert, Walter, and sundry unspecified de Folville brothers—who along with a number of other desperadoes were about to dispatch an unscrupulous tax collector, a baron of the Exchequer named Roger Bellers.

The similarity of the two periods is striking. In both, men (cowboys, knights) went about on horses fleeing outlaws and sheriffs alike, using spurs, drinking rotgut whiskey, playing cards—and facing death at every turn. In 1350 and in 1850 life was much the same.

The observation is not new. Back in 1965, UCLA historian Lynn White, Jr., wrote an essay in the medieval journal *Speculum* pointing out that most of the technology of the American West was derived directly from the Middle Ages without so much as a bow in the direction of the Renaissance or later times. After noting that most of the ideas and artifacts that helped settle the West were brought over by the European lower classes, White suggested that there is a modern fallout from this history: The United States is closer to the Middle Ages than Europe is.

This was a great revelation to me, but of course it made sense. White had taken a number of disparate facts about the West and fashioned them into a challenging, and riveting, thesis. Take the log cabin, for instance. This was not a new response to the American environment but a typical medieval Scandinavian construction, first brought to the shores of Delaware by the Swedes. Similarly, the Conestoga wagon was originally the *longa carretta* of the twelfth century. The stagecoach, a heavily sprung wagon without which long distances over bumpy roads would have been impossible, was first crudely depicted in an Anglo-Saxon manuscript of the eleventh century.

In 1931 the Great Plains chronicler Walter Prescott Webb showed how a mere three gadgets were critical to opening up our western frontier: the revolver, barbed wire, and the windmill. White agreed with this, but went on to demonstrate that all three inventions were dependent on technology essentially developed in Europe between 1100 and 1500. Or consider spurs. Modern Swedish archaeology shows that simple, pointed spurs were supplanted in the eleventh century by spurs with a loose ball and small plate and later by rowel spurs, with the disc first horizontal, then, by the thirteenth century, vertical. From this it's clear that the western buckaroo and the wandering knight both "jingled" as they rode.

The saloon of the Old West traditionally served whiskey, a fourteenth-century invention. Alcohol had been distilled from a wine base to make brandy in twelfth-century Salerno, and from a grain base as *usquebaugh* (whiskey) in Celtic lands. Scotch-Irish immigrants brought the technique to Pennsylvania in the eighteenth century and adapted it to distill maize or corn. To serve wine in American saloons would have harked back to ancient Roman roots.

The cowboy's staple pastime, the card game, was also a late medieval invention. Cards were a way of making chess more portable, faster, and more dependent on chance over skill. The face cards, for example, are simply two-dimensional views of the prominent chess pieces. The jack is equivalent to the chess knight, whose eccentric L-shaped move symbolized its roguish nature. So in the Old West the jack, especially one-eyed, was often a "wild" card.

In fact, it seems to me, it's when you consider the matter of knighthood that the two ages appear closest. On the American frontier, self was more important than community, personal codes of honor more important than law. It was just so in the deep forests and border country of England and on the high plains of Spain, to name two places.

The chivalric knights of the Middle Ages had their origins in a kind of buccaneering individualism well suited to a wide open countryside with sparse population. As technology, population patterns, and society changed in Europe, solitary knighthood went out of favor and style. But in the American West, those exact conditions arose again. Webb saw them like this: "The restraints of law could not make themselves felt in the rarefied population. Each man had to make his own law because there was no other to make it. He had to defend himself and protect his rights by his force of personality, courage, and skill at arms. All men went armed and moved over vast areas among other armed men. The six-shooter was the final arbiter, a court of last resort, and an executioner." After a hiatus of five hundred years, the wandering knight was back, transformed into hired gunslinger.

All this implied a toleration of violence in both societies. Take cattle rustling, or more exactly cattle raiding. In the West it was a scourge. But it was such a cultural commonplace among the Celts that stories about cattle rustling are an important element in Old Irish literature. The most famous of those stories, the *Tain* (rhymes with "lawn"), describes how the hero Cuchulainn (ka-**WHO**-lynn) goes single-handed about the business of keeping Ulster's cattle out of the hands of a raiding party from the other four provinces of Ireland.

A *tain* is a cattle raid. Although there are a number of *tana*, the *Cattle Raid of Cooley* is easily the best known because it introduced Cuchulainn, the Hound of Ulster. The tale begins when the king and queen of Connacht, Ailill and Medb (Maeve), in a domestic spat, decide to measure each other's possessions. Everything is weighed and found equal—except that King Ailill has a magnificent white bull. Only in Ulster is there a similar one, the Brown Bull of Cooley. Medb immediately sends emissaries to Cooley with a generous offer in return for a year's loan of the Brown Bull. The Ulstermen are amazed and readily accept—until they overhear one of Medb's messengers confide that it was a good thing the loan was agreed since Connacht would have stolen the bull in any case. The deal is off, and the epic dare has been hurled.

Because of a curse on the Ulstermen, however, only the solitary and valiant Cuchulainn is able to fight off the invaders, and much of the rest of the *Tain* simply presents the young hero hacking away at the Connacht warriors as they welter back and forth across the Irish landscape: "Cuchulainn went into the middle of them, and mowed down great ramparts of his enemies' corpses, circling completely around the armies three times, attacking them in hatred. They fell sole to sole and neck to headless neck, so dense was the destruction." Cuchulainn is Davy Crockett.

We like to think of the American West as the great frontier, as if this were a new challenge. But to medieval Spain and Portugal, the frontier was a major part of their heritage. Their no-man's-land was a huge zone between the Christian north and the Moorish-dominated south of the peninsula, a land that was bitterly contested for centuries. Curiously, this is a place that is reminiscent of the Americas, where the clash was not with the Moors but with the Indians. Certainly the landscape appeared the same: high plains, climate extremes, little water, mostly brush vegetation and grasses in season. In other words, it was ideally suited to cattle.

With the reconquest of Spain by Christianity, vast new areas were opened up to ranching, the first time that beef and hide raising was tried on a large scale in Europe. The twelfth-century experiment that began on the northern *meseta* flourished on the Andalusian plain, reaching its height in the sixteenth century. This, according to C. J. Bishko of the University of Virginia, gave rise in the Americas to the greatest cattle industry in history, ranging from Argentina to Canada. Andalusia, Bishko writes, gave us the essence of cattle ranching, with its long overland drives to new pasturage, its roundups for branding in the spring, slaughter in fall. Here, too, were the origins of the traditional cowpuncher's skills—roping, riding, bulldogging—displayed in periodical bullfights and rodeos.

There was a darker side, though. In medieval Spain the *vaqueros* (cowhands) were usually accompanied by pastoral military escorts who slept dressed and armed, ready to mount and ride after the raiding Moors, precisely like a western posse. Eventually, as the cattle industry prospered, not only the Moors needed controlling. A familiar litany of complaints began to appear: disputes over grazing rights, ownership of mountain passes, brand changing, crop damage, killing another's stock. Cattlemen and plainsmen began to fight among themselves, and a frontier system of justice and minor crossroads courts arose, administered by the vaqueros. There were penalties for rustling and misbranding. (The world's first brand, by the way, seems to be a heart-shaped mark drawn on the flanks of a bull and a horse in a tenth-century manuscript from León.) And when an animal was reported dead by a herdsman, its hide had to be produced in evidence.

It remains only for the badlands of medieval England to donate the single remaining element to this portrait of the Old West. That is the sheriff, or "shire reeve," a sort of tax official and justice of the peace, originally appointed by the king as his personal representative in the county (shire). Although the sheriff's title has been traced back to the reign of Ethelred the Unready (978–1016), he was most powerful in the twelfth century.

It was the sheriff who collected all revenues due the Crown, presided at the shire courts, proclaimed royal statutes, and acted as game warden for protected forests. More important, the sheriff also called out the *posse comitatus,* a force of county men whose duty was to round up and detain evildoers. There are thirteenth-century records of a sheriff and posse drawn from two shires who caught a murderer and decapitated him on the spot. Hanging was the more usual punishment, however, just as in the West. Thieves were only to be hanged in the presence of the sheriff, though, and in 1234 the people of Gretton in Northamptonshire had to be pardoned officially for erecting a gallows and hanging two criminals. It turned out that the king's constable had granted permission.

Unfortunately, corruption was one of the great hazards for medieval sheriffs. With so much power, they often fell under the control of a single influential family, and turned a blind eye to their affairs. Extortion was also common. In 1260 the people of Nottingham were paying one hundred marks annually to the sheriff to prevent him from exacting excess taxes or making false indictments.

Although no historical Robin Hood has been found, the sheriff of Nottingham in those folk ballads is a stock figure of grasping medieval officialdom. He is harsh toward the simple plowman and forester, and in collusion with the barons to crush the poor.

To be sure, the sheriff's job was a difficult one, for the fourteenth century was also the great age of outlaw gangs, some of which seem to have been little seminaries of crime. There was, for example, the Coterel gang—James, John, and Nicholas—who rode *armata potentia* through the forests and wolds of the Midlands, had at least twenty recruits at one point, including a university teacher and a counterfeiter, and were charged with numerous murders, robberies, and acts of wanton destruction. Sample: They were hired by a monastery to tear down the water mill of a competing house of monks. They were also charged with rustling £5,200 worth of livestock.

The Coterels occasionally joined forces with the Folvilles, the gang mentioned at the beginning. The Folvilles were a seven-brother crime wave that terrorized Leicestershire. Oddly, their father was a knight, one brother a priest, and another a keeper of the peace. On January 14, 1332, they captured Sir Richard Willoughby, an important justice of the King's Bench. A ransom of thirteen hundred marks was paid to release him. Yet in sixteen years of recorded crime, the Folvilles never appeared in court unless it was to brandish a pardon for past crimes, earned by soldiering for the king.

It was too much to bear. Although the turbulent years of rebellion and border wars are implicated in much of this violence, a more likely cause was official corruption in the wide open Midlands and the undependability of local justice. Willoughby, like Roger Bellers before him, was said to have been a scoundrel who "sold" the laws "like cows."

The world had to wait until the nineteenth century, on our western frontier, to see such conditions return. And then it was not the Coterels or Folvilles who would take matters into their hands, but people with names like James, Dalton, and Younger.

Notes and Further Reading

See especially Lynn White's seminal paper "The Legacy of the Middle Ages in the American Wild West," *Speculum* 40 (1965): 191–202. See also Luis Weckmann, "The Middle Ages in the Conquest of America," *Speculum* 26 (1951): 130–141. And consider now how apt was Richard Boone's gunslinger Paladin in the 1950s television series *Have Gun, Will Travel*. He carried a business card with a chess piece, a knight, printed on it.

For Spanish antecedents, see C. J. Bishko, "The Peninsular Background of Latin American Cattle Ranching," *The Hispanic American Historical Review* 32 (1952): 491–515, and his "The Castilian Plainsman: The Medieval Ranching Frontier in La Mancha and Estremadura," in *The New World Looks at Its History*, eds. A. R. Lewis and T. F. McGann (Austin: University of Texas Press, 1963), 47–69.

For the Folvilles, see E. L. G. Stones, "The Folvilles of Ashby-Folville, Leicestershire, and Their Associates in Crime, 1326–1347," *Transactions of the Royal Historical Society*, 5th series, VII (1957): 117–136. See also M. H. Keen, *The Outlaws of Medieval Legend* (London: Routledge, 1961), and William Alfred Morris, *The Medieval English Sheriff* (New York: Barnes & Noble, 1968). For the Coterels, see J. G. Bellamy, "The Coterel Gang: An Anatomy of a Band of Fourteenth-Century Criminals," *English Historical Review* 79 (1964): 698–717. Walter Prescott Webb's book is *The Great Plains* (1931; repr. Lincoln: University of Nebraska Press, 1959).

3. Celebrations

MARRIAGE

BIRTH

VACATION

HAZING

GRADUATION

APRIL FOOLS' DAY

Marriage

WEDDINGS—at least from the point of view of the species— may be the most crucial of all our elaborate rites. Rites of birth, adolescence, and death all have about them a tincture of certainty: Nature will bring them about whatever we do. But the process of taking a mate and engendering children is too important a matter to be left to Nature.

The propagation of the human race with any semblance of order or civilization has thus always demanded a suitable ritual. Across all cultural and geographic barriers, these rites have traditionally emphasized fertility, sought to ensure domestic peace, and even encouraged certain games and play to underscore the communal aspects of the coupling. The surprise is that marriage ceremonies still include a healthy dose of those early elements.

One of the first broad-scale catalogues of wedding rites appeared in England in 1822. Written by Lady Augusta Hamilton, it was modestly titled *Marriage Rites, Customs, and Ceremonies of all Nations of the Universe.* Travel journals, classical literature, diaries, and memoirs were Hamilton's sources, which she often reproduced verbatim with a charming lack of skepticism.

Her account of Athenian marriage customs contains most of the facets we have come to see as important. The bridal house was decked with flower garlands and a pestle was tied to the front door. The bride brought a sieve and a handful of barley to be ground, to show that she was ready for domestic life. Together the couple ate a quince, to signify that their talk should always be agreeable and peaceful. At the last, the axle of the bride's carriage was ceremonially burnt, severing the ties between her old and new lives.

In the century and a half since Lady Augusta, her work has been superseded by anthropologists, literary scholars, and folklorists. Not surprisingly, a great deal of their interest has centered on fertility. Consider the orange blossoms that are the chosen flowers for bridal bouquets in many cultures. Orange trees are a symbol of fertility and fruitfulness because they are both evergreen and ever blossoming. They have been seen in this light in western Europe since the Crusaders brought them back from the Holy Land.

Greeks and Romans believed that Jupiter gave Juno an orange at their wedding. More important, Juno would have thought of the orange as one of the "golden apples of the Hesperides," the fruit used to trick the prideful Atalanta into marriage. Atalanta, the legendary huntress who thought marriage beneath her dignity, had stipulated that any suitor must first defeat her in a footrace. She also demanded that losing suitors be executed. But Aphrodite, jealous of Atalanta's beauty and furious at her disdain for love, conspired to help the young suitor Hippomenes. Aphrodite gave him three of the divine "golden apples," or oranges, which he was to drop at strategic points in the race. Each time Atalanta drew abreast of him, Hippomenes tossed a single orange. Each time, the curious girl stopped to gather in the glittering prize. Although the race was close, the young man won and the love match was sealed.

Curiously, games that involve throwing things are often associated with weddings. Roman brides threw nuts at rejected suitors as they left the ceremonies. Today we throw the bouquet and rice (which, being a seed, is an obvious fertility symbol) and garters. The garter throw takes us to the Middle Ages, when a feature of the marriage festival was the throwing of stockings. In those days, it was a custom of the bridesmaids and groomsmen to accompany the wedded couple to the marriage chamber and tuck them in bed. They would then play a game with the recently removed stockings—turning away from the bedded couple, tossing the stockings over their shoulders, and trying to hit either the bride or groom. This game, recorded in fifteenth-century England, lasted until one of them hit the bride or groom on the head, or nose, with her or his own stocking. The winner was next to be married.

In old Germanic weddings, the slipper of the bride was thrown. Earlier, the bride's slipper or shoe had been an important part of the old English marriage feast. As part of the dowry, this token was handed over to the husband, who ritually knocked his bride on the head with it and took it home to be nailed to the wall over the marriage bed. Clearly, a symbol of power and sexual conquest. So later, throwing the slipper to the wedding guests was a lottery to decide the next couple to have connubial bliss awarded to them. Today, the tradition lives on only in the tying of boots to the rear bumper of the departing honeymoon car.

Another custom, dating from the sixteenth century, was the race for the ribbons that graced the bride's hair or her gown. Immediately after the ceremony, the wedding guests would tumble and grab for these simple prizes, which conferred upon the holders a special status. In fact, the tumult and racing started so soon after the last words of the ceremony that ecclesiastical authorities were hard pressed to keep the game out of the church and churchyard. The antecedents of this game were even more raucous, as the bride and groom were both attacked at the altar and stripped of their garters, which had been decorated with gaily colored ribbons.

As a further diversion, the custom of nuptial sports arose. Special bridal ribbons, not part of the bride's costume, were specifically created for the nubile among the wedding party to contend for. A parishioner in rural England was horrified in 1851 when he witnessed a group of stark naked village lads contending for these bridal prizes—but, as he soon learned, the custom had been going on for a long time, and thus enjoyed popular approval.

Marriages in the eighteenth century were celebrated with a race out the church door and on to the wedding feast at home, perhaps as much as ten miles distant. To the winner went the first piece of bridal cake, or cup of soup, or plate of cabbage—some restorative reward to the swiftest. The sixteenth century saw the association of the game of quintain with marriage festivals. Quintain was a medieval game that had taught proper lance handling to young knights. In it, a youngster missing a target was struck by a reciprocating arm weighted with a sandbag. Apparently, this game became a feature of rural weddings, in obvious parody of the royal tournaments that occupied the attention of the fashionable at aristocratic marriages.

The wedding ring is ancient. Originally, its circularity suggested endless constancy, and thus the longevity of the union. But a gold ring was also a valuable trophy, a token given the victor in some contest. As such, it was connected with games. A wedding custom among agricultural folk has been to dip with ladles for a golden ring dropped into a bucket of syllabub—a festive drink of milk, sweet cake, and wine. This has much of the lottery about it. The lucky milkmaid who found the ring could be assured of being next to go to the altar, where she would officially receive her trophy ring.

In England, tiny pieces of the wedding cake were sometimes pushed through the wedding ring, a custom brilliantly illustrated by Sir John Everett Millais in *The Bridesmaid*. The wedding cake itself also figures in a game of chance. A coin or ring would be mixed into the batter and baked into the cake. All things were possible for the bride or bridesmaid who was dealt out the lucky piece of cake containing the token.

Pushing chance to the limit, an old Russian wedding custom was for a bride to take off her husband's boots on the wedding night. One shoe contained a jewel, the other a whip. Her choice would determine whether a joyful partnership or a life under the husband's domination would ensue.

The tradition of "sixpence in my shoe" was thought to confer similar luck on English brides. As the full text of the verse reads:

Something old, something new,
Something borrowed, something blue,
And silver sixpence in your shoe.

This sounds like it has the wisdom of the ancients compressed in its three short lines, but actually it was first recorded in connection with weddings late in the nineteenth century, according to Ann Monsarrat. We can recognize the source of the color blue in the line from the adage "Married in blue, love ever true," and the old, new, and borrowed probably have to do with the financial vicissitudes and unpredictability of married life. The "silver" is easier, being associated with the moon and the huntress Diana, Roman patroness of unmarried girls and chastity. Silver was thus a bribe to buy off Diana's wrath at the impending loss of another virgin. In France, marriage couples were escorted to the church bound in silver chains; and in German villages, a bridal cake was baked with a silver coin in it and given to the oldest inhabitant to avoid the evil eye. In American folklore, a silver dime is either swallowed or worn about the neck or in the shoe.

Such may be the stuff of superstition, but the bottom line is that the customs persist to this day. In rural America, it is believed that the first of the bridal pair to step down from the altar will die first. And the idea of lifting the bride over the threshold can be seen worldwide. The rite has twin purposes: to show the bride's kinfolk that she is only unwillingly abandoning them, and to avoid stumbling over the threshold, a misstep that would mean a lifetime of bad luck.

Notes and Further Reading

This piece appeared in *Smithsonian* in October 1981. Soon after, Linda Johnson of New Orleans wrote to say that "two customs—ribbon pulling and the wedding cake aleatory game—survive, combined, in my hometown. Tiny charms attached to the ends of ribbons and concealed under sugar roses are arranged around the wedding cake. The bride selects certain single women to 'pull' from her cake. Each one chooses a ribbon and, at a given signal, pulls her charm. The charms include a fleur-de-lis (faith), an anchor (hope), a heart (love), a horseshoe and a four-leaf clover (good luck), a button and a thimble (forever unmarried), and a ring (next to be married)." *Smithsonian,* Letters, December 1981, 20.

For "the first person to leave the altar (bride or groom) is the first to die," see Brown, Item 4973. Item 4977, from Durham, N.C., says that the first "to step over the doorsill will die first," which may have something to do with lifting the bride over the threshold.

Showering the bride and groom meant throwing things at them; see Hazlitt, 627. For oranges, see Leach, 829. For wedding rings in syllabub, see Hazlitt, 627. For the Danby naked race and quintain, see Strutt, 190. On the ring and coin in cake, see Leach, 165 and 181. On racing and other contests for the bridal cake, see Hazlitt, 511.

For the Russian boots custom, see Lady Augusta Hamilton, *Marriage Rites, Customs, and Ceremonies of All Nations of the Universe* (London: Chapple, 1822), 99; for the Athenian customs, 63–65. Ann Monsarrat's *And the Bride Wore. . . . The Story of the White Wedding* (New York: Dodd, Mead, 1973) discusses "silver sixpence" on pp. 179 and 231 and the stocking toss on p. 36. For more on silver, see Leach, 165 and 1012. Leach discusses shoes in marriage and their sexual implications on pp. 1008–1009.

Birth

THERE IS something whimsical about seeing the immersion of the inventor of baptism. In a miniature in the fifteenth-century prayer book called *The Hours of Etienne Chevalier,* the infant St. John is about to receive his first bath, a soaking. The room is full of midwives and gossips: one smoothes the sheets, another tests the water, yet another takes the chill off the swaddling clothes. It's a very human moment, suggesting that even saints-to-be enter this life one toe at a time.

If the little one could only look down at the pictures below this scene, he'd notice that he would some day sprinkle water from the River Jordan over the adult Christ. To the right, he could also glimpse his own death.

That's the problem with birth celebrations the world around, the whiff of death is always in the air. *Et in arcadia ego,* it was said: We all have to go sometime. Which is why birth customs are so important. From the start, they bind us to members of a clan, make us a part of something greater than our own paltry lives.

Christians call it baptism, an initiation ritual that involves a little water over the head, a pinch of salt on the tongue, and sometimes an anointing with blessed oil. But baptism is but one of countless similar customs connected with entry into the world. Christians celebrate this rite of passage with cleansing, rejuvenating water. For Jews, a ritual circumcision (on the eighth day of life, according to *Genesis*) sends the child out into the world. For Eskimos, a shaman is called in to slip a tiny ivory carving of a whale into the child's mouth to make it a great hunter. Loud singing and drum beating help ensure the babe will be stouthearted.

As is the case with most rites, local culture and temperament have a way of intruding. The Welsh archdeacon Giraldus Cambrensis (1146–1220), who traveled widely in Ireland, noted the following about that land's inhabitants:

> At the baptizing of the infants of the wild Irish, their manner was not to dip their right arms into the water, that they might give a more deep and incurable blow.

The idea is commonplace. Mankind everywhere wants to be civilized. But not too civilized. A body still needs to instill fear and trembling in his enemies, still needs to be able to give a deep and incurable blow.

The entry of a baby into the world is universally considered a "blessed event." And with good reason. The passage from the relative safety of the womb to the whips and scorns of life on the outside has always been fraught with danger. Mother and child alike are subjected to a host of evils—medical, psychological, physical, social, environmental—that all too frequently combine to kill. The dangers are still there today, although the best of modern nutrition and technology have combined to diminish them.

Many ancient societies saw birth as yet another manifestation of the fertility of the earth. The earth's powers along those lines were everywhere abundant. Trees and grasses, springs and wells, all had their sources deep in the earth. So it was that infants were born from mothers who were encouraged to lie directly on the ground, making contact with the forces of growth. In time, this custom gave way to a ritual laying of the newborn infant on the ground.

Cultural historian Mircea Eliade has pointed out that the demotic Egyptian word for birth is actually a linguistic compression of the words for "sitting on the ground," suggesting that birthing was done in a squatting position. For the ancient Chinese, the laying of the baby on the ground prefigured the burial ritual in which the aged child would permanently return to the earth. And midwives in the Scottish Highlands used to feed their new charges a spoonful of earth and whiskey as their first food.

For the Romans, from the moment of birth, a series of minor gods called *numia* were invoked to oversee virtually every facet of the child's development. According to the classical historian J. P. V. D. Balsdon, the tiny one's first hours were tended to by Wailer, Cradler, and Breastfeeder—to be followed in their turn by the little gods Bedder, Eater, Drinker, Speaker, Stander. Perhaps the most renowned classical baptism is that of the hero Achilles, dipped into the river Styx by his concerned mother, Thetis. The act made him invulnerable to all weapons, save where his mother had clutched his tiny heel.

Another famous epic baptism is that of the Teutonic hero Siegfried, who bathed in the blood of a slain dragon. He too was to be made invulnerable, everywhere the blood touched. Unfortunately, as he showered beneath the beast's great wound, a tiny leaf fluttered down from a nearby tree and stuck to his back between his shoulder blades. Later, that single spot would be the site of the hero's mortal stabbing.

Baptism in purifying blood, like Siegfried's bath, is a holdover from the Roman cult of Mithras, which included a ritual baptism of its converts in the blood of a sacrificed bull or ox. The rite was called *Tauroboleum* and featured a special stage under which the communicant would stand while the animal was being killed above, the blood raining down. For a time this religion, which had roots in the Eastern empire, vied with Christianity as the most popular underground cult. Scholars believe that the trauma of its initiation ceremony, as well as its acceptance of only men as members, led to its decline.

Another important Roman custom was the showing of the child publicly. In this way, a few days after birth, the child's father would openly acknowledge his paternity. Among the Tartar tribes, an entirely opposite ceremony took place. When the village chief had a son, it would be taken round to all the local women who were breast-feeding. To promote a sense of unity and brotherhood, each woman would then briefly suckle the newborn prince.

The Baptist religion took its name directly from its adherents' insistence on total immersion as the method of initiating neophytes. Although the popular press and television make a spectacle of their rites—the common image usually includes rural streams and great flowing robes—it is known that total immersion was the rule for early Christians. The surviving baptismal fonts of those times, called *piscinae,* are all floor-level tanks into which the catechumens descended.

The change to elevated tubs reflects a shift in the average age of new Christians. In early times, most were adults, converts. By about A.D. 800 the majority were babies, and some way of bringing the water up to the level of the priest and godparents was needed. Also, consider this about baptismal fonts: They all have eight sides. In Christian iconography, the number eight stands for the start of a new life—the eighth day of the week, the day of the Easter resurrection. This is one of the most persistent symbols in sacred art.

Because the person at baptism is reborn—in imitation of his actual birth—he often takes a new name. It is a widespread custom in Christian circles to take the name of the saint on whose feast day the birth fell. A child born on February 14 might be called Valentine. Occasionally, this habit resulted in some odd names. A nineteenth-century divine once was bemused to be called upon to christen a child Simon-Jude. Since the child was born on October 28, the feast of Saints Simon *and* Jude, the child's parents felt it would be tempting fate to favor one saint over the other.

Naming-customs themselves are a distinct species of lore. In Scotland, the eldest son always bore the name of the paternal grandfather. A Jewish tradition is to name a child after a recently deceased relative. Eskimos also named their children after the last deceased person in the family, and if the mother was away from the village during birth, she named her child after the first thing she saw—a plant, a lake, a mountain. In Greece, a son never took his father's name because it was considered unlucky to do so. After the parent's death, however, the son was free to adopt his father's name, and thus honor his memory.

There is also a body of lore having to do with the baby's first appearance and with events on the birth or baptismal day. A child born with open hands was expected to have a good disposition; conversely, a "tightfisted" adult was simply born that way. To be christened by a left-handed priest was unlucky (according to Thomas Dekker's 1630 play *The Honest Whore*). A child who didn't cry during the baptism wouldn't live long; priests complained that nurses would sometimes try to thwart this outcome by pinching their charges. By contrast, a belief recorded in Lancashire was that an unbaptized child could not die. And in 1790 a minister in the Orkneys was cautioned about baptizing a female child before a male one during a joint ceremony: it was felt that this reversal would cause the girl to have a growth of beard in later years, while the boy would have none. A Glasgow contributor to *Notes and Queries,* writing in 1857, noted the following:

> The custom of persons, when carrying infants to church for baptism, taking with them bread and cheese to be given to the first individual met, is not yet gone into disuse. One Sunday forenoon, about two years ago, when walking along Can-

dleriggs, I saw the practice carried out, amid a little laughter, in all its entirety. On this occasion a *silver* coin was given in return for the eatables. I was told that the appearance of copper in such transactions was, if possible, to be avoided.

In our rural parishes, where the child to be baptized had sometimes to be carried a considerable distance before the church was reached, it was not an unusual sight, some sixty or seventy years ago, I have been told, to see a quantity of common table salt carried *withershins* (i.e., contrary to the course of the sun) round the baby before the baptismal company left the parental dwelling. This done, no harm, it was believed, would befal the little stranger in its unchristened state. I have conversed with an old woman, a native of Ayrshire, who had seen the custom put in practice when she was a girl.

That same salt is used in the Roman Catholic baptismal liturgy. It was the feeling of the early church that, since salt was a preservative of food, it could symbolically act to preserve the child from evil.

Even the physical concomitants of birth were enlisted in man's superstitious war with the unknown. In England in 1660, we read, "a piece of a child's navell string . . . is good against the falling sickness, the pains in the head, and the collick." But the strangest of customs are those associated with the caul, a section of the mother's amniotic sac that sometimes adheres to the child's head throughout birth. Those rare children born with the caul were thought to be unlucky if the membrane was dark, lucky if it was reddish. The possessor of the caul was also said to be immune from drowning, a conviction that caused cauls to be frequently advertised for sale. Thus, from the *London Morning Post,* August 21, 1779: "To the gentlemen of the Navy, and others going [on] long voyages to sea. To be disposed of, a child's caul. Enquire at the Bartlett Buildings Coffee House in Holborn. N.B. To avoid unnecessary trouble the price is Twenty Guineas."

Modern ideas about what godparents and relatives should give to infants are similarly antique. A silver cup or spoon does well today. But for several centuries, reaching a peak in the early nineteenth, it was customary to give silver "apostle spoons" to the newborn. These tiny spoons had handles cast in the shapes of saints with their symbols—St. James the Greater with his pilgrim staff, St. Peter with his keys. The Huntington Museum in California has a fine collection of such spoons. Although well-heeled godparents could afford to give the entire set of twelve, poor relations had to be content with giving just one, usually representing the name-saint of the baby (not necessarily an apostle). Shakespeare and several of his contemporary playwrights mention apostle spoons. The decline in the generosity of "gossips," a word that originally meant "godparents," is ridiculed in this eighteenth-century verse:

Especially since Gossips now
Eat more at christenings than bestow.
Formerly, when they us'd to trowl
Gilt bowls of sack [wine], they gave the bowl
Two spoons at least—an use ill kept—
'Tis well now if our own be left.

Another custom associated with christening parties was that the midwives and neighboring ladies could take home as much food as they could carry in their pockets. Conniving at this pilferage probably helped ensure a lucky lifetime for the child. Not surprisingly, christening parties, like funeral wakes, often got out of hand, and ecclesiastical authority had to be called in to curb the excesses. The following Nuremberg experience, described in 1565, was apparently typical:

When the child is eight days old a *Weissat* or *Kindschenk* must be held, accompanied by eating and drinking, at which more guldens are needlessly squandered. It is a flagrant shame and disgrace that the occasion should be so unsuitably kept and so much time wasted; for today it is at one neighbour's, to-morrow at another's, and there is seldom a village where two or three christenings are not held every week; this is a general misfortune, for in this way the people grow poor, squander God's gifts of food and drink, waste their time, and spend it sinfully in over-much eating, drinking, blaspheming and other iniquities.

The complaint could also take on a more personal cast. In 1631 a "jealous" father was greatly put out by the outlay for food at his new child's christening, especially since he questioned his own role in its engendering. Said a commentator at the time, "he is perswaded that he may eate his part of this babe, and never breake his fast."

Notes and Further Reading

Leach reminds us (p. 199) that David Copperfield was born with a caul, which was advertised in the newspapers "at the low price of fifteen guineas." See also Hazlitt, 100. For the vulnerable spots of Siegfried and Achilles, see Leach, 1163.

For Giraldus Cambrensis and Irish baptisms, see Hazlitt, 341. For left-handed baptism and open-hand births, see Hazlitt, 111–112. For the spoonful of earth given to infants, see Hazlitt, 380. For the Roman *piscina*, see Horn and Born, I:135. See also Smith, II:429.

The Glasgow rites on the way to baptism are described in *N&Q*, 2nd series, III:59 (January 17, 1857). For crying, see "Children Crying at Baptism," *N&Q*, 1st series, VII:96–97 (January 22, 1853). For baptizing boys first, see Clericus Rusticus, "Baptismal Superstition in Surrey," *N&Q*, 1st series, X:321 (October 21, 1854).

The shaman and the whale carving as well as other Eskimo lore is from Edward W. Nelson, *The Eskimo About Bering Strait* (1899; repr. Washington: Smithsonian Institution Press, 1983), 220. See also my article on Nelson and the Bering Strait Eskimos in *Smithsonian,* May 1982.

The complaint about Nuremberg christenings in 1565, from a political reformer named Berthold Holzschuher, is printed in Janssen, 405n. Charles G. Rupert's *Apostle Spoons: Their Evolution from Earlier Types, and the Emblems Used by Silversmiths for the Apostles* (Oxford: Oxford University Press, 1929) is the standard source.

◪ Vacation

THERE'S NO SUCH THING as a Volkswagen built in August. West German industry closes down for the month.

The institution of the paid vacation is in very good health and still attracts legislative and union attention. On January 16, 1982, the new French government under François Mitterrand granted a fifth week of vacation to Gallic workers, building on a tradition begun when Premier Leon Blum's Popular Front government handed out a week's vacation in 1936.

Around the world, it's much the same. In the United States, England, and Canada, the average is about three weeks. In Spain, Zimbabwe, and India, four weeks. Germans get about six weeks off.

All this seems so modern and indolent. But wait. To judge by a few early societies, the custom of lengthy summer vacations is an ancient and honorable one. A tribe of Indians living near Cape Flattery in Washington State were discovered by nineteenth-century anthropologists to refrain from work for the whole of the late summer—the equivalent of our month of August. No fish were caught, no berries picked. The yam farmers of Benin, in West Africa, were known to rest for the whole first month of the dry season, after the yam crop had been brought in. The Kikuyu of East Africa similarly rested for three months of the year as their crops were ripening in the fields.

By contrast, school vacations are a purely modern concept that is utterly changed from its historical model. Students today look forward to summer as a carefree and glorious hiatus—no more rulers, no more books. But the medieval view of vacation was far different and is still visible in the great paradigm of monastic life, *The Rule of St. Benedict*. Since the life of the monks was full to the brim with prayer and work, there was little time left over for what we would call "scholarly pursuits," pure reading or research. In A.D. 845, the commentator Hildemar of Corbie explained St. Benedict's idea of vacation in this way: *"Vacare* means to relinquish one thing and to replace it with some other preoccupation; it is in this sense that [St. Benedict] insists in this chapter that, manual work being set aside, the time thus released be used for study."

There you have it. Vacation time, people, is a time to fly to your books. In support of this thesis, the *Plan of St. Gall,* the ninth-century master plan for all monastic architecture, labels one of its large halls the *domus communis scolae, id [est] vacationis.* Architectural historians Walter Horn and Ernest Born explained the tag as "the common hall for learning, i.e., for the time relinquished from other obligations for the purpose of study."

Certainly this was an attitude Ben Franklin would have been in touch with. Almost a millennium later, his advice was clear: "Methinks I hear some of you say, Must a Man afford himself no Leisure? I will tell thee, my Friend, what Poor Richard says, Employ thy Time well if thou meanest to gain Leisure; and, since thou are not sure of a Minute, throw not away an Hour. Leisure, is Time for doing something useful."

Although Franklin doesn't suggest reading, something of that idea is still afoot. As the protagonist of Philip Roth's *Goodbye, Columbus* says, "Doris? She's the one who's always reading *War and Peace.* That's how I know it's the summer, when Doris is reading *War and Peace.*"

The idea of paid vacations for nonagricultural workers had to wait until the Industrial Revolution to find adherents. Before that, vacations and leisure time were dictated by the calendar of agricultural life.

In turn, the church calendar was attuned to the demands of spring planting and fall harvesting. Although there was no annual vacation as such, holidays were plentiful. In fact, the word holiday was originally *holy day,* a time when work was proscribed, a time when people would be better employed in relaxation, reflection, and prayer. At least that was the theory. But there were two problems.

First, there were so many ecclesiastical holidays that they threatened production. The twin-horned monster Profit-and-Efficiency reared its ugly head. An early writer noted: "If we calculate the number of holidays kept in Ireland, the working hands who keep them, and the value of their labor, the amount will be immense. The priests have it in their power to remedy this evil. . . . St. Chrysostom said that 'the Martyrs had no delight in being honoured at the expense of the tears of the poor, as also that instead of promoting religion and devotion, it had quite the opposite effect; and that piety should not trespass upon industry, nor industry upon piety.'"

In 1536, Henry VIII tried to compress the number of English holidays as follows: "All those feests or day holydays which shall happen to occurre in the harvest time, which is to be compted from the fyrst day of July unto the 29 day of Septembre . . . shall not be kepte or observed from henceforth as holydayes, but that it may be lawful for every man to go to his work or occupacyon upon the same as upon any other workyeday, excepte alwayes the feests of the apostles, of our blessed Lady, and of saynt George."

The second complaint about holidays was that they were often filled with violent or "lewd" (meaning low-class or indecorous) games. Football, cards, and dice are commonly mentioned. These distractions, as well as an abundance of food and drink, often led to riots and eventually called for special laws designed to protect Sundays and other holidays. The so-called "Peace of Sunday," observed at Chester (1086) and Manchester (1301) among other cities, greatly increased the fines for bloodshed or waylaying from Saturday noon until Monday morning. Countless other church decrees and civil statutes appeared on the books to staunch the violence and waste of the holidays.

Weekend dustups became so commonplace that they led to a literary genre, especially in Scotland and Germany, that detailed the wild times, not without a degree of satire. Poems like "Christis Kirk" and "Peblis to the Play" cover the familiar descent associated with communal festivals, plays, and sports. The line ran from merrymaking through drunkenness and fighting to riot, death, and finally the keening of the widowed females. It is probably not surprising that this parade was set in motion by mock battles to celebrate summer's victory over winter or high-jumping contests to make the plants grow taller.

Although the exaggerated cult of the saints fell out of favor with both Catholics and Protestants at the time of the Reformation, the secular observance of saints' days with raucous festivals—having nothing to do with church—was a source of annoyance for centuries. In 1640 playwright Barten Holiday was said to have addressed the English Puritans in this way:

> *'Tis not my person, nor my play,*
> *But my sirname, Holiday,*
> *That does offend thee, thy complaints*
> *Are not against me, but the Saints.*

Curiously enough, there was a siesta for English laborers and aristocrats in the Middle Ages. An hour-and-a-half nap was customary at midday from May through August in the fifteenth century, although the practice was eventually restricted by Parliament. It survives only in Mediterranean cultures.

The indefatigable promoter of secular holidays in England was Sir John Lubbock, the sponsor of the Bank Holidays Act of 1871, which established the first legal holidays. Through a series of bills over the next quarter century—the Holidays Extension Act (1875), the Shops Hours Regulation Act (1886), and the Early Closing Act (1904)—Lubbock managed to nudge the employers of the Industrial Revolution into the twentieth century.

In partial thanks for that beneficence, a grateful English public conferred a special title on those first Bank Holidays, one that conjured up a sense of medieval merriment. They called them St. Lubbock's Days.

Notes and Further Reading

On St. John Chrysostom, see "Lady Day in Harvest," *N&Q*, 1st series, VI:471 (November 13, 1852), and Clericus (D.), "Holidays," 1st series, XII:65 (July 28, 1855). See also T. J. Buckton, "Holidays," *N&Q*, 1st series, 113 (August 11, 1855).

For *vacare,* see Horn and Born, II:174. On naps, see Samuel Davey, *"The Paston Letters* with Special Reference to the Social Life of the 14th and 15th Centuries," in *Chaucer Memorial Lectures,* Royal Society of Literature of the United Kingdom, London (1900; repr. Philadelphia: Norwood, 1976), 45–69. See also Hutton Webster, *Rest Days: A Study in Early Law and Morality* (London: Macmillan, 1916).

For the weekend brawls, see Mary Bateson, *Borough Customs,* No. 21 (London: Selden Society, 1906), 46–47. On the brawl poems, see George Fenwick Jones, *"Christis Kirk, Peblis to the Play,* and the German Peasant Brawl," *PMLA* 68 (1953): 1101–1125. St. Lubbock's Days are discussed by John Vaughan in *The English Guide Book, c. 1780–1870* (Newton Abbot: David & Charles, 1974).

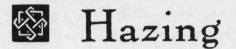 # Hazing

"THIS CEREMONY is intended to make you humble, so that you not be haughty and arrogant. . . . " The date: July 23, 1539. The speaker: Professor Martin Luther of the University of Wittenberg, addressing a group of new students about to undergo hazing.

Luther was right, of course. What has happened over the last four centuries is that people have stopped seeing metaphorically, so that a blow is a blow and pain must be real to have any meaning. In other words, what used to be ceremonies have sometimes been transformed, by the dull and the literal and the mean-spirited, into the thing itself. The result is that more than half of our state legislatures have recently passed antihazing laws.

Over the centuries, initiates have again and again been injured, maimed, and killed—all in the name of time-honored custom. And just as continually, civil, church, and scholastic authorities have tried to curb abuses of those rites.

One reason for the persistence of initiation ceremonies and hazings is that they have always served two sensible functions in society. First, they test the mettle of candidates. Second, they temper them against the buffets that life will surely send later. Every culture has initiation rites and ordeals, which usually amount to a formal induction into some position or club, or signify that the beginner has been granted some secret knowledge. Most often, it means a new understanding of hunting, warfare, survival, or religious or sexual rites.

The ordeal part of the initiation was always crucial, and often harsh and painful. The Indians of some California tribes, for example, had a puberty initiation rite that was notorious. It involved stinging with nettles until a child was immobile, then stinging with ants, and then fasting. In Brazil and Bolivia, pubescent girls were sewn into hammocks and hung from the roof timbers of their huts—for periods that ranged from four days to four months. They were beaten regularly to drive out evil spirits. In Guiana, the girls were also bitten by large ants while they were suspended in their hammocks.

In these, and in hundreds of similar examples from around the world, what we are supposed to see is the death of the old spirit and a rebirth of a new person inside the initiate. Even in the innocuous ceremony for sailors "passing the line"—the equator—for the first time, the initiation involves paying homage to old King Neptune, and then a ritual drowning or dunking. And the process of dubbing (as in "I dub thee knight") demands a light but symbolic blow against the old self. In every case, the violence results in new life.

Modern college fraternities and sororities too have their share of mystical elements in their initiation ceremonies. There is the making of paddles by the pledge class, and then the ritual spanking of the neophytes, in which their former evils and their immaturity are transferred into the wood. On some campuses, the paddles (or one symbolic paddle) are then burned in the fireplace, signifying the death of the old way of life, up the chimney with the smoke. This is homeopathic magic from the remote past of folklore: Rub your warts with a leaf, deposit the leaf in the notch of an old tree; when the leaf blows away, so will your warts!

The trouble that has arisen in the past has come not from the ceremonies themselves but from those who willingly confuse the literal with the symbolic nature of the ordeal. Such dolts have always been around. As the *Daily News* observed on October 16, 1894, "The freshman class of Princeton is smaller this autumn than last . . . due in part to the hazing outrages of recent years." This was printed at a time of lobbying to reform the system of hazing in colleges and military schools. Until recently, attempts at reducing the severity of hazing have been seen as products of namby-pamby twentieth-century liberalism. Consider, for instance, the following, from a booklet printed in Annapolis in 1906, ridiculing the attempts of Congress to change the Naval Academy:

H is for hazing, an art
That Congress has caused to depart;
Nowadays, if you'd talk
To a plebe on the walk,
Say "Please," with your hand on your heart.

The service academy custom of eating "squared-off" meals, in which all hand motions must be in rigid right angles, may perhaps be related to a late medieval drinking custom at English colleges. That custom was known as "salting and tucking" (nicking the chin until it bled, then stinging the wound with salt).

Of course, not every undergraduate has borne such indignities silently. In 1637, for instance, the earl of Shaftesbury, then a freshman at Oxford's Exeter College, helped end the reign of salting and tucking. He decided to resist that "foolish custom of great antiquity" and went on to describe what typically happened: "One of the seniors in the evening called the freshmen . . . to the fire, and made them hold out their chin, and they with the nail of their right thumb, left long for that purpose, grate off all the skin from the lip to the chin, and then cause them to drink a beer glass of water and salt." By prearrangement with other members of the freshman class, the earl and his followers incited a riot in the college hall at the time of the next ceremony and so defeated the custom.

Nevertheless, the practice was still observed at other Oxford colleges, notably at Merton, where writer Anthony Wood matriculated in 1647. Wood describes tucking as a nicking on the chin, "which sometimes would produce Blood," and salting as a sort of reward or punishment for a student's first college speech. On Shrove Tuesday each student would discard his college gown in favor of making himself "look like a Scoundrel." While the students were thus disguising themselves, the college cook would be preparing a caudle, a syrupy gruel with spices and wine or ale added. Each freshman would then be led before an assembly of upperclassmen in the college great hall, and made to stand on a box and deliver a speech. Wood says the salting would depend on how well the speech came off: "If well done, the person that spoke it was to have a Cup of Cawdle and no *salted Drinke;* if indifferently, some Cawdle and some *salted Drinke;* but if dull, nothing was given to him but *salted Drinke,* or *salt* put in College Bere." Afterwards, an oath was administered to all freshmen by the senior cook of the college "over an old shoe." Each new student would then kiss the shoe and could put on his gown as a full-fledged member of the upper class.

The emphasis on salt is not accidental. Since salt is a preservative, it was often used in far graver rituals. In baptism, for example, it symbolically preserves the infant against evil. A 1666 German volume on academic ceremonies contains a woodcut of a freshman about to receive a pinch of salt on his tongue. Nearby, a glass of wine stands ready to quench his thirst. The Latin text advises him to "taste the salt of Wisdom, drink the wine and rejoice!"

Although the hazing of freshmen is an ancient art, perhaps its fullest expression is available in an Anglo-Latin treatise, "The Dialogue of Jacobus Pontanus," which dates from the seventeenth century and yet has a surprisingly modern ring. The narrator is derisively hailed as Prince of Freshmen by his tormentors, and made to lie still while they all thrash him and mockingly chop at him with an ax. They then "wash" him with dirty water, shave him (although he is, as he says, "guiltless of a beard"), and comb him with a rake. Next, they ask him to write a letter, and roar with laughter when he is unable to open a fake inkwell.

But the cruelest joke was planting a forged letter from his mother, which was snatched from his pocket and read aloud before the assembly. Its contents: "My mother lamented my absence, and consoled me in the most silly and weak manner: saying how carefully she had nursed, how often kissed her sweetest child, how carefully she had brought me up, and how she had made me her darling all my life, calling me her little angel, her sweet lambkin, her chicabiddy sweeter than honey. Then she added that she could not sleep at night, and that she shed floods of tears every day on account of the torments she had heard I must suffer in this [initiation]. Of course this epistle was concocted and written by my tormentors themselves. How they enjoyed it—they almost burst with laughter. . . . How they knocked me about! I had rather die than go through it again. If I had known what I had to undergo, I would have gone where there are schools in which nothing of this sort is allowed."

In all this, it's clear that inculcating a sense of humility is the key, and that the blows, as in the case of the fraternity paddles, are simply remnants of honorable rites. A surprisingly candid commentator on all this was Martin Luther, officiating at that hazing of new Wittenberg students in July 1539. In Luther's day, the ceremony involved calling new students "yellow bills," attaching horns to their heads to symbolize their monstrous, uncivilized immaturity, and then pouring wine over them in a token baptism to cleanse them of their former unbridled natures.

"Learn to be patient," Luther advised his charges. "You'll be subjected to hazing all your life. When you hold important offices in the future, burghers, peasants, nobles, and your wives will harass you with various vexations. When this happens, don't go to pieces. Bear your cross with equanimity and your troubles without murmuring. . . . Say that you first began to be hazed in Wittenberg when you were a young man, that now that you have become a weightier person you have heavier vexations to bear. So this [test] is only a symbol of human life in its misfortunes and castigations."

Notes and Further Reading

The Naval Academy satire is from William O. Stevens, *An Annapolis Alphabet, Published at Crab-Town-on-the-Bay* (Baltimore: Lord Baltimore Press, 1906). A copy is in the Special Collections Room, Mullen Library, Catholic University of America.

On salting, see S. R. Maitland, "College Salting," *N&Q,* 1st series, I:261 (February 23, 1850). For giving salt to initiates at Eton, see Hazlitt, 213. For initiations, see Leach, 525. Other ethnographic and homeopathic magic details here are from Frazer. For definitions (initiation, hazing, etc.), see the *OED.*

✦ Graduation

DIGNIFIED AND STATELY. Those are the twin watchwords for commencement ceremonies. And that's as it should be, for the degree ceremony is an important one, substituting for any number of rites of passage that youths had to endure before they could be counted as members of a tribe or clan. The equivalent of vanquishing a fearsome opponent or surviving a solitary walkabout, the degree ceremony is nothing less than society's acknowledgment that a youngster has passed a hurdle in life.

Certainly degree ceremonies have been with us a long time, since the mid-twelfth century at the University of Bologna, shortly thereafter at Paris, Oxford, and Cambridge. The rites and dress to be seen at graduations all across America every spring are antique customs. Even the words have changed very little.

In Latin, *gradus* is a step or pace, and *degradus* a step on a stair or ladder. From the first we get our word graduation; from the second, degree. The sense of both words is closely connected to a step or a stage in life, not at all a resting point or climax but a beginning—a point that graduation speakers always flog to death.

Although graduation is the term generally used, the word that most closely approximates the original sense is commencement, the Cambridge University term for the ceremony of conferring master's and doctor's degrees. (The reason America is so fond of the word commencement is that the first American college to have one was Harvard, in 1642. Since John Harvard was a Cambridge man, the Cambridge term was used.) At Oxford, commencement was called the Act, and participants were called *inceptors* or beginners. Will Paston, writing to his parents in 1479—dutiful son to outraged parents—promised to be an inceptor at Oxford before midsummer.

Graduation ceremonies, originally consisting of two parts, have been greatly reduced since medieval times. Only the activities associated with the bachelor's degree still exist. According to Hastings Rashdall, whose monumental history of medieval universities was published in 1895, this was to be followed in six months by the candidate's inception and first formal lecture to the assembled faculty. After that, he received the teacher's cap (biretta) and a token book in recognition of his scholarship, whose essence was reading. That is why a book is the perfect graduation gift, and why Harvard, even in its early years, gave each graduate a book (which had to be returned right after commencement).

America's big change was that commencements (inceptions) were mainly for those taking only the bachelor's degree, like the nine graduated from Harvard in 1649 and a handful more at William and Mary in 1700. Back at Oxbridge, the B.A. remained merely a step in the road to teaching, which could begin in full only with a master's degree.

As for the meaning of bachelor and baccalaureate, history is cheerfully confused, probably because so many well-meaning but amateur etymologists have had a crack at it. Even the redoubtable Dr. Johnson was wrong in his *Dictionary* when he derived bachelor as a combination of *bacca* (Latin for "berry") and *laurus* (laurel). Said he: "Bachelors being young are of good hopes, like laurels in the berry."

Another highly suspect but nonetheless satisfying derivation insists the words came from French *bas chevalier,* those young squires in training who were forced to sit "below the knights" at table. Although this too is almost certainly wrong, it does communicate an impression of callow youth. Much more likely is that both bachelor and baccalaureate came from *baccalaria,* a small unit of land, and *baccalarius,* the Latin term for the impoverished tenants who worked such lands. So, beginning farmers rather than fledgling knights is the original sense.

Earning degrees by written examination is a modern practice. Originally, the graduation ceremony and the final exam were rolled into one. The examination part was called the *viva voce* (with the living voice) and was undertaken in full academic dress before a hall full of examiners and guests. B.A. candidates had to dispute a series of published questions and topics. Higher degrees were won by reading a thesis, followed by the answering of questions not only on that subject but also on any other the examiners might expect of a university graduate.

Disputation became an important part of colonial graduations in America. But here it served as an initiation ceremony, especially for those who never intended to teach. Lists of graduates and the topics they were to dispute were printed each spring. At Harvard in 1743, young Samuel Adams argued the affirmative on the question "Is it Lawful to resist the Supreme Magistrate, if the Commonwealth cannot otherwise be preserved?"

In England, the Oxford Act and Cambridge commencement became such fixtures of the social season that the best people wouldn't miss them for the world. And neither would the worst, apparently. In 1602, the Oxford festivities saw a "great confluence of cutpurses. . . . Master Bodley lost his clock, Sir Richard Lea two jewels of 200 marks . . . and divers other lost good sums of five, eight, and fourteen pounds . . . and one mad knave whether of malice or merriment took the advantage to pull off a gentlewoman's shoe and made the goose go home barefoot."

In America, commencement became the highlight of the summer and typically lasted several days, with entertainments, wrestlings, banquets, dances, and a great deal of public drinking. It was so popular in Williamsburg that local Indians were wont to attend, parading their native fashions just as the white men did their academic dress. It was so much fun, at last, that there were cries for commencement reform. But it took the Revolutionary War to accomplish that, as the growing popularity of the Independence Day celebrations crowded graduation week off the calendar.

Academic costume in general comes directly from common modes of dress in the late Middle Ages and Renaissance, with gowns based on Italian and Spanish models. Nearly all are made of black cloth, with the exception of some doctoral robes. The Oxford doctor of philosophy, for example, wears scarlet silk with blue sleeves and blue facings down the front.

Sleeves are key telltales. The bachelor's gown has long pointed sleeves that extend halfway to the hem of the garment. The master's has oblong sleeves open at the wrist, with a long, narrow pouch cut out of the remaining cloth. And doctors' sleeves are copious and bell-shaped, freighted with three bars of rich black velvet.

High school commencements have only been conducted in cap and gown since 1908. To distinguish them from the B.A. costume, the gowns were designed with short, full sleeves and usually made of gray cloth. The feeling at the time was that cap and gown would lend a solemn note to the event. Another often expressed reason was to prevent graduates and their families from trying to outdo each other with expensive suits and dresses.

Perhaps the most important element of academic regalia is the hood. The color of the doctor's hood indicates not only the wearer's field of study but his or her school as well. Throughout the United States, if the hood's velvet facing is green, the degree is in medicine; if dark blue, philosophy; orange, engineering; yellow, science; and so on through the rainbow. Likewise, the color of the hood's inside lining indicates the school. The University of Pennsylvania's, for instance, is red with a blue chevron slashing through it.

My own hood, a dark blue with a black and gold lining (University of Maryland), has never seriously been pulled over my head to keep off the elements. But if these were still the Middle Ages, it would have. Universities were created by banding together houses of religious study and instruction, and tonsured monks needed something over their heads on cold days. Academic costume was everyday wear.

The third element of academic dress is the cap, which as a symbol of liberty and attainment came down to us from the Romans. For them, the *pilleus* was a felt cap given to slaves at their manumission, a token of freedom. Shaped like half an egg and close-fitting, this cap played an important part in that ancient ceremony. Even freeborn people who had fallen into captivity wore it for a while after they'd been released. Victorious gladiators wore the hat after their discharge and so did off-duty Roman soldiers, so they would stay accustomed to the military helmet. So there's a real link between student caps and the hats of slaves, gladiators, and soldiers.

Today's scholastic cap began to appear in the sixteenth century. In Scottish universities, the trencher or square cap was called the John Knox cap or cater-cap, a reference to its four sides. In England it soon became a term of derision, as in this 1589 quotation: "There were none of these Catercaps, Graduates, nor Doctors." The name trencher arose (in 1721) because the inverted hat resembled a serving board or trencher with a bowl (the *pilleus*) upon it. Calling the whole a mortarboard is comparatively recent, first recorded in English no earlier than 1854.

With so much choice in academic fashion, abuses began to appear in no time. Dress had to be regulated by the University of Toulouse in 1314 because the competition in gowns and hoods had become a hindrance to education. Many scholars had to leave school because they were pawning their books to buy cloth and pay tailors. So the university rector set a ceiling price of twenty *solidi* for gowns. For people newly admitted to degrees, it was allowed that if they were unaware of the law, they might wear their overpriced new gowns for exactly one month. After that, they had to march to the same dress code as everyone else.

Earlier, at the University of Paris, new inceptors had to agree to a long list of obligations. Among them: to deliver lectures in the great round cope or *pallium;* also, "to incept in your own cope, not one borrowed or hired."

Academic dress codes have long been with us. In America, colleges met in 1895 to study these matters. They met again in 1935. Part of their mission was to settle once and for all that lingering silliness about the position of the tassel. The Ph.D.'s golden tassel, they suggested, should be fastened to hang over the left side of the mortarboard. If fastened at the center of the cap, however, its location should be determined by the whim of the local breezes. The persistent idea that the tassel should be moved to the left side of the cap just when the degree is conferred had, they said, "no warrant in precedent or in common sense."

What is far more important is receiving the gown itself, still a high point of the Oxford degree ceremony. This takes place in the Sheldonian Theatre, one of the finest baroque buildings in the world, designed by Sir Christopher Wren in 1667. It's the perfect setting for a ceremony shrouded in medieval custom, under a vast painted ceiling by Robert Streater (1669) that depicts Ignorance being cast out of heaven by Truth.

After the candidates "supplicate" for their degrees (that is, are presented a few at a time to the university vice-chancellor), they leave the Sheldonian by the side door, only to return a few moments later. During that interval, they dash across the paving stones to the Divinity School, put on their new gowns and hoods, and then reenter the building by the main entrance, where they are again led to the vice-chancellor. To him they bow for the first time in the robes of their new degrees. And then it's right out the side door again and on to life itself.

Very dignified and stately indeed. And not at all like what happened in this very same building in 1809. That June, out-of-work playwright and out-of-office politician Richard Brinsley Sheridan had been turned down for an Oxford honorary degree. Although crushed by the refusal, he came to the Sheldonian anyway and headed toward the guest seats in the balcony. When the students saw him, they immediately set up the cry "Sheridan among the doctors! Sheridan among the doctors!"

Dignified and stately got a special boost that day. And Truth— looking down from Streater's ceiling—must have been very pleased.

Notes and Further Reading

See D. R. Venables and R. E. Clifford, *Academic Dress of the University of Oxford* (Oxford: University of Oxford, 1957). For the U.S., see Mary Kemper Gunn, *A Guide to Academic Protocol* (New York: Columbia University Press, 1969).

On hoods, see J. W. G. Gatch, "University Hoods," *N&Q,* 2nd series, VI:211-212 (September 11, 1858). See also C. F. S. Warren, "University Degrees," *N&Q,* 7th series, X:335 (October 25, 1890), and J. H. I. Oakley, "Baccalaureus," *N&Q,* 4th series, IV:466-467 (November 27, 1869). The quotation about commencement crime is from Mark H. Curtis, *Oxford and Cambridge in Transition, 1558-1642* (Oxford: Clarendon Press, 1959), 4–5 and 89–93.

The standard sources on medieval university life are Hastings Rashdall, *The Universities of Europe in the Middle Ages,* eds. F. M. Powicke and A. B. Emden, 3 vols. (Oxford: Clarendon Press, 1934), and Lynn Thorndike, *University Records and Life in the Middle Ages* (New York: Columbia University Press, 1944). For Toulouse, see Thorndike, 150; for the cope, 105.

For America, see Samuel Eliot Morison, *Three Centuries of Harvard, 1636–1936* (Cambridge: Harvard University Press, 1936), 34, 91, 122, and

132. On the tassel controversy, see American Council on Education, *An Academic Costume Code,* July 1935, 3–5 and 7. For Indians at the William and Mary commencement, see Walter Crosby Ellis, *Baccalaureate Degrees Conferred by American Colleges in the 17th and 18th Centuries* (Washington: U.S. Office of Education, 1958), 57.

The "Sheridan among the doctors!" episode is in Jan Morris, *The Oxford Book of Oxford* (Oxford: Oxford University Press, 1978), 176. See also H. M. Colvin, *The Sheldonian Theatre and the Divinity School* (Oxford: printed for the Curators, 1964). See also the pamphlet *Guide to the Oxford Degree Ceremony* (Oxford: Oxford University Press, 1949).

▦ April Fools' Day

I SHOULD HAVE KNOWN something was up. It was a fine spring day and there was George Plimpton swinging for the fences inside *Sports Illustrated,* regaling his readers with the exploits of a new and unhittable fastball pitcher in the Mets training camp. The kid's name was Sidd Finch, and he came equipped with a Harvard education, a predilection for the French horn, and the habit of wearing a single hiking boot. He had a windup that was a cross between Goofy's and a cricket bowler's. More enticing, he possessed a fastball that was radar-clocked at 168 miles per hour!

Obviously, all this was too good to be true, especially since the magazine bore the publication date April 1, 1985. Actually, Plimpton's opening words should have been a dead giveaway: "He's a pitcher, part yogi and part recluse. Impressively liberated from our opulent life-style, Sidd's deciding about yoga—and his future in baseball." Now look again, reckoning just the first letter of each word: *Happy April Fools' Day—ah, fib.*

I, for one, was completely taken in by the charm of this sports fable. I wanted it to be true. Two weeks later, the editors and Plimpton 'fessed up. Even that was charming, for it seems that Plimpton was driven toward this hoax by another April Fools' sports fable that had appeared the year before in the London *Daily Mail.* That one was the tale of a Japanese long-distance runner who had so much trouble with English that he thought the object of a marathon was to run not for twenty-six miles but for twenty-six days!

Down through the ages, a kind of April Fools' Day has always been celebrated, either as a springtide fertility rite or as a simple release from the confining grip of winter. And perhaps the most frequently played trick has been the sending of an unwitting dupe on some false errand, often called a "sleeveless errand" since the eighteenth century. Oddly enough, this cruel tradition has a curiously pious source.

According to an English newspaper article of April 13, 1789, the custom was widely believed to have been started in *Genesis* by Noah, who blundered by sending forth his dove too early, before the waters had receded, on the first day of the same Hebrew month that answers to our April. It was thought entirely proper to revisit the bird's worthless flight, the original sleeveless errand, on anyone who failed to remember this bit of biblical lore. And therein lies an important distinction between April Fools' hoaxes and ordinary garden-variety tricks. If you've forgotten what day it is, you deserve to be hornswoggled.

The first recorded use of the phrase April Fool is in Congreve's play *The Old Bachelor* (1693), which also gets across the idea of a bootless mission: "That's one of Love's April-Fools, is always upon some errand that's to no purpose." Nor have the specific tricks visited on the unwary changed much over the years. Two centuries ago, people were sending patsies out to booksellers for *The History of Eve's Grandmother* or to bird keepers for a bottle of "pigeon's milk." These days, batboys are regularly sent out for an equally improbable "bucket of steam" or the "key to the batter's box."

Great men and great locales both have been caught up in April foolishness. In 1713 the magisterial satirist Jonathan Swift—*Dean*

Swift, in fact, for he was a man of the cloth—recorded in his journal on March 31 that he aimed to spread about town the rumor that a recently hanged criminal had been resuscitated and could be visited at the Black Swan Inn, Holborn, London. Next day, however, Swift was disappointed that so few gullibles took his April Fools' bait and came to gawk.

And great places? In March 1860, thousands of prominent Britons were sent an invitation, bearing all the hallmarks of officialdom, that read: "Tower of London.—Admit the Bearer and Friend to view the Annual Ceremony of Washing the White Lions, on *Sunday, April 1st,* 1860. Admitted only at the White Gate. It is particularly requested that no gratuities be given to the Wardens or their Assistants." The Tower has neither a White Gate nor White Lions, washed or unwashed. A commentator wrote that "cabs were rattling about Tower Hill all that Sunday morning, vainly endeavoring to discover the White Gate."

In another historic case, April 1 furnished the backdrop for a Great Escape. Around 1700, when the duke and duchess of Lorraine were imprisoned in Nantes, the pair decided to use the day's silliness to cover their departure through the garrisoned city gate. Disguised as laborers carrying hod and rubbish, the two cautiously set out. But when they were suddenly betrayed to the town guards, the information was treated as an April Fools' joke and the bedraggled and obviously unroyal couple were told to be on their way. Too late to prevent the escape, the ruse was discovered; there is no record of any punishment meted out to the unfortunate gatekeepers.

Doubtless the primary influence on April Fools' Day is Nature itself. The change in seasons is, in the northern hemisphere at least, truly welcome. In France, this is the season when fish, especially mackerel, are again easy to catch. So the phrase April Fool is in fact *poisson d'avril,* April fish. Perhaps the most august of those fish was none other than the emperor Napoleon, who so far forgot himself as to be married (for the second time) on April 1, 1810.

Among the Romans, the date was celebrated as the start of the festival called *Cerealia,* essentially a fertility rite devoted to the renewal of crops. The feast honors the goddess Ceres, whose beautiful daughter Proserpina was whisked off to Hades by Pluto one fine spring day as she was gathering flowers. Ceres, the goddess of grain, was so furious she put an immediate halt to all growing, and winter reclaimed the landscape. Eventually the gods allowed Proserpina to return. But because the girl had been so foolish as to eat a single pomegranate seed in the underworld, she must still, to this day, return to Pluto for six months every year. Which accounts for our seasons.

There's an April Fools' note to this legend as well. When Ceres first realized her daughter was missing, she sought her by following only an empty echo. That hopeless search for the source of the echo was the Latin original of the sleeveless errand.

Too, in the classical tale and in the French *poisson d'avril,* it should not be overlooked that both seeds and fish are universal fertility symbols. After all, it's spring, a time when a young man's fancy turns to more than baseball. Canadian poet Bliss Carman in 1905 cautioned us, "Fear not the mighty instinct, the great Aprilian Creed; the House of Spring is open and furnished for thy need." So it's entirely right that in Latin the *mensis Aprilis,* the month of April, is derived from the verb *aperire* as the time when the earth opens and softens in the sun.

While Shakespeare suggested that "men are April when they woo," Chaucer was more informed on the point. When he opened his *Canterbury Tales* with those lines about April's sweet showers piercing the drought of March to the root, he was relating that narrow springtime impulse to the general reawakening of all creation. And he was putting his medieval audience on notice that this would be a devotional, "serious" work of art.

With all this emphasis on natural stirrings, reawakening, and remembering—T. S. Eliot called April the cruelest month for just those reasons—clearly some sort of holiday respite was due. And in the old calendar, which held sway in Europe until late in the sixteenth century, there was indeed one. It was April 1, the eighth day—the gift-giving day—of a festival that started on March 25. In the old Julian calendar, March 25 was New Year's Day. But in 1564 in France, when Charles IX began promoting calendar reform, a basic task was to move New Year's from March to January 1.

Old habits, however, had a way of persisting, and conservatives who preserved the old gift-giving holiday on April 1 soon began to attract criticism. Eventually they began to attract mock gifts and sarcasm as well, and the cruelty of April Fools' Day was thoroughly entrenched. It was simply a matter of time before a twenty-six-day marathoner would trudge into view.

Notes and Further Reading

For Proserpina (or Persephone), see Leach, 859; for April Fools' Day, 36–37. On the connection with New Year's Day, see Hazlitt, 13. For *Aprilis*, see Lewis and Short, 145.

For Noah, see *N&Q*, 4th series, VI:409 (November 12, 1870); *N&Q*, 6th series, IX:340 (April 26, 1884); and *N&Q*, 7th series, XI:319 (April 18, 1891). The Tower of London episode is from Robert Chambers, *The Book of Days: A Miscellany of Popular Antiquities in Connection with the Calendar* (London: W. & R. Chambers, 1866), I:462. The full Shakespeare quotation, from *As You Like It* (IV.i.147), Rosalind speaking, is:

> No, no, Orlando. Men are April when they woo, December when they wed; maids are May when they are maids, but the sky changes when they are wives.

4. Implements & Symbols

TOOLS

LAWNS

TREES

KEYS

PETS

PLACE-NAMES

DIBS!

UMBRELLAS

 # Tools

Man is a tool-using animal. . . .
Without tools he is nothing, with tools he is all.

—THOMAS CARLYLE, *SARTOR RESARTUS*, 1833

IT'S THE SIGN that gets you. It hung outside the Newtown, Pennsylvania, shop of cabinetmaker Henry Van Horn (1796–1798) and was painted by the American master Edward Hicks, the same man who gave us *The Peaceable Kingdom.*

Hicks' eye is as Romantic as they come. He selects three products to stand for the range of Van Horn's world: a cradle, a chest, and a coffin. That is to say, from cradle to grave, craftsmen—and their tools—are fellow travelers with us through all the travails of life. Such a notion would have been commonplace in the 1790s, the decade when this sign swung lazily over the aroma of wood shavings and sawdust, the din of hammers and the sweet slide of molding planes. Something was a-building in North America. Tools were being used.

In a way, tools are immune to High-Style History, the sort that gets hijacked by nostalgia and good taste. Tools are about sweat equity and as such can be considered faintly not nice. They have dirt under their fingernails.

That's why it was so refreshing, in February 1994, to see Hicks' sign resurrected and hovering pointedly near the start of a surprising Williamsburg exhibit called *Tools: Working Wood in Eighteenth-Century America*. It represented nearly a decade of research and collecting under the direction of Jay Gaynor, curator of mechanical arts at Colonial Williamsburg. "I see our role as a museum being the preservation of chisels and saws and rusty things as well as the chairs and the silver and the ceramics," Gaynor says.

This was the first show of its kind, concentrating on eighteenth-century tools, the century *before* the explosion of information about the manufacture, marketing, and use of tools. For instance, only two dozen eighteenth-century English handsaws are known to survive. Seventeen of them were brought together for the show.

Traditionally, tradesmen at living-history museums have made a point of using old tools, but until recently these have been mid-nineteenth to early twentieth century in most cases. Over the last decade at Williamsburg, there's been a movement to try to replace them with reproductions of eighteenth-century tools. The thinking is that to recreate the eighteenth century you should use period tools. But because original eighteenth-century tools are rare, they must be copied. Among the sources: the few surviving tools themselves, engravings in tool manufacturers' catalogues or in books like Diderot's *Encyclopédie* (1751–1765) or Joseph Moxon's *Mechanick Exercises* (1677), and archaeological digs, which often yield tools, though frequently in a wasted state.

Reproduction tools turn out to have an unexpected side benefit. Today's craftsmen can feel free to modify these tools to suit their work habits or to drop them without having a heart attack. This is just how early workmen would have treated their tools. Too much reverence for tools—for the tool as a work of art—makes it impossible to work with them.

Tools are part of the everyday and certainly were for the American colonists. A 1622 broadside, printed in London at the start of the Virginia experiment, lists tools as vitally important to the commonweal on this new land, so important that budding colonists were to be outfitted with—exactly—ten broad and narrow hoes, seven broad- and felling axes, two handsaws and two two-man saws, a whipsaw, two hammers, three shovels, two spades, two augers, six chisels, two piercers (brace and bit), three gimlets (boring tools), two hatchets, two froes (for splitting wood), two handbills, a grindstone, nails, and two pickaxes.

I know a hawk from a handsaw.

—*HAMLET,* 1602

For several years, Gaynor and historian Nancy Hagedorn read in early Williamsburg and Pennsylvania newspapers that saws manufactured by White were very desirable: "White's Best Steel Plate Saws," said the ads. George Washington ordered them from England for his slave carpenters. White's saws were offered for sale in many shops, but no modern researcher had ever seen one—until Gaynor went to the Stanley-Whitman House in Farmington, Connecticut, to look at the surviving tools of a carpenter who worked there between the Seven Years' and the Revolutionary Wars.

"I was looking at his tools," says Gaynor, "and my gaze kept returning to one particular saw. It looked very old. If you looked closely, you could see a little stamp on it, but it was not quite legible. As I was getting ready to leave, the museum director, Jean Martin, asked me if there was anything else she could help me with. I casually picked up the saw, handed it to her, and said, 'Sure, tell me about this mark.'

"As I did that, the light hit the saw at just the right angle and both of us could see immediately that it was marked 'White.' This was just a piece of the tools story, but it gave us an artifact to tie in with all the textual evidence. Turns out, this is also the earliest documented English backsaw."

A backsaw is designed for close-tolerance work; its blade is usually so thin it must be reinforced—or backed—with a bar of iron or brass across its top. More literally a "backed handsaw," it was soon called simply a backsaw. The sole known White backsaw is exhibited today at Williamsburg. It's a confident and well-fashioned implement, fit for making refined joints in wood, for making things that will last a long time. How many, you wonder, have survived with this fine engine itself?

Another saw mystery has to do with handsaw teeth. In the nineteenth century it was well established that the teeth on saws meant to cut *with* the grain should be shaped like tiny chisels that chip out the wood, while saws that cut *across* the grain should have teeth like knives to sever it. When you look at earlier saws—since you can't know if the tooth patterns were altered by resharpening in the nineteenth century—you can't figure out if that distinction held true for eighteenth-century saws. It's a tiny detail, but vital to saw history. And although saws are an ancient invention, we have no idea when this particular distinction was first made. "I have a sneaking suspicion," Gaynor says, "that the different tooth shaping was so well known that no one bothered to write about it."

There are design puzzles as well. Handsaws often seem to have a little metal nib on their far end, opposite the handle. Why? It's not a leftover product of the saw's manufacture, nor does it offer any special purchase as the saw bites its way through wood. But many eighteenth-century saws have that nib, a feature that continues until the early twentieth century. Often the nib breaks off in use, leaving a tiny vestigial stump in tribute to all the work the saw has seen.

Or take the rounded knob on the end of the wedge that holds the cutting blade in place on hand planes. Purely a decorative detail? It's not until you begin working regularly with planes that you notice how convenient the knob is for pulling the wedge back out when it's time to change the bite of the blade or to sharpen it. Same with the "chamfering" or rounding you see along the edges of planes. Although it's a graceful detail, it also makes the plane easier to use and thus contributes to efficiency. Centuries of use and experience are shrouded in such details.

The granddaddy of old saws was the pitsaw, a four- to eight-foot monster worked by two men. One of them stood in a muddy pit below a great log meant to be sawn into boards; the other stood directly on the log itself. When Hieronymus Wierix depicted the Holy Family in 1600, it was as a typical carpenter's family using a pitsaw—St. Joseph in the pit, the Christ child atop the log. Angels carted off the sawn boards. An old pitsaw from the Virginia plantation called Blandfield in Essex County still survives. In the 1760s, Blandfield's owner, Robert Beverley, wrote to England for a saw "for sawing [in] a Pitt." It may be that same eighteenth-century tool.

The idea that lies behind artifact trades is "archaeology by experiment," the use of antique implements in historical contexts, with the hope that using them will teach us about past lives and cultures. Into the bargain, such activities are picturesque and contribute to the eighteenth-century ambiance of living-history museums. But that is not enough.

Pitsaws, for one thing, teach us about muscle. "Since we've been using pitsaws," says Gaynor, "our woodworkers have learned how to use their bodies to make them work. So we've come to a fuller understanding of apprenticeship. It's not only about acquiring mechanical knowledge and tricks and shortcuts, but it's also developing your body in ways that allow you to use tools safely and efficiently. It's about muscle groups and eye-hand coordination. If you do basically one task from the time you are thirteen until you are twenty-one, you end up being a far different person from someone learning how to use such tools at age thirty-two as part of an academic exercise or a historical enterprise.

"There's often a negative reaction to the reintroduction of an old tool," Gaynor continues. "Then people actually start using it and they say, 'This works. This really makes sense.' It's a conversion. Equip a shop with *all* correct tools, and it changes how people go about their work. When you move the whole clock back two hundred years, the cumulative visual and technological effect is huge. The tools, while functionally similar to their late-nineteenth- or early-twentieth-century counterparts, are different enough that suddenly you realize your techniques are changing."

Mack Headley has been a cabinetmaker for twenty-seven years, the last seventeen of them using reproduction hand tools at Colonial Williamsburg. Earlier, he worked in a shop that depended on hand tools for fine work but machines for surfacing lumber or for rough-sizing. On this bright morning, a generous sun streams into his shop, gilding a few random motes of dust that hover in the warm air. Mack Headley is talking about what he loves to do, about his planes and saws and chisels. Although it's 1994, it could as well be 1796 and the costumed joiner standing before you could be not Headley at all but Edward Hicks' friend Henry Van Horn. He has sawdust in his mane.

"When I came to the Anthony Hay shop and began working completely with hand tools," Headley notes, "I was shocked at how much I'd missed. It takes far longer to hand plane your lumber, but you get to know the material. Machines largely ignore the nature of the wood, its variances and personality. You never feel the wood. You're outside the whole question of grain and quality."

It's clear from Headley that cabinetmakers are often more interested in the personality of the wood than in its working properties. This penchant complicates woodworking and means that the right historical tools must be found and copied. "Hand tools are slower," says Headley, "but they have a great deal more flexibility. Machines are very efficient at a few things, but there are a lot of things they don't do or don't do easily. There's not much you can't do with a hand tool—working with curly material is no problem.

"For a harpsichord, we recently needed an extremely broad

sheet of veneer, seventeen and a half inches wide, about three thirty-seconds thick. It obviously would have been hand sawn in the eighteenth century. We did it. Not on the first go, but still. It called for a lot of finesse and fine-tuning the veneer saw, but it worked. Try to do that in a typical modern shop. No way."

> *. . . my sword [is] hacked like a hand-saw.*
> —*HENRY IV*, 1597

With those words, lying Jack Falstaff insinuates that he's been in the fight of his life. His sword, he swears, has received so many dints, it's as toothed as a handsaw.

The visual arts of the eighteenth century have been surprisingly fertile for tool historians. There is, famously, Hogarth's popular print from the series *Gin Lane* (1751). In it, a carpenter and his wife pawn a saw to buy liquor. The awful reality behind such scenes helped create laws that would prevent a debtor's tools from being confiscated from him. (Tools could still be stolen, of course. An early saw is engraved "JAS PAGE BOAT BUILDER 1789. IF OFFER'D TO BE SOLD OR PAWN'D, STOP THE PARTY." Think about that: it's the same momentous year as the French Revolution. But how much would that mean to a boatbuilder up a creek without his saw?)

Then there is a creamware jug displaying the arms of the coopers' guild of London. Made in Liverpool between 1790 and 1810, it's a model of grace and precision—except that it depicts carpenter's tools, not those of a barrel maker. The house-building and furniture-making hierarchy was clear: a *carpenter* was a rough-framer, a builder; a *joiner* did finishing work—doors, windows, moldings; a *cabinetmaker* worked to the closest tolerances of all. (The distinction was more rigid in England. In the colonies, a man might do all three jobs.) The cooper was associated with a totally different kind of woodworking and devised highly specialized tools germane to his work only. The cooper's side ax, with its blade tilted off center, was used to shape barrel staves. The cooper's croze or "crow" did nothing but cut the groove inside a barrel for the head to snap into.

Consider too the Bucktrout chair, one of the treasures of Williamsburg. Built in the 1760s by local craftsman Benjamin Bucktrout, it served as the seat of honor in some unknown Masonic lodge. The chair is a virtual throne, its back sprinkled with carved tools. It displays not only the symbolic compass and square that are the hallmarks of Freemasonry but also plumbs, level, trowel, mallet, hammer. There's also a carpenter's ruler on the chair back. For a long time, scholars thought that a hint of gilt in the center of the ruler had to do with the golden mean. Jay Gaynor had another idea: "It struck me this was supposed to be a joiner's *folding* rule, in the standard twenty-four-inch length. We stared at it and realized there was a wooden half circle broken off in the center that would have been the rule's hinge. The gilt represented the brass of the hinge."

Similarly, George Forster's 1816 painting of an English woodworking shop is important because it's one of the earliest realistic interiors of a trade shop, either English or American. We can't identify the location, but like shops in the colonies they're doing a little bit of everything. There's an armchair hanging on the wall, shutters up in the rafters, a wing chair up there as well, picture frames, a violin back, patterns, and countless meticulously depicted tools: planes, saws, squares, a brace and bit, vises and clamps, a hammer, a broadax, and the traditional woven basket for carrying carpenter's tools.

Forster's workers wear paper hats, a custom that may have started late in the eighteenth century. There is no colonial record of such hats, but in England they became traditional for a number of trades, notably printers. One theory is that when hairstyles changed and men started pomading their hair, they desperately needed to keep sawdust out.

In addition to art, two other kinds of evidence contribute to the history of tools: probate inventories and records of court proceedings. For instance, when Major Edmund Dickenson of Virginia was killed at the Battle of Monmouth, his estate included a remarkably complete set of joiner's tools. He left, among many other things, no less than eighty-one planes and a copy of *Longinus on the Sublime.* Dickenson's sudden death meant his collection was in sharp contrast to those of other carpenters, who either gave away tools to their relatives or slowly sold them off to raise cash during retirement. The estate was probated in York County Court on August 17, 1778.

Jonathan Parish, a joiner's apprentice, was forced to sue his master's estate for certain tools promised him, to wit: "a good froe, broad ax, handsaw, adz, Inch auger, hamer, drawing knife, two Chisells, gouge, a rule & a pair of Compasses, & two Gimblets. . ." The suit succeeded and appears in the Lancaster County, Virginia, court order book on March 8, 1727.

Cabinetmaker (and accused murderer) John Owen of Raleigh, North Carolina, used one of his chisels to cut through the floor of his jail cell. The escape appears in the *Raleigh Star,* August 9, 1811. And Alexander Crookshanks used a plane to cosh in the skull of William Wheeler of Virginia. He and his blunt instrument make a brief appearance in the Spotsylvania County order book on January 13, 1749.

It's this *heft* of old tools that's so surprising. These are big-shouldered things—a large crown-molding plane that takes two people to push and pull, for instance. And yet, on close inspection, many tools also have details that have little to do with utility and everything to do with art. Many eighteenth-century squares have a charming little ogee curve on their ends, carefully filed there by a busy toolmaker. Heart and head are fused in these tools in an organic way that gets lost in the industrialism of the next century.

The philosopher and craftsman Eric Gill once said you could tell the moral stance of a nation by looking at its pots and pans. For eighteenth-century Anglo-America, Gill could have used tools as his measure. There is, for instance, a 1790 English tool chest with an elaborately inlaid lid depicting a cabinetmaker amid his tools. The owner of the chest was likely a Mason because of the telltale overlaid compass and square on the end of the bench. He was also adept at veneer work; the fine inlaid top says so, brilliantly, and so does a veneer tea caddy on the workbench and a copper glue pot dangling below it. Most important, however, there's a huge compass that frames his head, an allusion to the maxim "Keep within compass"—stay centered, alert, and sensible. If he did so, prosperity would surely follow.

In fact, that's probably why tools have acquired such symbolic rank: if handled properly, tools confer prosperity and status. This may date from the medieval guilds and the mysteries associated with apprenticeship and membership among people who all worked with similar tools. The implements themselves became a common bond.

It's our distance in time from many tools that makes them so arcane. Consider planes, which near the end of the eighteenth century had evolved into the hundreds, each designed to do particular, minute jobs. Major Dickenson, remember, had eighty-one planes at his death. This is exactly what Adam Smith predicted—as population increases, people are driven to specialize. More than anything else, specialization requires special tools.

Until recently, no one paid much attention to woodworking planes, even though many of them were easily identifiable. They were stamped, often on the toe, with makers' marks that enabled the provenience and age of the tool to be traced.

Once the history of the planes began to be sorted out, people began wondering just what they did. There appears to be an infinite variety of planes: ones designed to cut grooves, rabbet planes for putting a step on the side of a board, makers of hollows and rounds, and planes used in combination to turn out complex molding or to shape the edge of raised paneling. Bench planes took wood down to the size you wanted it and made sure it was flat. They were used in series—short planes rode up and down hills, but long planes shaved off the tops of hills. The longer the plane, the smoother the result.

Many planes were not difficult to make, and were made by the joiners themselves. Among specialists, by far the most interesting was Caesor Chelor, a slave belonging to Francis Nicholson of Wrentham, Massachusetts. Nicholson happens to have been the earliest documented American plane maker, and Chelor our first documented black toolmaker. When Nicholson died in 1753, he freed Chelor, who continued to make planes until his death in 1784.

Since planes are datable, the moldings they produced have become a valuable tool for historians wanting to accurately date a building. Molding fashions changed with dependable regularity: Greek Revival followed neoclassical, which followed Roman. Planes were sometimes labeled "Roman ogee" or "Greek ogee" after the curves they produced.

"Planes are so useful," says architectural historian Edward Chappell. "If someone suggests a mantel is seventeenth century, I can say, 'Actually, no, these Greek moldings were not made before 1790. There might have been a mantel here before, but this one was changed after 1790.' "

[Virginia's] best commoditie was iron, which we made into little chissels.

—CAPTAIN JOHN SMITH, 1607

Iron was one of the first exports from Jamestown to England. In part, this explains why the seven Anderson forges have so prominent a place in Colonial Williamsburg, right off Duke of Gloucester Street. The modern equivalent would be plunking down a Ford plant on Fifth Avenue.

Working at the forges today is Ken Schwarz, a blacksmith who reproduces period tools. He represents a critical juncture between the archaeologists and historians who research tools and the craftsmen who use them.

"From archaeology," says Schwarz, "we can look at a finished chisel and figure out the best way to reproduce it. It helps to be able to compare the corroded piece from the ground with illustrations in old catalogues and with surviving chisels. Because iron has a grain to it much like wood, even a deeply rusted piece can allow us to read the grain structure. Rust follows that structure as it attacks the metal. By looking at that we can see just how the straight grain of the iron has been deformed on the anvil to create a shape."

Corroded chisels from Jamestown and other Virginia sites told Schwarz that the tool was basically made from one piece. "Although some chisels are made with a collar that's welded on to form a bolster for the wooden handle to push against," he says, "we were after the one-piece version. Our job was to develop the tooling and skills to be able to make that shape—blade, shank, collar, and tang— in one piece."

From the Hewlett chest, a gentleman's set of tools sold on February 13, 1773—which perhaps was never used and is still pristine— the blacksmiths were able to examine a chisel in mint condition. "It had scratches in places that told us where it had been filed after being hot forged," Schwarz says. "Other parts appeared to have been ground on a grindstone."

Another telltale is the metal near the edge of chisels. Iron is not hardenable, so it cannot keep an edge. Steel (iron with a tiny admixture of carbon) can be hardened but is more expensive. So when blacksmiths consider an old chisel closely, they find that the bulk of it is iron, with a piece of steel welded onto its business end.

The Anderson forges are called upon to make a surprising range of tools, from anvils to tiny springs for gunlocks. They've even made a tool we hardly consider a tool at all these days—cowbells. Consider them agricultural implements.

"The bells were actually copied from an archaeological example found in an eighteenth-century context at Trebell's Landing on the James River," says Schwarz. "Bells were of sheet iron covered with copper or brass to enhance their musical tone. To make one you forge an iron bell, cover it with borax as a flux, and encase it in a clay box along with some scrap brass. Then you poke a hole in it. Throw the whole thing in the fire and heat it until you see the zinc of the brass burning and shooting out the hole. That means the brass is molten. You then pull it out of the fire and roll it around on the floor so the brass coats everything. Works like a charm."

One of the myths the study of eighteenth-century tools helps dispel is that old tools were crude. In fact they were subtle and refined. Says Schwarz: "What I enjoy most about making old tools is how natural the evolution of every piece is. It just becomes a fast, fluid shaping of materials. Until we get to that stage, we always assume we're doing something wrong. If it's a struggle, then we haven't figured it out yet. Chisels are a great example. We start at the tang end and then create the bolster. Once you cut it off the bar and turn it around and start shaping the blade, you've got it made. They knew what they were doing."

Studying tools also crushes the myth that woodworking was a spiritual and leisurely activity. Not so. The past was under constant pressure to produce. Evidence of the compromise between quality and production is everywhere. The parts of a fine cabinet that aren't visible are made with vernacular woods and with far less refinement. Practicality ruled. Corners were cut to save time.

"Historical accounts document the astounding productivity of woodworkers," says Jay Gaynor, "such as turning out five thousand chair parts in five or six months. Using period tools, Williamsburg's tradesmen are confirming such times. When David Salisbury was turning balusters for the courthouse, he could crank one out in about six or seven minutes."

There are other museums that make use of old tools, but Williamsburg is unusual in that it focuses on the eighteenth century. There's a quantum leap from that century to the next. For one thing, there's much more published information about toolmakers after 1810. Before that, you're in the dark ages. But there is another reason for looking at eighteenth-century tools:

"The eighteenth century is the best time for woodworking ever," says Mack Headley. "There are more tools in more people's hands than ever before—or than would be shortly after, because of the decline into industrialism. It's an intriguing point in history."

George Eliot had it just right in *Adam Bede* (1859), her tale of a country carpenter that opens on June 18, 1799. This is from the novel's first page:

The afternoon sun was warm on the five workmen there, busy upon doors and window-frames and wainscoting. A scent of pine-wood from a tent-like pile of planks outside the open door mingled itself with the scent of the elder-bushes which were spreading their summer snow close to the open window opposite; the slanting sunbeams shone through the transparent shavings that flew before the steady plane, and lit up the fine grain of the oak panelling which stood propped against the wall. On a heap of those soft shavings a rough grey shepherd-dog had made himself a pleasant bed.

There are attics and odd corners of old houses, historical societies, and small museums all over the world that have unconsidered—or under-considered—tools. It is not too much to say that in them resides a real part of our past. Such things are worth looking at.

Notes and Further Reading

An earlier version of this appeared in *Colonial Williamsburg,* Winter 1994–95. Thanks to Jay Gaynor, Ken Schwarz, Mack Headley, and Ed Chappell for sharing their research with me. The article was published in conjunction with an antique tools exhibit at the DeWitt Wallace Decorative Arts Gallery. The catalogue from that show, by James M. Gaynor and Nancy L. Hagedorn, was published as *Tools: Working Wood in Eighteenth-Century America* (Williamsburg: CWF, 1993).

See also Jay Gaynor, "Mr. Hewlett's Tool Chest—Part I," *Chronicle of the Early American Industries Association,* 38 (1985): 57–60, and "Part II," *Chronicle,* 39 (1986): 4–12.

The cowbells were originally made for the music program at Williamsburg's African-American Programs Office; see Ken Schwarz, working drawing of Trebell's Landing cowbell, CWF blacksmith office files, n.d.

See also Harold Gill, *The Blacksmith in Colonial Virginia,* CWF research report, October 1965, and Richard T. DeAvila, "Caesor Chelor and the World He Lived In," *Chronicle of the Early American Industries Association,* 46 (1993): 39–42 and 91–97.

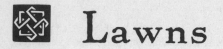 # Lawns

IN 1883, the traveling circus passed through Pulaski, Tennessee, putting on its show in one of the town's grass lots. When it departed a few days later, its only legacy was a series of three great circles etched into the turf by its tents, with a curious bare spot in the center of one. Over the next century, the locals would point to that spot, shake their heads, and claim it was where "the acrobat fell and killed himself." In the mind of the folk, grass refuses to grow on the spot of a murder, a lynching, or any violent death.

This is good news if your lawn isn't quite the pride of the neighborhood and you're casting about for an excuse. Mention the starcrossed lovers who came to grief in that patch on your front yard.

As a nation, we seem to go at this lawn business with colossal determination, throwing mountains of natural resources—fertilizer, lime, water—at the task. But why? Certainly lawns do not occur in Nature. The grasses are all there, to be sure, but not in staggeringly huge plots that exclude all other plants. Even on the Great Plains and in the savannas and the veldt, where there were herds of grazing animals to keep down the woody vegetation, countless other plants have always competed with the grass.

Face it, modern lawns are unnatural. In the mid-1800s, when Nathaniel Hawthorne visited England—where the rage for solid green lawns was in full cry—he was driven to distraction by the artificiality of it all. In vain he searched for a weed, a nettle, anything to break the spell of unrelieved greenness.

Novelist W. H. Hudson (1841–1922), who wrote prose poems on the eloquence of South America's rain forests, truly *saw* grass. Said he: "I am not a lover of lawns; on the contrary, I regard them, next to gardens, as the least interesting adjuncts of the country house. Grass, albeit the commonest, is yet one of the most beautiful things in Nature when allowed to grow as Nature intended, or when not too carefully trimmed and brushed. Rather would I see daisies in their thousands, ground ivy, hawkweed, and even the hated plantain with tall stems, and dandelions with splendid flowers and fairy down, than the too-well-tended lawn grass."

It is said that great areas of green fill some psychological need in us. But that apparently wasn't always the case. Ancient and classical gardeners had smallish green plots in mind, but plots that were dotted with flowers, as if they were replicating meadows.

The first man celebrated for flowery greenswards was King Cyrus of Persia (ca. 500 B.C.). His style of green interspersed with blossoms can still be seen in the design of Persian garden carpets. And the concept lives on in our word "paradise," derived directly from the Old Persian word for an enclosed garden. This idea of the flowery mead was so seductive that the Romans looked to Sanskrit for their word for meadow, *pratum,* which they then transformed into *pratulum,* the little meadow in the midst of a garden. That is to say, a lawn. In the illuminated manuscripts of the Middle Ages, lawns are consistently shown sprinkled with delicate wildflowers, and are again called the enclosed garden *(hortus conclusus),* as by the Persians. Except that this is the Judeo-Christian garden, representing both the old Eden and the paradise yet to come. In any case, flowers are the key.

With or without flowers, however, our ancestors invested grass with a great deal of symbolic importance. Consider the legend of medieval St. Begha, a seventh-century virgin who lived and died at St. Bee's Head, on England's Cumbrian coastline. Although she was born an Irish princess, she left that land to sail across the Irish Sea to her lifelong eponymous home. Begha's boat? A piece of green Irish sod, which she cut, threw onto the waves, and stood on for the seventy-five-mile trip due east.

The folk seem to find sod useful. In North Carolina, folklorists have heard that to keep a dog from "treeing," you should cut out a turf the shape of your foot from beneath the tree in question, turn it upside down, and replace it. Your dog will avoid the tree until the grass grows back up through the sod again. In Denmark, as late as the nineteenth century, it was reported that a cure for infant illness was to pass the child through a sort of doughnut of sod cut at midnight from a churchyard cemetery. The parent must then return the sod to the church and watch for it to reroot. If it did so, the babe would be cured. If the grass died, the child's condition was hopeless. It's easy to see the primitive reasoning behind this. Its object was to pull the spirit and body of the moribund infant back through death's door, the hole in the sod of the burial ground.

Much more widespread, however, are a number of other beliefs about grass. It's bad luck to see a dog eat grass. If a cat eats grass, it will rain soon. In Illinois, it is said that a cat that eats grass is sick. This belief is related to the Pennsylvania saying that grass is cat medicine. Likewise, expect rain if the grass is dry in the morning. Conversely, if the grass is bedewed in the morning, the rest of the day should be fair.

Farmers who follow folk wisdom never plant grass seed when the horns of the moon are pointing up, lest the seed hop up out of the ground. If it snows on Christmas, the grass will be green on Easter. But if you see grass in January, "lock up your barn," as the folk advice has it, because spring will be very late.

Another commonplace of folklore and literature is that grass is the lush, green hair of the grave, as both Walt Whitman and James Joyce suggested. If they were alive today, they'd be thrilled to learn that Koreans prize their zoysia grass not for its green but for the way it covers graves with a coat of golden straw in winter. Since Korean tombs are simple mounds of earth covered with grass, part of the national funerary ritual is for the deceased's family to pick out the straw hue of the zoysia strains that will cover their loved one for eternity. Royal graves there have been so covered—without fertilizer or irrigation—since the year 1200.

This knowledge prompted the USDA's Agricultural Research Center at Beltsville, Maryland, to send a team of agronomists to the Orient to find new varieties of grass—zoysias mainly—that could be adapted to American lawns and playing fields. The project was directed by Jack Murray, who went there for two months in 1982 and came back with some eight hundred new specimens (the first brought back since shortly after World War II, when the zoysia craze first hit). The goal was to infuse the drought-tolerant, low-fertilizer, and low-maintenance characteristics of some of these plants into new U.S. varieties. "The big push today," Murray explains, "is for minimum maintenance grasses. The need to conserve water and fertilizer is just too great to divert these national resources to lawns, which after all are largely ornamental."

Although he found some cultivars that were still green when snow was on the ground (at a time when most American varieties would have been dormant), a more surprising finding was the overall range of zoysias, including a seashore variety that had a genetic tolerance for salt and could conceivably be irrigated with sea water over here. "I noticed we were spending a lot of time in cemeteries taking grass samples," says Murray. "Cemeteries and golf courses. The Koreans love their golf and play it all year long—in winter on a carpet of golden zoysia straw." Any cultural anthropologist worth his salt ought to be able to tell us what all this means. In both East and West, it seems our adolescent games and our graves alike are intimately associated with verdant, prolific grass.

Actually, the history of two games—bowling and golf—is closely connected with lawns. Bowling was originally an outdoor game played on turfs so fine that subtle discontinuities in the ball's shape—called the bias—could come into play. And the bowling allée was a lane among the trees, a vista in a landscaped park. British Admiral Sir Francis Drake is said to have been bowling at Plymouth when the Spanish Armada was first sighted. He finished the game.

Golf was first played in Holland, Scotland, and England, wherever there were naturally close turfs caused by grazing, drought, or shallow soils. Lawn tennis was not invented until the nineteenth century when "real" tennis or "court" tennis, an indoor game, was finally moved outside to be played on a chalked turf.

But the rise of golf and bowling are only part of the problem for us and our lawns. Better by far to blame it all on Edwin Budding, the man who invented the lawn mower in 1830. Budding, a clever foreman in an English textile plant, saw how the machine for cutting the nap off cloth could be transformed into one that would cut lawns. Without lawn mowers—or grazing sheep or tenants wielding scythes—we could scarcely have taken all this lawn business on board. Said Budding at the time: "Country gentlemen will find in using my machine an amusing, useful and healthful exercise."

Notes and Further Reading

The American Association of Plant Food Control Officials says we spread about a million tons of chemical fertilizer on our lawns, parks, and playing fields to keep them green each year. The National Limestone Institute reckons we put down a like amount of lime to fix our collective soil pH. And the Water Resources Division of the U.S. Geological Survey throws up its hands when it comes to estimating the volume of water wasted on lawns. They do note, however, that each American citizen uses 183 gallons of water per day around the home.

Special thanks to Jack Murray of USDA Beltsville for talking to me about zoysia grass. My article on plant science and modern agricultural research at Beltsville appeared in *Smithsonian,* March 1982. See also J. Jack Murray and M. C. Engelke, "Exploring for Zoysiagrass in Eastern Asia," unpubl. paper, USDA, Field Crops Laboratory, Beltsville Agricultural Research Center, n.d. [1983].

For the Pulaski incident, see Brown, Item 7925; see also Items 6114, 6381, 6663, 7173, 7400, and 7425. For *pratum,* see Lewis and Short, 1439. There is some interesting lawn history in Eleanour Sinclair Rohde's "The Garden: Part II, Lawns" in *The Nineteenth Century and After* 104 (1928): 200-209. The story of the Danish cemetery sod is in "Balder the Beautiful," Frazer, II:191. St. Begha is found in *Butler's Lives of the Saints* under her day, November 1.

Edwin Budding appears in James B. Beard's *Turfgrass: Science and Culture* (Englewood Cliffs, N.J.: Prentice-Hall, 1973), 3, and in F. J. Reed's *Lawns and Playing Fields* (London: Faber and Faber, n.d. [1950]), 16.

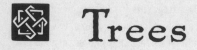 # Trees

MEN ARE AT WORK. Arriving at dawn bearing chain saws
and axes, they are right now chopping and buzzing, mulching and
humbling a hundred-year-old tulip poplar. All this in the name of
progress. Okay, road widening.

Not that the road ran into the woods. It did not. It's just that
some day a speeding car might have careered off the verges and into
that solemn tulip poplar, the sort of thing that crash reports call a
"large fixed object."

Large fixed objects called trees have been much on my mind
lately. As a race, we love our trees and have long depended on them
to give us timber and firewood, fruit and nuts, shelter and shade.
(King George III once mistook an oak tree for an ambassador; His
Majesty shook one of its branches.) All this bounty, in fact, has
caused trees to be given a large role in our spiritual and emotional
and aesthetic existence.

Susanne and Jake Page, who lived among the Hopi in the mid-
1970s, note that spruce is a major part of tribal religion. The
kachina dancers of the May ceremony wear manes of spruce
boughs and have spruce shoots all over their costumes. Each

dancer's left hand also brandishes a spruce sprig. At the beginning of the world, according to Hopi legend, magically growing trees—spruce, fir pine, long-needle pine, and bamboo—were called on by mankind to elevate us from out of the underworld. The sky, the Hopi believed, was like a round hole in the top of an immense kiva. You needed a very tall tree to get out. Trees were thus instruments of salvation and deliverance.

The tree of life is a widespreading one. Buddha's first test occurred under the shade of the bo tree, or Tree of Enlightenment. There, on the Immovable Spot, he faced down the fearsome god of life and death, Kama-Mara. Joseph Campbell regarded this encounter as "the most important single moment in Oriental mythology, a counterpart to the crucifixion in the West. The Buddha beneath the Tree of Enlightenment (the Bo Tree) and Christ on Holy Rood (the Tree of Redemption) are analogous figures, incorporating an archetypal World Savior, World Tree motif, which is of immemorial antiquity."

In Scandinavian myth, the great world tree is called Yggdrasil. It's evergreen, it stretches from heaven to hell—from Valhalla to the underworld. The invincible spear of the chief god, Odin, was fashioned from a sliver of its wood. The Yakut of Siberia tell of a huge tree of life growing on the summit of a great hill. Its topmost branches reach to the dwelling place of the high god. Its roots descend to the forbidding passages of the netherworld. From the milky dew of this tree Yakut heroes derive their character and strength.

Across all cultures, people sing of such nurturing trees, their trees of life. According to Campbell, such trees only exist at the center of the world, the World Axis he calls it. The Garden of Eden was a World Axis. Here "the wish-fulfilling, fruitful aspects of trees are paramount." The impulse to honor an important and magical tree is what deeply underlies our Christmas tree.

Yet we know, and a comparison of worldwide myths confirms,

that there were always two trees in the Garden of Eden story. The Tree of Life was the nourishing one that could confer immortality on Adam and Eve. The Tree of Knowledge of Good and Evil, however, was the forbidden one. In prompting the hapless pair to choose the latter tree, the serpent robbed them of eternal life.

This sense of evil is clear in the Greek and Latin. The word *malus* denotes an apple tree, the Tree of Life. But the same word does double duty as "evil." Note too how serpents or dragons jealously guard the fruits of these trees. In the classical tale of the Golden Apples of the Hesperides, a dragon named Ladon tended the forbidden fruits. The twelfth labor of Hercules was to slay him and pilfer the goods.

Can there be evil trees? The Romantic poets were quite taken with the image of the upas tree of Java, which was rumored—in Europe at least—to rain a sap of death and destruction in all directions. Poet Erasmus Darwin, the grandfather of Charles, wrote in his fantastical *Loves of the Plants* (1789), "Fierce in dread silence on the blasted heath/ Fell Upas sits, the Hydra-Tree of death." Moreover, the early Christians regarded the wooden Holy Cross as a symbol of defeat that only a God—and his son's death—could transform into a symbol of victory.

It comes as no surprise that the Egyptians, in parched North Africa, would hold a special reverence for trees. When a pharaoh died, for example, it was believed that he went to dwell with the gods and ate of the Tree of Life. At Heliopolis grew a sacred tree on which Thoth and the goddess Sefchet wrote the names of the monarchs and all the other important dead. (Scholars believe this tree to be the model for Islam's Lote Tree of Paradise, whose leaves bear the names of every person who ever lived.)

Osiris himself was worshiped as a tree spirit in one of his many manifestations. Pottery and carnelian amulets representing the Tree of Osiris, looking for all the world like tiny watchtowers bound with four rows of palm fronds, were always draped around the necks of

the dead in honor of Osiris. The tree symbolized stability. It signified that the bearer could enter the realm of the dead and eat from
the blessed tree.

The Egyptians were also among the first people to try their hand
at arboriculture, at least in royal gardens. Exotic tree varieties were
brought from all over the kingdom in the Eighteenth Dynasty to
grace the garden at Thebes. There and elsewhere, the sycamore
was a particular favorite. The sun god Ra was said by the *Book of
the Dead* to rise each morning in the east between two turquoise
sycamores.

A sycamore is easy to love. It grows to great heights, has massive
leaves with downy undersides, and boasts an always staggering
bark, mottled brown and white. Actually, the sycamore of the ancients must have been the *Platanus orientalis,* the eastern plane
tree. The American sycamore, *Platanus occidentalis,* was brought
to Europe early in the seventeenth century. There the two
sycamores were hybridized into the magnificent London plane, *P.
acerifolia,* a tree that became the standard along the grand avenues
of cities the world over.

"I am exalted as a plane tree," the Old Testament prophet Ecclesiasticus declared. And in the Gospel of Luke, it is a sycamore that
Zacchaeus the reformed publican climbs to get a better glimpse of
his Lord in the madding crowd. In the mid-thirteenth century,
Marco Polo marveled at a huge, solitary plane tree he came across
on the desert borders of Persia. There were no other trees for a
hundred miles in one direction, ten miles in another, he said. "Its
leaves are green on one side, white on the other." Anyone who has
handled a sycamore leaf will see the accuracy of that observation.

Sycamores seek water in the depths of the earth, and the folk
have always attributed an almost human thirst to them. Nomadic
tribes, dusty from traveling, learned to look for a great sycamore. Its
roots would often lead them to a spring. And the sycamores along
the Wabash, far away, gave Indiana a state tree—and song.

The classical world was also devoted to trees. The fluting on Greek and Roman columns was originally intended to simulate tree bark—art imitating Nature, as if the roofs of their temples were supported by ranks of great trees. There is some aptness in that image as well, since the world's first temples were nothing more than sacred groves in the woods. Indeed, the Latin *templum* is simply an open space among the trees.

Groves dedicated to Apollo were lined with laurel trees, in remembrance of Daphne, the god's first love. Rather than submit to his advances, however, Daphne was metamorphosed into a tree. "Her soft sides," says Ovid, "were begirt with thin bark. Her hair was changed to leaves, her arms to branches. Her feet grew fast in sluggish roots. . . . Her gleaming beauty alone remained." Later, Greek and Roman athletes were awarded laurel wreaths in honor of Apollo and his sacred groves. And before making their predictions, Greek oracles chewed sacred laurel leaves from the Olympian and Delphic slopes.

Despite the popularity of laurel and sycamore in art and literature, however, it is the lofty oak that stands tall at the head of the tree kingdom.

Clearly the most famous of oak trees was the English one near Worcester in whose branches King Charles II hid after a resounding defeat at the hands of the Parliamentary forces on September 6, 1651. The tree stood on land called Boscobel, farmed by a family named Penderel. After the tenants tossed up some comfy pillows, both the young king and his aide Colonel William Carlos spent the night in the Boscobel oak. With Roundheads combing the area and Charles dead asleep against the colonel's numb arm, it is said that Carlos so far forgot himself as to rouse His Majesty with a sharp pinch. In the end the oak played its part in the king's salvation, and down to this day Englishmen have worn oak apples (oak galls) in their caps every year on May 29, the date of Charles II's restoration. (For their part, the Penderels won a royal stipend in perpetuity. In

1931 it was revealed that the claimant was a retired laundry worker named George Penderell of Brooklyn, New York.) In the English colonies in North America, a number of towns were named Royal Oak in memory of the event, and that name also served with distinction as the name of a line of English warships, from the first in 1674 down through today's Royal Navy.

The greatest efflorescence of trees and leaves in art occurred in the medieval cathedral. Stone carvings in England and on the Continent consistently show botanically detailed views of oak, hawthorn, holly, woodbine, hazel, laurel, plane, maple, cherry, and fig. The finest such leaf collection is in the chapter house connected to England's Southwell Minster. The small building dates from the end of the thirteenth century and was celebrated by Nikolaus Pevsner in his 1945 study of church decoration *The Leaves of Southwell.* Pevsner regarded Southwell as one of the highest moments in medieval carving, and a tribute to the carvers' scientific skills as well.

Although medieval Christianity had a special affinity for plants, surely no tree received more attention in religion and folklore than the tree, or cross, of Christianity. For the Middle Ages, a basic tenet of faith was that since the Eden tree had brought mankind low, so the wooden tree of Calvary was to raise us up again.

What is not so clear is what wood the true cross was made of. Medieval theologians reasoned it would have been fabricated from four woods, representing the four points of the compass, thus indicting all mankind in the crime. Others suggested instead that four incorruptible woods were chosen: palm, cypress, cedar, and olive. A Middle Eastern myth held that King Solomon cut down a cedar and buried it near what would later be called the Pool of Bethesda. Centuries later, during Passion week, it floated to the surface and was used to fashion the cross. An associated myth has it that Seth placed apple seeds under the tongue of the corpse of Adam. The trees that sprouted eventually furnished the wood of the cross.

In modern thought, trees also have had very broad influence. A solitary aspen, for instance, had a profound effect on the first of the modern art critics, the Victorian John Ruskin (1819–1900). The particular epiphany I have in mind occurred in 1842, when Ruskin was just embarking on his long career. On the grand tour through France and Switzerland, he found himself alone on a cart road near Fontainebleau, resting to recover his strength. Lying on the road bank, he was transfixed by a little aspen tree:

> Languidly, but not idly, I began to draw it; and as I drew, the languor passed away: the beautiful lines insisted on being traced—without weariness. More and more beautiful they became, as each rose out of the rest, and took its place in the air. With wonder increasing every instant, I saw that they "composed" themselves, by finer laws than any known of men. At last, the tree was there, and everything I had thought before about trees, nowhere.
>
> But that all the trees of the wood (for I saw surely that my little aspen was only one of their millions) should be beautiful—more than Gothic tracery, more than Greek vase-imagery, more than the daintiest embroiderers of the East could embroider, or the artfullest painters of the West could limn—this was indeed an end to all former thoughts with more, an insight into a new sylvan world.

Ruskin thereafter practiced "careful botany." During the course of the century he became one of the great philosophers of the age, the mouthpiece for the art of the Pre-Raphaelite Brotherhood, the sole enthusiast for the paintings of the neglected J. M. W. Turner, the instigator of the Gothic Revival in architecture, and a social reformer. It's not too much to say that it all started with the Fontainebleau aspen.

Like Ruskin, I too have a single favorite tree. Unfortunately, it no longer exists. Nor have I ever laid eyes on it. The tree appears only in one of my faded books, an 1895 red guidebook to south Devon and south Cornwall. Its entry on the tiny village of Moreton Hampstead "on the Edge of Dart Moor" speaks of a lime tree in the center of town. (This is the English lime, or linden, a *Tilia* species, not the citrus lime.) "This tree," says the guidebook, "has had its top flattened and its branches trained into the shape of a bowl, the bottom of which once formed a fiddler's platform." By 1896, however, when the guide was reissued, the publisher was forced to bind in a small correction sheet on coarse paper facing that page:

The lime tree in the Moreton Cross has been blown down.

I've been turning that forlorn slip of paper over and over in my mind lately. Our love affair with trees has been a very fine thing. So perhaps it's good that the Moreton Hampstead lime went down in the rude storms of the winter of 1896. Had it survived Nature's onslaught, traffic planners would even now be going at it with chain saws, just another large fixed object in the path of progress.

Notes and Further Reading

The lime tree appears in C. S. Ward and M. J. B. Baddeley, *Thorough Guides Series: South Devon and South Cornwall* (London: Dulau, 1896), 94. The Fontainebleau aspen is in Ruskin's *Praeterita: Outlines of Scenes and Thoughts, Perhaps Worthy of Memory, in My Past Life* (Boston: Dana Estes, 1905), 62 and 252–254.

For spruce customs, see Susanne and Jake Page, *Hopi* (New York: Harry N. Abrams, 1982), 152–154. For some lively lists of botanical symbolism and folklore, see Mackenzie Walcott, "Notes on Trees and Flowers," *N&Q,* 1st series, XI:460–462 (June 16, 1855). An addendum was contributed by W. Denton, "Notes on Trees and Flowers," *N&Q,* 1st series, XII:70–71 (July 28, 1855).

On planes and limes, see B. E. Nicholson, *The Oxford Book of Trees* (Oxford: Oxford University Press, 1975), 194. On Yggdrasil, see Leach, 1190. On the upas tree, see *The Oxford Companion to English Literature,* ed. Margaret Drabble (Oxford: Oxford University Press, 1985), 848.

On trees of life, see Joseph Campbell, *The Hero with a Thousand Faces* (Princeton: Princeton University Press, 1949), 31–33, 61–63, 213, and 334–336. See also Nikolaus Pevsner, *The Leaves of Southwell* (London: Penguin, 1945). The plane tree is in the Old Testament in Ecclesiasticus 14; compare Luke 19:4. On *malus,* see Lewis and Short, 1104. See also *The Travels of Marco Polo,* trans. Ronald Latham (New York: Penguin, 1975), 70.

 # Keys

IF YOU HAVE EVER bought a house or a car, or even rented an apartment, at the moment you were handed the keys you took part in an ageless ceremony. Receiving the keys meant you were in charge. It's stunning how something as simple and utilitarian as a key can wield so much symbolic weight.

Item: A visiting dignitary—politician, astronaut, Olympic hero—is presented with a huge, obviously bogus, but nevertheless herrih-boned, key to the city. This in spite of the fact that the town is no longer, or never was, protected by walls with lockable gates.

Item: Writer Alex Shoumatoff, reporting from deep in the Ituri Forest in Zaire, notes that a local policeman there does not wear a badge, but rather sports a set of four keys as symbols of his civic authority. Two open desks at the station; another is for the policeman's house. The last is a skeleton. That key ring is all the badge he ever needs.

Item: It is every child's fiction, between the ages of eight and ten, that a magical key exists somewhere. That solitary key, it is fervently believed, can open every lock on earth.

How did all this profound silliness come about? And why is it still going on?

In America, the key as a symbol of power extends back to colonial times. William Penn first arrived in the New World to lead his colony on October 27, 1682. After his great ship *Welcome* dropped anchor off New Castle, Delaware, Penn proceeded directly to the town's fort for an elaborate ritual in which he was given the key to the defensive works, as well as a piece of turf with a twig in it and a porringer of river water and soil. He was indeed in charge.

In Williamsburg, Virginia, a like ceremony, in which keys were featured performers, was acted out on Friday, November 30, 1705, signaling the completion of the first capitol building. On that day, the four keys to the structure's four doors were called in from master builder Henry Cary and theatrically smashed in the presence of the speaker and several members of the House of Burgesses. Cary no longer had the run of the building; it was now officially Virginia's.

A "ceremony of the keys" has been played out every evening for some seven hundred years at the Tower of London. At precisely 9:53 each night, the chief warder makes symbolic rounds of the castle to lock all the gates in turn. Finally at Bloody Tower archway a stern sentry demands, "Who goes there?" Answer: "The keys." "Whose keys?" "Queen Elizabeth's keys." The ritual's last words: "Advance, Queen Elizabeth's keys, all's well."

The Constable of the Tower—a dignified and stately office held by military heroes and other important personages, once by the duke of Wellington himself—is known by his insignia, a pair of gold master keys. On his installation, each new incumbent receives the keys on a velvet pillow directly from the Lord Chamberlain, who intones: "I have the honor in the Queen's name and on the Queen's behalf, to hand to you the keys of the Tower of London and to charge you with the custody of the Tower itself."

Since the symbolic force of all keys lies in their power to lock and unlock, a number of English words and phrases have come to depend on that image. The "king's keys," for example, were the crowbars and hammers legally used by royal constables to break down the doors of outlaws and scofflaws. And when a scurrying Dickens character, Job Trotter *(Pickwick Papers)*, arrives at Gray's Inn after the gates have been locked for the night, he is told: "You've got the key of the street, my friend."

In Latin a key is *clavis.* Thus your clavicle (from *clavicula,* little key) is your collarbone, so called because this double-curved bone is slightly key-shaped and helps to gird together the upper body.

There is a whole train of meaning from *clavis* that has to do with music. In 1609, English composer John Dowland defined the keynote by observing that "A key is the opening of a Song, because like as a Key opens a dore, so doth it the Song." The clavichord, a forebear of the modern piano, is an instrument in which a *clavis* makes a musical note by striking a *chorda* or string. The keyboard is a collection of such keys. A *clavier* originally meant a man who was a keybearer; in time the word came to mean yet another keyboard instrument.

Consider also the musical *clef,* similarly derived via the French from *clavis.* As an anonymous Victorian writing in 1856 noted: "The object of the cleff is to divide off and enchain the sounds within a certain confined compass. That which locks, unlocks; that which closes, discloses; hence the key makes clear the proposed confinement or compass of the sounds." This solid connection with locking, confining, and closing leads naturally to the concept of the keystone, the wedge-shaped block that holds together the other stones or bricks in an arch.

It is a matter of some debate just when the first lock and key were made, but it is known that the Egyptians, Greeks, and Romans had keys. Essentially, these came in two varieties: sliding or turning keys. The sliding type entered through a hole in the door and was used to pull a bar or bolt into position. (This type continued into the medieval period as a "latch lifter." An archaeological dig in East Anglia recently uncovered a Saxon woman buried with her sword and her latch lifter.) Turning keys were similar to those still being manufactured today, and included fused pins or pierced bits attached to a round (sometimes square) shaft. They opened chests and padlocks as well as doors. Ancient keys were made of iron and wood as well as gold, silver, and bronze, and keys of all these materials have been uncovered throughout the classical Mediterranean. The moral philosopher Augustine was attacking the Roman love of opulence when he demanded: "Of what use is a gold key if it will not open what we wish? Or what objection is there to a wooden one . . . when we seek nothing except to open what is closed?"

Trouble was, the early key and lock technology was so simple that it could be defeated easily. Skeleton keys, called *adulterae*, were common among the Romans. The solution: to lock valuables away and then seal the door or chest with wax. For just this reason, a number of sets of keys from the classical and medieval periods also have bronze seals dangling from the chain. These were used for making a monogram impression in soft wax. One of the finest pieces at the Dumbarton Oaks Center for Medieval and Byzantine Studies is a gold signet ring (for making the wax impression) with a tiny key swinging from the inside of the ring's hoop. The design allowed the key to be hidden in the palm of the closed hand. This signet key ring is the only one of its kind in gold to survive from Byzantium.

To the Greco-Roman world goes the credit for depicting gods with keys representing their powers. Athena is shown with the keys of Athens, Hecate with the key to Hades. Janus, the doorkeeper god, holds keys in both hands. We derive the name of our first month, January, from him because with his two faces he looks both to the future and the past, and holds the door into the next year. But we also get "janitor" from the same source and from the word for the slave who held the keys to a Roman estate. A nice arc of coincidence from those days to ours is provided by the fact that janitors are still recognized by their pendulous key rings.

Of course, the figure most often associated with keys through the ages is St. Peter. His connection with keys comes directly from the Gospel of Matthew: "And I will give unto thee the keys of the kingdom of heaven." Ever since, painters and sculptors have made those keys the symbol of St. Peter. The image is so robust that Milton, in a famous couplet from "Lycidas," could describe St. Peter without having to name him outright:

Two massy keys he bore of metals twain
(The golden opes, the iron shuts amain).

That's all it took, although the distinction between the two metals is apparently the poet's own poetic invention. (The tradition is that the golden key is for heaven, the iron for hell.)

That is the great benefit of symbol, in fact. Those keys are as vocal as a sign around the saint's neck declaring his name in neon. The imagery even extended to tavern signs. In old England, a Cross-Keys Inn is often located near a cathedral or church of St. Peter.

Keys are also an important symbol of domestic authority. Foremost among the figures freighted with this notion is St. Martha, who was revered by the early Christians for her devotion to home and hearth. Because Martha was also the sister of the resurrected Lazarus, it was to her that Christ addressed the words "I am the resurrection and the life" in the Gospel of John. But despite that lofty fame, her symbol in art quickly became the housewife's bunch of keys. When a Roman bride first entered her husband's home, she received the keys to all his storerooms. An important part of a Roman divorce was the demand that those same keys be returned. Martha's keys are in touch with this tradition.

The notion of the housewife or the maid being recognized through her keys is commonplace in our culture. Oliver Goldsmith used it as a plot device in *She Stoops to Conquer* (1773), where the character Marlow falls in love with his host's daughter, mistaking her for a maid. Says he: "Didn't you see the tempting, brisk, lovely little thing that runs about the house with a bunch of keys to its girdle?"

But bunched keys were not just feminine accoutrements. The head butler of Governor Botetourt of the Virginia Colony, William Marshman, for example, was never far from his keys. He was not only in charge of all the Palace accounts but also in direct control of all the supplies, glass, and plate needed to run that huge entertaining and governing enterprise. As if to formally declare Marshman's domestic power and authority, the restored Governor's Palace at Williamsburg prominently displays a large key ring hanging on the door to Marshman's pantry-office.

The last word on keys in bunches, however, properly belongs to English poet Harry Graham (1874–1936), whose grim eye once detailed the tribulations of a "Mr. Jones" and his keys:

"There's been an accident!" they said,
"Your servant's cut in half; he's dead!"
"Indeed!" said Mr. Jones, "and please
Send me the half that's got my keys."

Notes and Further Reading

The power of the housewife's keys has been appropriated to represent the mastery that madams and whores have over their clients, as in a 1993 production of William Wycherley's *The Country Wife* (1675) at the Swan Theatre, Stratford-upon-Avon. Said a reviewer at the time: "A night-town interlude with whores parading the stage, fanning their crotches with jingling keys, suggests the harsh grip of pleasure, more challenge than invitation." See John Stokes, "Ugly Pleasures," *TLS,* August 20, 1993. Keys and sports? When golfer Bobby Jones played in his last British Open at St. Andrews, Scotland, he was given the keys to the city. He was only the second American, after Ben Franklin, to be so honored.

Archaeology is not our only source for old keys. For an example of medieval keys that appear as graffiti, see Pritchard, 30. St. Martha and her keys are discussed in Ferguson, 132–133. The Augustine quotation is from *On Christian Doctrine,* trans. D. W. Robertson, Jr. (Indianapolis: Bobbs-Merrill, 1958), 136. For *clavis,* see Smith, I:450–452. For the quotation on *clef,* see "Key and Treble: Etymology," *N&Q,* 2nd series, I:195 (March 8, 1856). See also R. St. John Tyrwhitt, "The Cross Keys," *N&Q,* 6th series, VII:172 (March 3, 1883), and Mackenzie Walcott, "Custom at Feasts," *N&Q,* 1st series, XI:255 (March 31, 1855).

The "Lycidas" quotation is from lines 110–111. The Goldsmith quotation is from near the start of Act IV. On the destruction of the keys to the first capitol building at Williamsburg, see Marcus Wiffen, *The Public Buildings of Williamsburg* (Williamsburg: CWF, 1958), 46–47. Alex Shoumatoff's "A Reporter at Large: The Ituri Forest" appeared in the *New Yorker,* February 6, 1984.

✸ Pets

I HAVE ALWAYS THOUGHT it nothing short of spectacular, in the way of Kindness to Animals, that the Egyptians mummified their cats. What is somewhat problematic is the question of whether they were properly dead cats, or merely those made ceremonially defunct in order to accompany their masters to the afterlife. Anyway, there they are, in virtually every Egyptology exhibit in the world, rows of tightly bound and casketed cats, looking as contented as bowling pins.

Still, never mind the quibble, for in the history of mankind there seems to have always been room for all the tamed animals we now consider pets. Pets of old were tolerated and encouraged because they gave their masters comfort, protection, and at times instruction—the same reasons we keep them today. The medieval period even brought forth a pantheon of saints specially associated with domestic animals. There was St. Dominic for dogs; St. Anthony of Egypt for pigs; St. Loy, a French saint, for cattle and horses; and St. Gertrude for mice.

By the secular and enlightened eighteenth century, the celebrated English hermit Mrs. Celestina Collins would never think of dining without her two favorite pets—a huge and aged rooster with three-inch spurs and a cozy rat. These three took meals together in Coventry for many years until the night the rat ate the rooster and Mrs. Collins was forced to deal the rodent a mortal blow, possibly with her soup ladle.

The great pet in history and legend is, of course, the cat. A cat cult existed among Egyptians of the late dynasties, and its best-known goddess was named Bastet. Cats were mummified in her honor at Bubastis in the Nile delta. The Romans had *Felis catus* to help with mousing and to play with around the hearth. (The designation *Felix domesticus* is a modern popular term, not a scientific one.) This pet appears again and again in Roman art, coins, and literature. There is even a Latin word, *murmare,* meaning "to purr."

The colossal Italian poet Petrarch is remembered, for, among other things, some fugitive lines in Latin attributed to his cat, who it seems was as beloved as his human heartthrob, Laura. The feline narrator of the verse suggests that he was rewarded by Petrarch for his fidelity even as Laura was for grace and beauty:

She first inspired the poet's lay,
But since I drove the mice away,
His love repaid my duty.

The cat has nowhere been the subject of more fascination and respect than in the British Isles, where it seems that centuries of folklore and observation have recorded all the pet's habits, real and imagined. A cat washing its face is often a sign of rain. In nineteenth-century Anglesey, the same face-washing meant a visitor would call. If the face only was washed, the caller would come in the indefinite future; if the paw went over the ear, the visit would be that day. Similarly, desperate cats were thought to feast on coals, and a cat's sneeze was a good-luck omen for a bride. A kitten born in May will never be a good mouser, but will instead bring in glow-

worms. In other locales, people tell the time of day, or the tides, by
the dilation of a cat's eyes. The pupils are said to be open at high
tide, tiny slits at low.

Among the most charming of folk devices, though perhaps associated with overmuch kindness to kitties, is one reported in *Notes
and Queries* in 1858:

> Upon a recent occasion, on bringing a full-grown cat home, I
> desired my servant to take every precaution to prevent puss
> attempting to return to her old domicile. This my servant in-
> formed me could be effected by buttering the cat's feet! Ac-
> cordingly pussy's feet were smeared with butter; and being
> kindly treated, she never "imitated" (to use a Norfolk expres-
> sion) straying away.

An attractive story, but easily topped by one sent a decade later to
the same journal by a correspondent who was intrigued by brainy
cats:

> We were talking about the sagacity shown by some animals,
> when I mentioned the story which I think Archbishop
> Whately tells in some of his writings, of his cat ringing the
> doorbell. This anecdote brought out a still better one from my
> neighbour, who had come in to see me for a chat. He said that
> when he was about twenty-five years of age, there was belong-
> ing to his house a certain cat, which up to that time had not at-
> tracted notice for any particular sagacity. But the pantry
> window of the old-fashioned house was found to be repeat-
> edly broken. Time after time the broken square—for one only
> was broken at a time—was repaired. At length my friend,
> growing tired of mending, made up his mind to have a board
> nailed over the lower row of the window-panes. Not very long
> after this precaution had been taken, being awake one night,

he heard in his bedroom, which was close by, several distinct taps, as of a stone, upon glass. Getting out of bed, and looking down from the window, he saw then and there his cat resting with her hind feet upon the window-sill, her left paw clinging to the top of the new board, and with her other paw, in which she held a pebble, she was tapping the glass, in order no doubt to break it. He shouted out, and the cat jumped down, dropping the pebble—about the size of a marble—which in the morning he picked up. I have only to add that my neighbour is a man of his word, and assures me that this is literally true. I have told it as he told me.

But life was not, and is not, always so pleasant for cats. Even today, people are admonished for not taking black cats seriously, an unacknowledged bow in the direction of times when black cats were seen as demons, ghosts, or witches' familiars. In eighteenth-century Scotland, a cat that jumped over a laid-out corpse would cause the funeral to be stopped while the mourners caught and killed it, lest the deceased become a vampire. White cats, by contrast, were universally thought to be stupid, and frequently deaf as well.

Such beliefs likely gave rise to the world's dismal catalogue of cruelty to cats. The municipal records of Colchester, England, detail the 1651 trial of William Beard, who was alleged to have cut off the tail of Tom Burgis's cat. (For their part, the Burgis family retaliated by either poisoning or bewitching their pet's tormentor.)

Medieval students are known to have gambled with cats. As a result, medieval schools regularly forbade the keeping of pets of any kind (dogs, hawks, ferrets, birds), but apparently to little avail. Students at the University of Paris in the thirteenth century are known to have diced with stray cats, by balancing the cubes on their paws. Winning cats were fed; losers had their skins sold. On one occasion a group of gamblers playing for dinner grabbed a regularly freeloading cat and made him dice with them because he had never paid for his food. After he lost, they sent him home to his master with the dinner bill tied round his neck, claiming his skin if it was not paid.

Dogs occasionally suffered similarly cruel fates—including, incredibly, being executed along with their criminal masters or as examples to other animals. There was a late Roman custom of crucifying dogs, annually, to repay them for their failure to warn the city of approaching Gauls. Among the Danes wolves were hung along with parricides, and elsewhere in Scandinavia and in Germany criminals were hanged with dogs to show the enormity of their disgrace. A sixteenth-century cleric, Rorarius, noted that it was the custom to crucify lions to dissuade them from entering North African towns, and that wolves were still being hanged at that time in German forests as an example to their obdurate brothers.

The folklore associated with dogs, as with cats, is rich and varied. A belief in East Anglia was that if a dog turned around three times, a stranger would call. A person should never handle children's teeth that were accidentally knocked out; otherwise, that person would grow dog's teeth. Nor should one point to the spot of sky where lightning came from, for fear of the immediate appearance of dog's teeth in the mouth of the pointer. All these superstitions were current in the nineteenth century.

Dogs were thought to howl at night because they alone could see ghosts. Dogs were also, well into Elizabethan times, associated with the myths surrounding the mandrake. This plant, you will remember from Shakespeare, had a large root that was held to resemble a human body. When it was plucked from the earth, it would issue a bloodcurdling scream, a sound that meant sure death to whoever heard it. As a result, a dog was enlisted in its harvesting—for the root was valuable and conferred great powers of sorcery on its possessor. The harvest drill went like this: Find a hungry dog, tie it to a mandrake root, and then call it for dinner. When it dashes for its meal, it pulls up the root, hears the scream, and so sacrifices its life for the enrichment of its master.

The reputation of dogs for faithfulness gave rise to their being a symbol of fidelity, and to their being selected to appear on tomb effigies with ladies and knights of great stature. Bishops' tombs also have dogs under the prelates' feet. In one celebrated thirteenth-century case, a dog was actually buried along with the bishop. The reasoning was obvious. As the shepherd of a flock, a bishop has a fit companion in his dog.

As for the "pet" saints of medieval Christianity, their stories are as memorable as they are charming, a good antidote to cynical disbelief. For example, St. Dominic is symbolized by a dog—at his birth his mother dreamt she had brought forth a whelp with a torch in its mouth— and fittingly founded the religious order called the Dominicans (from the Latin *Domini canes,* "hounds of the Lord").

St. Anthony of Egypt (251–356) was the saint of swineherds, and is often shown in medieval illustrations with a tiny pig at his side, a symbol of man's triumph over gluttony. The pig also functions as a symbol of St. Anthony's role as a hospitaler saint, for pork fat was used to dress the wounds of St. Anthony's fire, a frightful skin disease prevalent in the late Middle Ages. A recurrent plaint in medieval villages concerned people letting their pigs wander loose. Most towns, again and again, enacted laws aimed at this nuisance. Only the St. Anthony pigs, belonging to local monks—and equipped with bells around their necks—were exempted from such strictures.

The legend of St. Gertrude (626–659) is much the same. In iconography she is often shown so absorbed in prayer that she is able to ignore a tiny mouse that gambols about her feet and runs up her abbess's crozier. In time, water from the well of her chapel in Nivelles, France, was prized as a mouse eradicator, and tiny cakes baked at her convent were sold as ratsbane.

Although Aristotle flatly states that fish are the only creatures that cannot be tamed, St. Anthony of Padua (1195–1231) seems to give him the lie. The legend records that at a time when a group of heretics refused to be moved by his preaching, Anthony turned his voice to the shore of the Adriatic and addressed the multitude of fishes, which obliged him and arranged themselves neatly according to their species. When the saint pointed out that God had spared fish alone from the destruction of the deluge, and that they were also insensible to the vicissitudes of weather and seasons that attack the world above water, "the fish, as though they had been endowed with reason, bowed down their heads with all the marks of a profound humility and devotion, moving their bodies up and down with a kind of fondness." Such was the tale presented to Padua tourists in 1705, when the English essayist Joseph Addison traveled to Italy and recorded it.

A similar legend is attached to St. Patrick, on whose feast day the fish were expected to rise from the sea and parade before his altar. St. Patrick might well have sent the snakes away, as every true Irishman knows, but to my mind bringing the fish back was a much bigger deal.

Notes and Further Reading

Recent archaeology has revealed that cats were often sacrificed in Bronze Age mines; see, for instance, for Wales, "The Great Orme Mine," *Current Archaeology* 130 (Fall 1992): 404–409. A sample:

> They were also very superstitious about cats for a cat was considered to be a bad omen down the mines. Thus whenever a cat entered a mine by mistake, they sacrificed it. Three skeletons of cats have so far been discovered, neatly laid out for sacrifice. One of them was surrounded by a circle of organic material and when samples were taken to Bangor University they turned out to be blackberries.

St. Anthony of Padua is in Ferguson, 105. His sermon to the fish is in Addison's *Remarks on Italy* (1705; repr. London, 1864), 324–325. For the Petrarch quotation, see "The Last Lay of Petrarch's Cat," *N&Q*, 1st series, V:174 (February 21, 1852). Mrs. Celestina Collins and her rat and rooster are in Sitwell, 65–66. For gambling cats, see Charles Homer Haskins, "The University of Paris in the Sermons of the Thirteenth Century," *American Historical Review* 10 (1904): 1–27.

See also the following, all from *N&Q*:

"L.," "Execution of Domestic Animals for Murder," *N&Q*, 2nd series, VII:343 (April 23, 1859).

A. De Morgan, "Dog's Teeth: Pointing at Lightning," *N&Q*, 3rd series, II:342 (November 1, 1862).

"W.H.S.," "A Cat Breaking Glass," *N&Q*, 4th series, I:531 (June 6, 1868).

Richard Spencer (on Tom Burgis cutting off a cat's tail), "Extracts from Colchester Corporation Records," *N&Q*, 1st series, VIII:464–465 (November 12, 1853).

William Harrison, "Dogs Buried at the Feet of Bishops," *N&Q*, 4th series, VIII:537 (December 23, 1871), and (on finding the remains of a dog buried along with Bishop Simon, who rebuilt the Cathedral of St. German on the Isle of Man and who died there in 1245), "Dogs Buried at the Foot of Bishops," *N&Q*, 4th series, VIII:222 (September 16, 1871).

♦ Place-Names

TO BEGIN WITH, there's Crackpot in Yorkshire. Not *a* crack-pot, just Crackpot, a small village off the B-6270 from Richmond. But Crackpot has nothing to do with harebrains. From the old Viking word for crow, *kraka,* and the medieval English for a hollow in the landscape, *potte,* it simply means a ravine where crows used to gather to drink.

It doesn't mean that anymore, of course. As with so many other place-names, the word has outlived its original significance. It's just a place. Still, it's a fine place-name, uniting as it did two languages and two cultures, probably a thousand years ago.

Actually, the study of place-names has a distinguished past and is an important tool in linguistic, archaeological, and historical research. American Indian, say, or Scottish place-names are frequently the sole remains of long-lost languages, the only vestiges of past inhabitants.

For example, the Old English suffix *-tun* meant an enclosure, so a name like Thornton originally signified a place surrounded by thorn trees of some sort. And Bickerton signified a beekeeper's enclosure or farm. Gradually the suffix progressed from enclosure to farm to village to town, and we have a name like Sutton meaning south town.

Likewise, *wic* meant a farm, or more specifically a dairy farm, so that Fenwick was a dairy farm in the marsh *(fen)*. Since a *leah* was a wood or a clearing in a wood, Healey was a clearing high on a hill, and Briarley one where briars grew. Such suffixes are medieval survivals on the Old World landscape, spread to America by immigrants fondly recalling the British Isles.

The dean of American place-name studies was George R. Stewart (1895–1980), whose classic *Names on the Land* celebrates the ingenuity, struggle, and just plain luck connected with our geography. Did you know, for example, that in 1847 a pitched battle was fought to change the name of San Francisco to Yerba Buena, or good herb, after a mintlike plant that grew there? Or that in 1777, when Vermont got its name on the wings of enthusiasm for French support in the Revolution, there was another uproar? Many people rightly complained that the name sounded more like "worm mountain" than "green mountain." In French, worm is *ver*, green *vert*.

By contrast, a river that passed through Vermont's Green Mountains, called *les Monts Verts* and correctly pronounced *lay moan vair*, was anglicized into the Lemon Fair River. This is an almost mystical name, and one impossible to account for without a bit of fractured French.

First published in 1946, *Names on the Land* has often been reprinted and deserves a spot on every American bookshelf. A companion volume by Stewart, *American Place-Names* (1970), is arranged like a dictionary and is a browser's delight. There you'll find a Faith, a Hope, and a Charity Branch. Faith (NC) was named in honor of a tyro businessman who opened a quarry with no experience, Hope (OR) is taken from a personal name, and Charity Branch (KY) recalls an early church on that site. Hook, line, and sinker can also be found. Hook Brook (NJ) comes from the Dutch word for corner, *hoek*. Line Creek is situated near the Kansas-

Nebraska border. And Sinker Mountain, Oregon, owes its name to several hunters who were overcome by eating heavy biscuits called sinkers.

A more widespread knowledge of Stewart's work and of place-name studies in general might be a good antidote to those commercial developers who insist on giving names like Whispering Pines and Rose Haven to places that have seen neither pine nor rose. But that may be too much to hope for. False etymology and folk etymology can be rampant even among those who should know better.

You sometimes hear, for example, that Brooklyn, New York, means a place where the land was so irregular on its first maps that it was termed a "broken land." Or that it contained countless "brooks." Actually, the Algonquin Indians had called it Meryckawick, meaning a sandy place. In 1638 the Dutch settlers called the sandy place their *bruijkleen,* derived from two words meaning free and loan; the resulting compound meant homestead or tenanted land. Inside the larger colony, the homesick Dutch simply named Breukelen Village after a small town near Amsterdam. When the British took charge of the area in 1664, the name began to shift according to its sound. Unable to get their tongues around the Hollanders' pronunciation, the English began using Brookland. Later, the switch to Brooklyn was dictated solely by a very subtle change in sound—much as many people today say the name of my home state, Maryland, as Marilyn.

Another of the five boroughs of New York City, the Bronx is unique as a place-name that includes the definite article. (In English, that is. There are many Spanish and French examples; think of Los Angeles and La Crosse, Wisconsin.) Anyway, it's always "the Bronx," never just a naked Bronx. According to Stewart, this usage dates from the seventeenth century, a time when a man named Jonas Bronck farmed the land north of Manhattan. When people back then said they were going to the Broncks', they really meant it. But even after the English settlement, when the family was long gone, the Manhattan phraseology still referred to traveling north. Only a slight spelling simplification followed in time.

Most often, place-name study is a matter of linguistics, or philology, as it used to be called. Especially in the Old World. In England, the landscape has frequently been likened to a palimpsest, a medieval parchment that has had old ink scraped off and new words overlaid on top. Look closely enough, and you can sometimes see those old layers of meaning.

The land has seen a succession of peoples. Prehistoric Britons and then the Celts were conquered by the Romans, who were supplanted by the Saxons and other Germanic tribes, who were invaded and subdued by the Vikings, who were overcome by the Normans in 1066. They all spoke different languages and had different ways of referring to the same landmarks.

Consider the city of York. This settlement, at the junction of the Foss and Ouse Rivers, must have been noted for its great yew trees at one time because the Celts called the spot Eboros, after their word for yew. The Romans, following them, called the place Eboracum. The Saxons, innocent of the ways of Celtic and Latin, saw the place as a compound word, but one entirely different in meaning. Using Old English, they translated the spot into their *eofor* (boar) and *wic* (village). Viking invaders, who made the town a royal enclave in the ninth century, compressed the Old English into Jorvik, which later became Iork, and finally York.

Listen closely to Hamlet's speech "Alas poor Yorick" the next time you go to that play. Yorick and York are indeed the same name, and that two-thousand-year run from Eboros to York, with intermediate stops at Eboracum, Eoforwic, and Jorvik, is almost palpable in Hamlet's remembrance of a boyhood friend from the north of England.

Prefixes, suffixes, and other root words are critical in place-name research. *Wic, tun,* and *leah* we have already seen, but there are countless others. From Old Norse, Cheswick meant cheese farm.

From Latin, Pontefract meant broken bridge, changed by the Normans to Pomfret.

Similarly, any place that ends in -*ness* is literally a nose, a promontory jutting out into an ocean, river, or lake—as in Dungeness. In fact, *ness* was not just a place-name suffix but also an English verb meaning "poke out." Writing in 1535–1543, John Leland said "betwixt Rumney town and Lyd the marsch land beginneth to nesse . . . yn the sea."

The early written forms of town names in charters, the *Domesday Book,* and other legal documents are vital. Otherwise the English village of Fawler would rightly be associated with people who hunted birds. But a 1205 document shows the town as Fauflor, an Old English phrase for a colored or variegated floor, *fagan flore.* Why? No one knew until 1865, when an old Roman villa with a mosaic pavement was unearthed. It had been lost since the early Middle Ages, a time when the first Saxon villagers were presumably astounded by the richness of that already old floor. But once the floor was slowly covered again by the grime and dust of centuries, the village name and spelling shifted to something that made sense to the average farmer, hunter, or fowler.

Is this imperfect process of naming still going on? The answer is yes: the best name changes continue to be created by our need to attach name tags to everything, and then to corrupt them through repetition, familiarity, and, indeed, even through lazy listening.

Evidence to this effect was recently uncovered by the sharp ears of English writer Richard Jerred. Near his village in Devon he heard two boys talking about a crop being harvested in Enklefield, clearly a geographical reference that implied a nearby site. Trouble was, local historian Jerred had never heard of such a place. When he questioned them, the boys pointed across a valley to an area that had always been known to him as Quarter-Mile Field. Then Jerred remembered: in April 1941 a Nazi bomber had crash-landed on that spot, and the rusting carcass of the behemoth had remained long on the minds of the locals. So long, in fact, that the name Quarter-Mile had been supplanted by Enklefield. And all because of that infamous bomber, a Heinkel 111.

Notes and Further Reading

O. G. S. Crawford's essay "Place-Names and Archaeology," Chapter VIII in *Introduction to the Study of English Place-Names* (Cambridge: Cambridge University Press, 1925), is remarkably lucid and consistently interesting. That last, of course, is the great appeal of considering place-names; it constantly challenges—and satisfies—our curiosity. The *fagan flore* of this essay comes from Crawford, 143.

Similarly, W. F. H. Nicolaisen's *Scottish Place-Names* (London: Batsford, 1976) is a mine of dependable information, gracefully expressed. John Field's pocket guide *Discovering Place-names* (Princes Risborough: Shire Publications, 1984) is also dependable (and portable) for travelers to England. William Thurlow's *Yorkshire Place-Names* (York: Dalesman Books, 1979) is also a fine book; Crackpot is on p. 46. For a more comprehensive look, see A. D. Mills, *A Dictionary of English Place Names* (Oxford: Oxford University Press, 1992). Two other important figures in this field are Kenneth Cameron and Margaret Gelling; see Cameron's *English Place-Names* (London: Batsford, 1977) and Gelling's *Place-Names of Berkshire* (Cambridge: Cambridge University Press, 1973) and *Place-Names of Shropshire* (Nottingham: English Place-Name Society, 1990).

The American Name Society has published a quarterly journal called *Names* since the 1950s. Like *Notes and Queries,* it's addictive. In my discussion of Brooklyn here, for example, I drew on Carl M. Weisman's "Brooklyn from *Breukelen* and *Bruijkleen,*" *Names* I (1953): 39–40.

The standard source for American towns is George R. Stewart's *American Place-Names* (New York: Oxford University Press, 1970). The Yerba Buena story is from his *Names on the Land* (New York: Random House, 1945), 263.

For the Heinkel-field, see Richard Jerred, "The Legend of Enklefield," *The Countryman,* April 1984, 71–74. A wonderful book on Britain's lost agricultural life, George Ewart Evans's *Ask the Fellows Who Cut the Hay* (1956; repr. London: Faber and Faber, 1972), has a fine chapter on how fields are named by the folk (pp. 201–205).

Contributors to *Notes and Queries* have long been interested in place-names. Some citations: "W.C.W.," "Field-Names," *N&Q*, 8th series, XI:246 (September 24, 1892); George Nelson, "The Material for Barrows Carried in Baskets," *N&Q*, 8th series, IX:513 (June 27, 1896); W. Fraser, "Rhymes Connected with Places," *N&Q*, 1st series, V:293 (March 27, 1852). Mackenzie Walcott's "Diamond Rock," *N&Q*, 2nd series, III:59 (January 17, 1857), has to do with the rocky outcrop off the south coast of Martinique that was registered as a "sloop of war" in the British Navy in 1804 (the only non-ship to be so recognized). To this day, I am told, ships of the Royal Navy still salute the rock as they sail past it.

After this article appeared in *Smithsonian*, March 1986, a letter in the May issue from Kenneth N. Phillips of Portland, Oregon, mentioned another common element in place-naming: incompetence. Said he: "In Alaska, before Nome was a town, a coast survey showed a cape nearby. The mapper did not know its name, so, after CAPE he added in light pencil '?NAME,' which the map tracer misread as NOME."

 # Dibs!

DIBS . . . it's coming back. A grade-school word, I used to hear it a lot back in the 1950s. Since then, dibs seems to have fallen into disuse. Which is too bad, because the word is a marvel of meaning and etymological compression, born of centuries of observation and living. Studying its etymology opens up a lane to our own past and that of our culture as well.

Today, "dibs" is only rarely used. When it is, it's a single-word expression signifying "That belongs to me!" People who use the word are usually trying to infuse their speech with a bit of informality. So a newscaster will point out that a politician has dibs on a certain bloc of votes. Or a sportswriter will note that a team has its dibs on players in the professional draft. I once heard some Maine fishermen say they had dibs on certain places for dropping their lobster pots.

Although adults will often expand "Dibs!" to the full "I got dibs on that," children seldom do. Why? Because they realize time is of the essence. It takes longer to say the complete sentence; you snooze, you lose.

In a very real way, dibs is the social contract in little. When we hear the expression, we're listening in on the origins of our species—a message in a bottle from a time when there were no lawyers or paper to sanctify ownership. If I say "dibs" first, it's mine. And there's an end to it. That is also why almost the only place you're likely to hear the word regularly is in the company of children. Despite computers and television, children are still among the most conservative of societies, and among the first to preserve old ways and distrust the new.

Fundamentally, the verb "to dib" has to do with looking down, bending down, or delving into water. In 1869, in *Lorna Doone*, R. D. Blackmore fixed in aspic for all time a squad of ducks: "It is a fine sight to behold them walk, poddling one after the other, with their toes out, like soldiers drilling . . . they dib with their bills, and dabble, and throw up their heads and enjoy something."

The association of the word with water comes from a corruption of "dip," a transformation recorded in 1325 and still in use in 1570: "Dib the shirt in the water, and so hang it upon a hedge all night." Meaning to jiggle the bait lightly on the water's surface, the word was thus an obvious choice for the jargon of fishing. "Put one on the point of a Dub-fly Hook," advised *The Angler's Vade-Mecum* in 1689, "and dib with it, or dib with the Ash-fly."

In swimming pools all across the nation, American children today play a game called dibbles. The rules are simple. Take a tiny sliver of wood, or a twig, and toss it into the water. The child who's "it" then does a huge cannonball of a dive, right on top. As he and the piece of wood come bobbing to the surface, all the other players—now straining their eyes to see the bit of wood—are poised at the pool's edge. The first child to see it screams "dibbles!" and jumps in after it, followed instantly by every remaining child—in the county, it often seems. It's all great, splashy, wild fun. The player who finally comes up with the dibble, as the wooden prize is called, gets to be "it" for the next go-round.

But if "to dibble" was to fish on the surface and dibbles is a child's diving game, a "dibble stick" is another matter altogether. For centuries farmers used this device to punch holes in the plowed earth, especially for a crop like potatoes, where large eyes and not seeds have to be planted. A foot dibber was critical to cultivation before the plow was invented. In his lyrical *Endymion,* John Keats noted the importance of the dibber, as well as the vital necessity of planting seeds by the light of the fertile moon. Said he: "In sowing time ne'er would I dibble take,/ Or drop a seed till [the Moon] wast wide awake." Nowadays the dibber has been replaced by a great whopping machine that not only drills holes in the ground but parcels out a solitary seed to each hole at the same time.

These then are the major components of "dibs": all the uses have a sense of looking down, as ducks and fishermen and swimming-pool children do. Moreover, all of them somehow communicate a sort of primordial respect for the earth. A dib is a small hollow in the earth; in Scotland, it's a puddle that fills up that hollow after rain. And dibstones are sheep knucklebones or small pebbles used for playing gambling games in the dirt, which gets hollowed out with repeated use.

Counting-out rhymes are metrical ways of deciding unpopular roles in games. "Eeny, meeny, miney, moe" may be the most familiar to us. But one that started with "Dip! Ickery, ahry, oary, ah," written down in Cornwall in 1897, was of special interest to folklorists. They suspected that children somehow intuitively felt that, if the first word was directed to the ground, then the rest of the rhyme would be fair, free from compromise by the speaker. So popular was the word "dip" that it appeared in numerous rhymes, and in time children simply began using the term "dipping" for what we now call counting out.

And then there's the expression "king's dibs." The two great scholars of the folklore of childhood, Iona and Peter Opie, classify this as a "truce term." Such terms are part of the "code of oral legislation" in children's games, according to the Opies, and include not only phrases but actions as well, such as crossing your fingers to signal all bets are off, or making a *T* with your palms to signify time-out.

There are a multitude of these magic phrases or words. Some of them carry a precise meaning derived from ordinary daily use. So "quits" means that the game should cease for a time, and "parley" means that we should stop playing at a breakneck speed now and rest, or *parlez,* from the French for talk. Truce terms can crop up in any game, although they are obviously most useful in games that have no time or space limits, like tag or prisoner's base (also known as capture-the-flag).

There's a class of seemingly incomprehensible terms as well. Kids who exclaim "barley" are merely using a corruption of parley. Those who shout "locks" or "eggshell" are claiming to be se-questered, out of the game for a time. Other children may say "nix" or "free" to remove themselves.

A number of terms seem to be describing the action of crossing fingers or legs. These include saying "crosses," "exes," "cruces," or even "twigs," a reference to the act of holding up two bits of wood forming a cross. Youngsters who received some training in Latin quickly learned to say *"pax"* for peace. The derivation of "keppies" may never be solved. Nor will "fains" or "fens"—though they seem to be related to "forfend" or the second syllable of "defend," mean-ing to forbid.

Nor are such words merely cute expressions of childhood. "Bar-ley" was used in this way in the major fourteenth-century poem *Sir Gawain and the Green Knight.* "Fains" was used by Chaucer in the Clerk's Tale. And one expression, "cree," is in daily use in America and Britain in the latter-day word "crease," the charmed circle around the goalie in hockey and lacrosse. Without recourse to ety-mology from the diction of childhood, "crease" in the sports con-text makes no sense, for it has nothing to do with folding cloth.

Perhaps the most natural of the magical terms for claiming precedence is "kings." Although probably used by children forever, it was first recorded in print in 1854. An English girl told the Opies: "If one gets a stitch while playing chase, one crosses one's fingers and says 'Kings' and the person who is 'he' does not chase until one is ready." Versions of this truce recorded in the nineteenth century include "kings to rest," "kings out," and "kings up." Kings are regal characters; their word supersedes all others.

In Canada, children say "kings ex" when they want an immediate, if temporary, truce. In the United States, we've spurned the idea of royalty, but our children top an ordinary "dibs" with a kinged version.

Had I known all this back in 1953, I would have got to keep that lost pack of gum I spied one day on the grass behind Rock Creek Forest Elementary. As soon as I recognized it as an unopened pack of Juicyfruit, I shouted, "Dibs." But an older, wiser head prevailed. Well after I'd spoken, he flatly intoned, "King's dibs"—and got to keep the gum.

It was no use my protesting I'd never heard of such a thing. An English folklorist, writing in 1864, once noted near Nottingham that whenever kings are invoked "unusual confidence and honesty are shown by both sides." Also, the other kid was much bigger.

Notes and Further Reading

After this appeared in *Smithsonian,* September 1986, Noah Lichterman wrote from Missoula, Montana, to urge that "dibs" mainly has to do with "dividing" spoils and derives from that verb: "If Billy hollers 'Fen dibs!' and picks up the penny, he has undisputed, exclusive rights to it." That is, "Billy fends off division." (Letters, November 1986, 24)

Another reader, Robert W. Buck of Waban, Massachusetts, wrote to take issue with the Lichterman letter and went on to say that he was born in 1893 and could recall dibs, king's ex, and fens being "current in Dayton, Ohio, about 1903." (Unprinted letter, November 4, 1986)

From New Orleans, Rosalind Joffe wrote to say that she'd heard the word in Kansas City in 1951, in Arkansas in 1962, and Louisiana in 1972, noting that it gradually lost all sense of sharing or dividing over those years: "Somewhere the concept of sharing has disappeared from the word (and our society?)." (Unprinted letter, undated [September 1986].)

Christine Darby wrote that while "growing up in the Fifties in small-town exurban Massachusetts, my friends and I did use the term 'dibs' or its fancier form 'dibsies.' Much more frequently, however, we'd say 'I hosey this,' as in to claim or reserve for future use." The word has not appeared in the literature before this. (Unprinted letter, September 6, 1986.)

James Watrous of Madison, Wisconsin, noted that the article "reminded [him] of a cartoon drawn over a half century ago for the *Wisconsin Octopus* during the heyday of college comics." The cartoon shows two huge football players about to tackle a tiny player with the ball; he is holding up two fingers in the king's ex sign; see *Octopus,* October 1933, 46. "One must have assumed that every reader had used 'King's X' when a kid in order to forestall disaster." (Unprinted letter, October 24, 1986.)

For definitions, see the *OED*. See also S. F. Creswell, "Kings!" *N&Q,* 3rd series, V:456 (June 4, 1864). For the "code of oral legislation," see Opie, 142–145 and 150–153; see also 26, 29, and 35.

Dorothy Hartley's *Lost Country Life* (New York: Pantheon, 1979) details the use of a foot dibber (p. 71). The *Lorna Doone* quotation is from Chapter X. The Chaucer quotation is from line 529. The Keats line from *Endymion* is 153.

Umbrellas

IT'S 1885 and *The Magistrate,* a farce by Arthur Wing Pinero, is
the toast of the world stage. The play's central figure, a Mr. Posket,
presides over a London police court and is a character of certified
probity and a genuine liberal outlook. We know this for two reasons. For one thing, Posket has no first name. Second, the generous
Posket has several ex-convicts in his employ, including one dimwit
"who abstracted four silk umbrellas from the Army and Navy
Stores . . . and on a fine day too!"

A funny line, but one that prompts questions. How long have
umbrellas been around? They're practical, but why are they so important symbolically? W. P. Kinsella uses umbrellas four times in
his great baseball novel *Shoeless Joe* (1982), prominently in connection with a magical old-time player: "He holds an umbrella, gently
as he might a fencing foil, and swishes it vigorously with each step."
An umbrella is a brave utensil, a surrogate bat, Excalibur.

First things first. Umbrella comes from the Latin *umbra,* meaning shadow, and the diminutive suffix *-ulum,* meaning little. The resulting *umbraculum* or "little shadow" signified a sunshade or
parasol.

Ovid said that Hercules held a golden *umbraculum* to keep the sun off his beloved Omphale, the princess of Lydia. And the epigrammatist Martial elevated the umbrella to a work of art in one of his bright two-liners. He saw the umbraculum as Everyman's personal awning, even when the wind was up. Which only goes to show that Martial never tried to maneuver one through a city downpour.

Earlier, for the Greeks, the umbrella was a *skiadeion,* a sunshade like those carried in processions by the daughters of foreigners living in Athens. Their job: to hold umbrellas over the heads of legitimate city maidens. A sign of respect. More to the point, the shadows would protect the nubile maidens from the view of either amorous or jealous gods. Similarly, in Aristophanes' play *The Birds,* Prometheus agrees to divulge everything that goes on behind the scenes at Olympus—but only if he can hide from Zeus under a *skiadeion.*

The sunshade seems to have come to Greece from Egypt and the Orient, where the idea of the gods looking down was common. It was also a way of deflecting the blinding sun from the head of the royal personage. Ceremonially, it meant that not even the sun should blanch the divine king's presence. In Egyptian art the pharaoh's umbrella is common, and both Assyrian and Persian bas-relief sculptures from Nineveh and Persepolis show the monarch protected by an umbrella. Again, the common sunlight that falls on us all must not descend on royalty as well.

So umbrellas had to do with power. No wonder they came to be the essential accoutrement of the British power broker, the businessman. And even as his Empire waned, his symbols—brolly and bowler—remained.

But this was nothing new, even for earlier empires. The Roman emperor Heliogabalus adopted the umbrella as the symbol of his reign (A.D. 218–222). Indeed, there is plenty of evidence that he identified himself with the sun god, hence the *helios* in his name.

On his coins and in his art, the point of his umbrella was that he too radiated power.

In China, India, tropical Africa, and Mexico, princes and cult leaders were always protected in ceremonies—investitures, marriages, state processions—by umbrella-like devices, often held by special retainers. In fact, one of the eight glorious symbols of Buddha is the umbrella. Scholars think this derives from the solar wheel usually depicted over the Buddha's head.

Predictably, it was in America that the symbolic umbrella was debunked. The weapon was "bumbershoot," a morsel of American regional slang derived from "bumberella," first recorded in New York and Ohio in 1896. (The second half of the word, "shoot," is likely related to the French *chute* or fall, as in parachute.)

"Bumbersol" and "bumbrella" are similar variants from the turn of the century that failed to catch on—though both are heard occasionally today in the South. People who chronicle language call such words "humorous alternatives." You can raise an umbrella over a king, but hardly a bumbershoot.

It appears that the classical umbrella was meant primarily as a sunshade, or parasol, owing to the Mediterranean and Oriental origins of the device. For the rest of Europe, sun was much less a problem. Damp was the killer.

Starting in the seventeenth century, umbrellas are mentioned in connection with rain more frequently. English travel writer Thomas Coryate saw them in Italy. Writing about the town of Cremona in 1611, he observed that "many do carry a thing which they call in the Italian tongue *umbrellaes*. These are made of something answerable to the form of a little canopy, and hooped inside with divers little wooden hoops." And Dr. Johnson had them in his *Dictionary* (1755) as "a screen used in hot countries to keep off the sun, and in others to bear off the rain."

For a time, both *parapluie,* a perfumed French derivation, and *parasol,* a dandified Latinate word, made claims on well-bred English diction. A travel book of 1790 made the distinction between the two clear: "He that takes the East side of the mountain should carry his *paraplue* [sic], while he that takes the West would have occasion for his *parasol*."

What were eighteenth-century umbrellas like? Of wood, covered by leather or oiled silk. This last we know from some lines by John Gay, author of *The Beggar's Opera:*

> *Good housewives all the winter's rage despise,*
> *Defended by the riding-hood's disguise,*
> *Or underneath th' umbrella's oily shed.*
> —*TRIVIA, OR THE ART OF WALKING THE STREETS OF LONDON,* 1716

Jonathan Swift had the same vision:

> *The tuck'd up seamstress walks with hasty strides,*
> *While streams run down her oiled umbrella's sides.*
> —*A DESCRIPTION OF A CITY SHOWER,* 1710

Clearly, the umbrella's heyday occurred in eighteenth-century England. Robinson Crusoe carried one in Defoe's 1719 novel, and years later big black umbrellas were called Robinsons. Defoe wrote that Crusoe had seen umbrellas on his stopover in Brazil, and thus while shipwrecked was able to fashion one of animal skins, "the hair outwards, so that it cast off the rain like a penthouse, and kept off the sun so effectually that I could walk out in the hottest of the weather with greater advantage than I could before in the coolest."

Hanway, however, was the umbrella nickname that almost took hold. This was a bow in the direction of the world traveler and writer Jonas Hanway (1712–1786). He had seen the strange but effective implements on his rounds in the Middle East and Portugal, and knew they were made for London weather.

Hanway cut a ridiculous figure on the streets of London—

eighteenth-century umbrellas were huge, ungainly things—and he took plenty of abuse from cab drivers because he was also taking money out of their pockets. A taxi ride is what God intended to keep off the rain and chill, not an absurd portable contraption. And in any case, everyone could afford an umbrella—even people who didn't deserve to be dry. After Hanway's death a monument to his memory was erected in Westminster Abbey.

But there were other matters for which Jonas was not well liked. When he attacked the "pernicious" custom of drinking tea in an infamous essay, he angered Dr. Johnson, who noted that Hanway "acquired some reputation by travelling abroad, but lost it all by travelling at home."

Hanway lived in London's Red Lion Square, and guidebooks to this day still point out his address, Number 13. Here lived, they say, the first Englishman never to be seen without his umbrella. Presumably, if he left it at his coffeehouse or pub, people knew where to return it.

Why then is the umbrella a utensil of mirth or derision? Doubtless because people who take themselves seriously when they carry one seem to cry out for parody. After all, the universe is in decline. What started out as the king's scepter became just another umbrella. Humbling thought. On the other hand, Charlie Chaplin, the little tramp, used a cane or umbrella as a symbol of defeated—but still unquenchable—pride. His character is all the more human and attractive because of the persistence of that symbol in the face of obvious pain.

How about this then for a crossword clue? "23 across—The single largest category of abandoned property on the New York City subway system (9 letters)." So umbrellas are still engines of humility. Because it's hard to stay prideful when you're consistently losing something. Especially a symbol.

Notes and Further Reading

For Jonas Hanway, see the *DNB*, 1196–1199. For Hanway and guidebooks, see Findlay Muirhead, *The Blue Guides: London and Its Environs* (London: Macmillan, 1927), 186.

For bumbershoot, see Frederic G. Cassidy, *Dictionary of American Regional English* (Cambridge: Harvard University Press, 1985), I:455. T. S. Crawford's *A History of the Umbrella* (New York: Taplinger, 1970) is a good overview of the topic, as is Robert Chambers's essay (for February 10) in his *Book of Days: A Miscellany of Popular Antiquities in Connection with the Calendar* (London: W. & R. Chambers, 1866), I:241–244.

The Thomas Coryate quotation is commented on by J. Foster Palmer, "Umbrellas," *N&Q*, 10th series, VIII:94 (August 3, 1907). See also Edward Parfitt, "Gay's *Trivia*," *N&Q*, 3rd series, VI:532 (December 31, 1864) and P. W. Trepolpen, "Umbrellas: Pattens," *N&Q*, 3rd series, VII:66 (January 21, 1865). The Pinero quotation is from p. 10 of *The Magistrate* (London: Samuel French, 1920).

For *skiadeion* or σκιαδειον, see Liddell and Scott, *Greek-English Lexicon* (1889: repr. Oxford, 1978), 1610. By the way, H. G. Liddell, coauthor of that volume, is—somewhat more famously—the father of Alice Liddell, for whom Lewis Carroll wrote the book from which the epigraph to this essay is taken.